Library of
Davidson College

subversions of desire

subversions of desire
PROLEGOMENA TO NICK JOAQUIN

E. SAN JUAN, JR.

 University of Hawaii Press • Honolulu

Handog sa aking Ina, Loreto Samia-San Juan

Published in North America by
University of Hawaii Press
2840 Kolowalu Street
Honolulu, Hawaii 96822

Simultaneously published in
the Philippines by
Ateneo de Manila University Press
Bellarmine Hall, Loyola Heights
Quezon City
P.O. Box 154, Manila

Copyright 1988 by Ateneo de Manila
ALL RIGHTS RESERVED

Photograph of the young Joaquin on the cover is
taken from Bienvenido Lumbera's "Towards a
Revised History of Philippine Literature," in
Book of the Philippines 1976, edited by Yen Makabenta
(Manila: The Research and Analysis Center for
Communications, 1976).

Library of Congress Cataloging-in-Publication Data

San Juan, E. (Epifanio), 1938–
    Subversions of desire.

    Includes index.
    1. Joaquin, Nick–Criticism and interpretation.
2. Philippines in literature. I. Title.
PR9550.9.J6Z88 1988   828   88–17088
ISBN 0–8248–1129–1

Printed in the Philippines

Contents

Preface vii

1 Celebrating the Virgin and Her City 1
2 Strategies of Compromising Truth and Power 17
3 From the Terror of History to the Return/
   Doubling of the Repressed 65
4 Simulacra of the Sublime: Deconstructing
   Joaquin's Poetics 104
5 Joaquin's Theater of Transgression and Sacrifice 117
6 The Woman Who Had Two Navels: Fable of
   Patriarchy "Salvaged" 143
7 Cave and Shadows: Toward the Production of
   Utopian Discourse 169
8 Demystifying the Past, Unfetishizing the Present,
   Reinventing the Future 192

Notes 204

Index 209

Preface

FULFILLING THE PROMISE made at the end of my essay on *The Woman Who Had Two Navels* in *Toward A People's Literature* (1984), this critical reading and interpretation of Nick Joaquin's fiction, poetry and drama looks forward to a project still in the distant horizon for the simple reason that, like the narrator of *Tristram Shandy*, I am faced with the enigmatic problem of how to catch up with the multiplication of texts that in their wake are modifying, altering and reshuffling the Joaquin corpus. Just like Hegel's owl, I am bound to complete that undertaking, *deo volens*, when the dusk has settled and the litter of texts lies on the field of battle ready to be gathered. The reader-critic then becomes the funeral-attendant, looking forward to dawn and the expected resurrection of his subject.

Why Nick Joaquin of all writers?

Why, especially at the present transitional moment (circa 1985) when the conjunctural phase of the struggle has become more pivotal and decisive amid the unprecedented advance in the consensual field of civil society, particularly after Ninoy Aquino's death?

We are, I trust, far removed now from the positivist and mechanical reflection theory of the sixties and early seventies when comrades had the peremptory habit of assigning immediate class values to artistic forms and themes. Progressive critical theory needs to be more sensitive and open to the complex overdetermined effects of various aesthetic and cultural practices, especially in the context of coalition struggles. While the essays here do not shirk making judgments about aspects of the texts invested with progressive or reactionary tendencies, I must add that on the whole Joaquin's textual power, however that is calculated, cannot be summarily explained by identifying such ideological tendencies (which I do here) because their reception by a necessarily limited audience of the middle strata is conditioned by the utopian, subversive pleasure necessarily embedded in them.

What I would emphasize then is the perspective and method of construing both critic and author as subjects-in-process, subjects-on-trial. From a dialectical standpoint, all of Joaquin's texts may be seen as overdetermined by multiple sociohistoric contradictions which affect all of us, without *exception*. And so it is the task of a creative oppositional criticism to interpellate these texts in order to let them speak an emancipatory message, and to articulate such message in a way diametrically opposed to the hegemonic ethicopolitical commentaries that have exploited Joaquin to maintain and legitimize class rule. "Joaquin" then may be conceived as the sign of multiple contractions outside/inside the texts. Let Joaquin speak to/for the masses.

My project is basically one of "historicizing" Joaquin, of trying to reappropriate the discursive, agitational power of certain texts which have been used earlier to propagandize certain reactionary or obscurantist interests. This study can therefore be viewed as a contribution to the cultural movement to constitute a national-popular consensus on behalf of the struggle of the Filipino people for social justice, true democracy, and genuine independence. This effort is, to be sure, part of the larger necessary task of completing the unfinished 1896 Revolution of Rizal, Bonifacio and Mabini—a task of ethical, political and cultural reconstruction. Critical praxis here derives its rationale from Gramsci's view (elaborated in *Prison Notebooks*, 1977) that such activity is not just purely theoretical but it is above all "a cultural battle to transform the popular 'mentality' and to diffuse the philosophical innovations which will demonstrate themselves to be 'historically true' to the extent that they become concretely—i.e., historically and socially—universal" (p. 51). The critic so engaged, "understood both individually and as an entire social group, not merely grasps the contradictions [of life] but posits himself as an element of the contradiction and elevates this element to a principle of knowledge and therefore of action (p. 418)." From individual texts and discourse to collective action: such is the configuration of Desire inscribed here.

This study is an entirely new estimate of Joaquin's achievement, supplementing and rectifying the particular judgments that I have proposed before, such as those in "For Whom Are We Writing?" (*Two Perspectives in Philippine Literature and Society*, University of Hawaii, 1981). It is perhaps superfluous to remind the reader that ideas, all theoretical practices, change their function and worth on the impact of events, under the pressure of fluid circumstances and unpredictable protean forces, so that we need constantly to revise, correct, and reformulate our thoughts not for the sake of some essential or universal truth immanent in them but for the sake of critiquing power and privileged elites that use their claim to absolute truth as a mask and weapon of torture and domination. If this work succeeds in inciting controversy and debate, or even some interest in the burning questions of cultural politics (via Joaquin) so crucial to the ongoing struggle, then it shall have accomplished its limited purpose.

I suggest that "Nick Joaquin" be considered here as a descriptive name of the total effect generated by the following texts from which I quote, all published in Manila except one: *Prose and Poems* (1952, reissued 1963), *Tropical Gothic* (St. Lucia, Queensland, 1972), *The Woman Who Had Two Navels* (1961, reissued 1972), *La Naval de Manila and Other Essays* (1964), *Tropical Baroque* (1979), and *Cave and Shadows* (1983). In my opinion, the two novels constitute the most substantial achievement of Joaquin's art.

Although the first book-length analysis of and metacommentary on Joaquin's oeuvre, this work does not by choice deal—except by allusion and references here and there—with the prose discourses particularly, *Almanac for Manileños* (1979), *A Question of Heroes* (1977), and *The Aquinos of Tarlac* (1983), and the voluminous collection of his journalistic pieces published under the name of Quijano de Manila. I hope to cover all of the works omitted here, including critical studies and reviews on Joaquin, in the project I mentioned at the beginning when and after the present assessment shall have produced its effect.

Given the continuing involvement of the subject of this book in the urgent issues and happenings of our country, what can be said here is obviously tentative and provisional, subject to changes as the future reveals.

It is somewhat of a historical curiosity to note that the raging critical controversy in 1952 on Joaquin involved the critic Armando Manalo and Professor Dolores Feria on the question of Joaquin's "realism." With a few exceptions, practically all the extant critical studies on Joaquin belong to the realm of hagiography: uncritical panegyrics on Joaquin's "genius," religiosity, etc. No doubt it would have been more worthwhile if the energies expended on such labors were devoted to three endeavors: a scholarly editing of all the texts by Joaquin toward a definitive version of the canon; second, an exhaustive bibliography of all of Joaquin's published writings; and, finally, a scrupulous biography or studies leading to a historicobiographical account. Owing to the author's quite healthy parsimony about his personal life, the last job might have to wait a while; but preliminary research and investigation can be made now. What is of utmost necessity, in my experience while writing this book, is an exact dating of all the texts and the location of their first and subsequent publications.

There are three major intellectual influences I would like to mention here as a kind of orientation for the reader: first, the tradition of oppositional criticism dating back to the prophetic biblical voices up to its contemporary articulations by Camilo Torres, Ernesto Cardenal, Father Edicio de la Torre, and others; second, the revolutionary feminist movement; and finally, Antonio Gramsci, the theoretician of hegemony *par excellence*, whose *Prison Notebooks* and other writings comprise a repository of insights for forging a socialist cultural politics in the Third World; and Georg Lukács, whose key concepts of totality and reification (in *History and Class Consciousness*)—reification grasped as a process of homogenizing and fragmenting life and the world—open up a space for a prefigurative and transformative theoretical practice insofar as such concepts implicate their users in action and are thus reinscribed in the inexhaustible richness of people's concrete struggles in the Philippines and elsewhere.

In response to queries by the publisher's referees and, more especially, to the unexpected victory of "people power" in the February 1986 uprising against the Marcos dictatorship, I would like to add the following clarification to what this project on Joaquin aims to do.

Given the poststructuralist deconstruction of the self-identical Cartesian ego or self, its displacement from the still pervasive Western analytic of knowledge and truth, the point of departure for any progressive critical hermeneutics today is by consensus the "text" in contrast to the "work" or *oeuvre* in Roland Barthes' terminology, or more precisely, discourse, discursive process and practice. The sign has now become, in Bakhtin's prophetic words, "the site of class struggle" (*Marxism and the Philosophy of Language*, 1930). There is no longer any neutral space quarantined from partisan conflicts and ideological contestation. It is now axiomatic that language incarnates what Pierre Bourdieu calls "symbolic violence" (*Reproduction in Education, Society and Culture*, 1977), inscribed in an individual's *habitus*, or system of dispositions which mediates between social structures and concrete practices. One goal of this study is to articulate Joaquin's *habitus* of discourse, the matrix of enunciation in his texts which generates configurations of meaning. Whatever meanings may be derived from this metacommentary I am engaged in, a commentary which strives to define the parameters within which the text produces meaning, can only be grasped in relation to the various positions the speaker (narrator or point of view, as the case may be) or the subject of enunciation occupies. And these positions in turn cannot be fully understood without reference to the specific historical formations, contexts reconstructed by the act of interpretation itself, whose force and pressure have registered their impact in the polysemic contours of Joaquin's texts.

It should be emphasized at the outset that this study rejects the mechanical and reductionist reading of texts and discourses as mere superstructural phenomena parasitic on a narrowly economic or class foundation (base/superstructure metaphor), a vulgar notion permanently refuted by Raymond Williams, Julia Kristeva, Fredric Jameson and others following a renaissance of the theoretical praxis of Gramsci, Brecht, Mao, Althusser, and others. If the February uprising in Manila has taught us anything, it would be nothing else but a reconfirmation of the fundamental insight crystallized in the Chinese cultural revolution (to cite one modern example) that ideas exert a tremendous material force when lived, applied and enacted by the masses.

Would it be superfluous to remind ourselves again that Marxism is nothing if not the unity of theory and practice realized in mass struggles where the critic or intellectual participates in wielding the weapon of criticism?

Engaged with exploring the thematic of ideology conceived less as a system of ideas or "false consciousness" and more as a strategic practice which constructs subject-positions (the internal psychological moment of the social process involved in reproducing production-relations), this inquiry confronts the task of how Joaquin's texts can be recuperated for the totalizing collective project of the radical transformation of Philippine culture and society. The fulfillment of this task of course exceeds the boundary of this book, but its beginnings can be initiated here, via a cultural critique of Joaquin's writings, in the analysis of the constitution of the subject in discourse. For class determination, as well as gender and racial interpellations, is displaced in language and in discursive practices where the Other (culture, sign-system) speaks. Thus the antinomies of social relations cannot be properly comprehended without mapping the overdetermined economy of the psyche, its complex and wily dialectics. Ultimately, this task of reading and rewriting posits the Filipino proletariat within the concept "people/nation" as the "political unconscious," the immanent mobilizing agent of change, in the discourse of this study as well as in Joaquin's art.

Before addressing the mode of recuperating Joaquin's political unconscious and its revolutionary utopian potential, I would like to review a tactical means used in the program of deconstructing the "metaphysics of presence," namely, Lacan's reinterpretation of Freud.

Lacan divides the psychic economy into the Imaginary, the realm of the mirror-stage characterized by spatial homologies, correspondences, ambivalent equations and doubling identifications; and the Symbolic, the realm of culture and social order where desire is sublimated and pleasure outlawed. In Joaquin's fiction, we encounter figures of ambiguous redoubling, mirror reflections and repetitions in plot, character, rhetorical *topoi* and maneuvers (from "Three Generations" to *Cave and Shadows* and *The Aquinos of Tarlac*) drawn from the Imaginary register invading and disintegrating the Symbolic: the patriarchal regime, the phallocentric dispensation.

Lacan's theory of the formation of the unconscious through a socially defined castration complex, through the subject's accession to language and its repression of love-objects (or their signifiers) associated with the now tabooed maternal presence, can be considered as the allegorical masternarrative of Joaquin's initiation rituals, psychodramas of the youthful experience of loss and the educational ordeal leading to acceptance of a world saddled with painful ironies, paradoxes and contradictions. Since the unconscious, for Lacan, is structured like a language and operates through the tropes of metaphor (condensation) and metonymy (displacement), the narrative strategies of the texts I have examined here can be seen to construct the subject in the peculiar dialectic charted by Lacan between need (biological), demand (interpersonal claims mediated by language and social conventions), and desire (recognition by the Other).

In Joaquin's universe, the key signifier that structures the unconscious and produces/reproduces the subject—the contemporary Filipino consciousness—is the unfinished 1896 Revolution and its effects throughout twentieth-century Filipino life. Its defeat by U.S. imperialism, crudely posed here as the castration of the fathers, triggers a movement where all the norms and values of Hispanic culture and medieval folk-Christianity suffer a crisis whose catastrophic and perverse consequence we still experience everyday. It is this crisis of the epochal struggle for national sovereignty and cultural independence—the desire of the collective subject—that Joaquin's art translates into various concrete individual demands, whether a woman's gesture of defiance and self-assertion, or a young man's spiritual ordeal and quest for maturity, whereby the subject is decentered by his/her ineluctable participation in the historical process itself. When this drive for the satisfaction of demands encounters resistance from the existing social relations and its code of language use and sexuality, it leads to the production of Desire: the return of the repressed, the perpetual metonymic displacement of the subject which recapitulates and captures the drama of its alienation. Hence the book's title: "subversions of desire."

By that rubric I want to foreground the textual or figural disruptions of the Symbolic (semicolonial and semifeudal dependency) based on a mythical Oedipal triangulation, unfolding the contradictory and heterogeneous potential of the dominant patriarchal discourse—the feminist project—and revealing the unconditioned sphere of communal justice. This justice can only be realized in a future city (emblem of a classless society) which has overcome the private ownership of property (e.g., land) and women's bodies conceived as locus of meaning and use-value, a city inaugurated around the cave of the virgin's sacrifice. Desire's subversions occur in the dialectic between necessity, the revolutions defeat, and freedom: the experience of defeat as release into a new stage of the struggle qualitatively more advanced and self-aware insofar as women, peasants, workers, etc. have assumed autonomous, decisive roles in the national-popular bloc of revolutionary forces.

In performing this symptomatic reading of Joaquin's texts, I have found the notion of the subject-in-process formulated by Julia Kristeva heuristic and catalyzing. For what we perceive in the moral and ethical predicaments staged in Joaquin's plays and fiction, the moment of existential or psychological interiority in modernist art, can be grasped as the articulation of social contradiction in the investment of drives. The libidinal drive decenters the subject as it rejects the old social structure, opening up a space for a symbolic "linkage component" which will "constitute in language the new object which the subject-in-process, whilst rejecting, produces across the moment of rejection" (*Revolution in Poetic Language*, 1974). Kristeva argues that the Marxist concept of practice "contains, as its fundamental moment, the heterogeneous contradiction which places a subject thrown into process by a natural or social exterior that is not yet symbolized, in struggle with old theses (that is, with systems of representation which differ from the rejection and blunt its violence)." What Kristeva stresses here (see *The Kristeva Reader*, 1986, pp. 80-83) is precisely the process in the unconscious where social contradictions rearticulate themselves; this unconscious is nothing else but the signifying practices, the material conditions of possibility of a text, in particular the distantiation and defamiliarizing effects contrived to annul and replace the illusionistic and fetishizing effects of bourgeois realism. Not so much in the earlier fiction as in *Tropical Baroque* and in *Cave and Shadows* do we encounter quasi-Brechtian parabolic gestures which disrupt illusionism and generate all those estrangement-effects so inimical to what Henry Lefevbre calls "the bureaucratic society of controlled consumption."

In *Almanac for Manileños* and in some of the journalistic essays, Joaquin deploys an allegorical strategy that mobilizes heteroglossia, polyphony, and various heterogeneous techniques to explode the homogeneous, terroristic and hierarchical discourse which has characterized neocolonial politics and culture from the U.S. colonial period through the Philippine Commonwealth to the early decades of the Republic. In effect, Joaquin's utopian impulse can be recuperated for the popular struggle by an outflanking hermeneutic move that I try to execute here. Using Gramsci's concept of hegemony—the moral-intellectual leadership of a class over a historic bloc of national-democractic forces directed to a certain historic goal—we can construe all of Joaquin's texts as cultural production of the Filipino *ilustrado* stratum suppressed by U.S. corporate hegemony, forced to ally itself with the oppressed and marginalized sectors (tribal elements, women, nativist sects, etc.) in trying to recover its already forfeited claim to national leadership.

Given the fate of enduring a perpetual metonymy of Desire—the *ilustrado* consciousness glorified in *A Question of Heroes* becomes a floating if opportunist signifier attaching itself to any anarchic guerilla attack on capitalist hegemony—the populist *ilustrado* becomes both victim and enemy of what Lukács calls a "reification," the general reduction of human social relations to commodity-relations and the cash-nexus. In this project to emancipate alienated labor from capitalist, neocolonial bondage, to alter production-relations by a change in the economy of the subject, Joaquin reinscribes the unconscious (the patriarchal order of language and society) into the ethical and moral conflicts of his protagonists and in doing so inadvertently exposes the class determination of sexuality, law, property, state, and routine practices of everyday life.

The recuperation of the other Joaquin, then, is what this study seeks to accomplish in the present context of a profound, relentless politicization of meaning when language cannot help but disclose its complicity with forms of power and institutions of symbolic violence. To reiterate our cardinal premise: No one can begin from a blank slate. The innocent reader is a myth. Locked in a war of meanings and signs, the critic necessarily engages in all the manifestations of the class struggle in our society, inducing and provoking the crisis of the dominant codes and rules of communication by historicizing everything, especially the discourse of the liberal conscience which condemns difference, obscures contradiction, and trumpets its claim of possessing/owning the transcendental phallus of Unity.

In the same breath, I hasten to add that this critique valorizing the utopian moment in the texts takes cognizance of Joaquin's potential and actual usefulness to the reactionary elite and, as National Artist, to the overthrown Marcos dictatorship and its imperialist patron. The most egregious example of this unconscionable tribute of the artist to the Minotaur is the *Reportage on the Marcoses, 1964-1970* by Quijano de Manila, published by the government's National Media Production Center in 1979 (reprinted in 1981). The recent biographies of Benigno Aquino, Jr. and Salvador Laurel exhibit once again Joaquin's versatile mythopoeic virtuosity in the service of oligarchic interests. "People Power" has surely overtaken this exemplary apology for the Marcoses, perhaps reducing it to an antiquarian document and exemplum. But what insights can we gain from reflecting on it that may partly illustrate the methodology of this book?

Viewed from the perspective of socialist feminism, *Reportage* has clearly apotheosized the figure of Imelda Marcos, "Aphrodite as the Dolorosa," and obscured gender antagonisms within the reconciling fetish of the "New Filipina." Its exorbitant rhetoric, camouflaged by the skillful juxtaposition of self-validating quotes and Wagnerian-like arias, defies even the bounds of journalistic decorum. Viewed from the theology of liberation, *Reportage* privileges the paradigmatic role of the imperial (read: neocolonial) elite and relegates the poor to speechless spectators of a colossal drama of Roman patricians and their virtuous ladies transported to the tropics.

Compensating for art's impotence and subservience to wealth and official power, *Reportage* in effect demonstrates the triumph of the symbolic order based on the will of the patriarchs (Marcos and his tribal cohort) where the *quaestio quid juris*, the question of right, becomes simply a *quaestio quid facti*, a question of fact. What is right is what exists. But whose fact? For whom?

As the February "festival of the oppressed" has shown, the truth of what exists can be grasped only in the process of its historical supersession and overcoming. In *Dialectic of Nihilism* (1984), Gillian Rose points out how, in Heidegger's reading, the Greek figure of Dike changes its meaning as "justice" of "the way of the world" celebrated by the organic community of the polis to Dike as "goddess of Vengeance" in a new stage of social development where individuals separate, collide and violate "the way." In *Reportage*, Dike is the elite way: the welfare of the polis to which Joaquin ascribes priority in his other writings becomes reduced to the Event, or series of events (from May 1964 to March 1970) when Marcos, the *Fuhrer*, ascends to power. Everything else dates from those founding, inaugural events.

Ultimately, however, the Marcoses for Joaquin (or his mask) personify an artificial geography of interests which flattens out complex mutations in time into the archetypal antagonism between North and South. Joaquin's version of history is quite idiosyncratic and sectarian at the same time:

> In every history there has been this collision between North and South, with the languorous South too often suffering ravishment. The Spanish reconquista of the fifteenth century was actually a civil war between a Faustian North obsessed with nationalism and uniformity and a Magian South that favored a cosmopolitan outlook and a pluralistic society. The American civil war pitted an industrial North moving toward a machine society against an agrarian South that based its graces on a slave culture. In both Spain and the United States, the South was crushed, but survives as a ghost muse—a haunted, agonized, tragic land that produces great beauties, great poets, and those sad songs bewailing a way of life gone under, a civilization put to the torch. But from the ashes, like a phoenix, perpetually rises, in Southern womanhood, an image of beauty.
>
> In the Philippines, this civil war between North and South constitutes our politics. The entire period of our political development, from the 1900s to the Pacific War, is a history of the contest for power between the North, as represented by Quezon, and the South, as symbolized by Osmeña, with the North gaining the victory during the Commonwealth, a victory expressed most resoundingly in the imposition of Tagalog as the "national language" on the defeated South.
>
> This is the drama that Imelda Romualdez Marcos, in whom North and South refought their classic battle, so uncannily embodies, both in her person and in her personal history. The image of Imelda is an Image of the South. (p. 26)

If I may borrow the terms used by Jacques Attali in his *Noise: The Political Economy of Music* (1985), Joaquin's *Reportage*, as well as his other historical essays and journalistic pieces, may be compared to music as "a simulacrum of the ritual sacrifice," creating and affirming the possibility of social order. By channeling violence and the imaginary through a "ritualization of a murder substituted for the general violence," Joaquin's texts affirm that Philippine society is possible if "the imaginary of individuals is sublimated." In the quoted passage, the establishment and preservation of hierarchy is founded on the ritual sacrifice of the scapegoat, the South (Imelda) charged with danger and guilt, so that the whole text can then be read as a prayer to the North (Marcos) which monopolizes the castrating power of the father. With this spatialization of time (in the Imaginary orbit), *Reportage* thus promises and also enacts a reconciliation of North and South in a hierarchical polity, purging all conflicts and contradictions under a regime of martial law.

Apprehended dialectically, however, the text self-deconstructs in our reading. For instead of the sacrificial ritual centralizing the elements of the social field, we perceive what Attali calls the network of "representation" of the spectacle whose emblem here is Malacañang Palace; the conjugal rulers' exchange-value as spectacle (Imelda Marcos constructed here as paragon of beauty and taste) ushers in the reign of money, art-fetishism, and competitive capital metamorphosing later into crony racketeering. Repetition, individualized consumption of acts of charity by Imelda and sycophants, ensues. Sociality dissolves; reified surrogates, mediated through the mass media (of which Quijano de Manila is one instrument or channel), take over. *Reportage* now no longer copies or imitates its live models but instead reproduces simulacra and quotations; and, as postmodernist artifact, replicates them endlessly. We find the Marcoses conducting endless monologues, always justified and confirmed, the text becoming an analogue to a society controlled and manipulated by transnational corporations and the IMF-World Bank, guardians of the repetitive and recycled mass production of all social relations.

Like Minerva's owl bolting from chthonic depths and surveying the carnage in the battlefield after the four-day February insurrection, Joaquin seeks to cancel *Reportage* from the canon with *The Quartet of the Tiger Moon: Scenes from the People Power Apocalypse* (1986) published under his *alter nomen* "Quijano de Manila."

My initial response is that Quijano's performance is vintage Joaquin with all his ludic wit and carnivalesque gusto. Chinese ritual and astrology (the tiger icon for 1986 and the New Year Moon of February reminiscent of the lunar climax in *The Woman Who Had Two Navels*) are conflated with Christian myth to produce a classless society. The satire on the Marcos Empire powerfully delivers a Rabelaisean knockout blow, with the help of the Virgin Mary and *vox populi*.

In sum, Joaquin's discourse rhetorically constructs "the people"—Filipinos "in totality," not any hegemonic class or coalition of classes—as the agent of the EDSA upheaval, fruit of a *kapit-bisig* populist culture. But the photomontage, interviews, and focal personalitites all foreground the elite and petty bourgeois strata, with a sprinkling of plebeians. The floating or empty signifier is the ghost of Ninoy and other victims of the Marcos regime. Patrician fetishism of the household gods and goddesses (*lares* and *penates*) coalesces with folklore, citations from *Time*, quotes from "beautiful" souls, rumor, flashbacks, and prophecy. The semiotic strategy is the conventional novelistic articulation of background summary with scenic drama. Its implicit metaphysics posits an intrinsic quality characterizing Filipinos: "the regular, the everyday, the traditional" for the Filipino, Joaquin insists, is the revolt against tyranny (p. 106). Consequently, what is non-Filipino was the acquiescence to fascism, the subservience to the U.S.-Marcos dictatorship. This, to be sure, is the essentialist thesis of *The Quartet* which remains hypothetical and undemonstrated.

Ultimately Joaquin is compelled to invoke our native tradition of Jacobin insurrectionism to explain the February uprising. But he makes the tiger moon's cabalistic numen a banal commercial advertisement for a few privileged actors/actresses. We confront in his theatrical rendering of epic material the *aporia* of populist myth. What deconstructs this attempt of the moribund *ilustrado* elite to impose its hegemony on this transitional conjuncture of Philippine society is the unintentionally ironic juxtaposition of Chesterton and Belloc to the archheathen Wordsworth who, in his youth, extolled the Jacobin radicals of the French Revolution who guillotined the kingly representative of God on earth and overthrew the Church as the political bastion of hierarchy.

If Joaquin atones here for the excessive glorification of the First Family and the Marcos ethos in *Reportage*, it is only to replace them with the cult of the Makati aristocracy, their military and bureaucratic entourage, and the church of the *ancien régime*—not the ecclesia of Fathers Edicio de la Torre and Francisco Navarro. So then, the "morning after" groans with the malignant, insidious cancer of the past not yet completely purged from the body politic, a past the revolutionary hope of the future will permanently exorcise.

It is obviously not possible in this brief excursus into method to do justice to Joaquin's voluminous polemical and journalistic prose—an integral part of the canon still in the making, an artistic achievement in its own right that needs to be assayed in another appropriate conjuncture, when circumstances and needs warrant.

Suffice it for now to sum up the target and trajectory of this work. One can discern three dialectically interlocked approaches orienting this interpretation and appraisal of Joaquin's writing: a scientific one based on the principles of historical materialism refracted through Lukács, Gramsci and poststructuralist semiotics which tries to historicize the problematic of the artist's signifying practice and connect it, in one degree or another, to the overdetermining influences of the ideological, political and economic instances; a feminist one which insists on an apocalyptic responsibility of negating patriarchal tyranny in feudal and bourgeois cultures; and, finally, a prophetic or eschatological one which affirms Desire and calls for the restoration of difference and contradictions and their ultimate resolution in revolutionary transformation of social practices. We have thus brought to bear on a Filipino writer the entire apparatus of contemporary global theorizing, particularly the oppositional critique of humanist essentialism, now just beginning to be Filipinized and absorbed in the autochthonous tradition. Perhaps from this exchange and dialogue, quite the opposite of transnational profit-taking, may emerge a distinctly Filipino theoretical praxis organically fused with the concrete political and cultural projects now proceeding apace in city and countryside, analogous to the *kairos* or epiphanic rupture born from the labors of Rizal and his compatriots in Spain in the 1890s, their practical memory of the sacrifices and struggles of their people harnessed to convert space into time—the time of the 1896 Revolution against Spanish colonialism. With the closing of this century, a new opportunity arises for exiles like myself to contribute their share in this transitional period to the rebirth of the whole Filipino nation and its impending entrance into the arena of world history.

I want to record here my deep gratitude to the following *kasama*, friends and colleagues for their help in various ways while the book was in the process of composition: Delia D. Aguilar, Petronilo Bn. Daroy, Doreen G. Fernandez, Elmer and Elenita Ordoñez, Marra Pl. Lanot, Emmanuel T. Santos, Roger and Fe Mangahas, Nicanor G. Tiongson, Francisco and Ana Maria Nemenzo, Soledad S. Reyes, Joseph Lim, Delfin Tolentino, Jr.; and especially Esther Mendoza-Pacheco, director of the Ateneo de Manila University Press, for warmly encouraging me to complete the manuscript of this book. In particular, I want to thank Maria Luisa F. Torres for her painstaking editing of the manuscript.

ONLY THE MESSIAH HIMSELF consummates all history, in the sense that he alone redeems, completes, creates its relation to the Messianic. For this reason nothing historical can relate itself on its own account to anything Messianic. Therefore the Kingdom of God is not the telos *of the historical dynamic; it cannot be set as a goal. From the standpoint of history it is not the goal, but the end.*

Therefore the order of the profane cannot be built up on the idea of the Divine Kingdom, and therefore theocracy has no political but only a religious meaning. To have repudiated with utmost vehemence the political significance of theocracy is the cardinal merit of Bloch's Spirit of Utopia.

The order of the profane should be erected on the idea of happiness. The relation of this order to the Messianic is one of the essential teachings of the philosophy of history. It is the precondition of a mystical conception of history, containing a problem that can be represented figuratively. If one arrow points to the goal toward which the profane dynamic acts, and another marks the direction of Messianic intensity, then certainly the quest of free humanity for happiness runs counter to the Messianic direction; but just as a force can, through acting, increase another that is acting in the opposite direction, so the order of the profane assists, through being profane, the coming of the Messianic kingdom.

The profane, therefore, although not itself a category of this Kingdom, is a decisive category of its quietest approach. For in happiness all that is earthly seeks its downfall, and only in good fortune is its downfall destined to find it. Whereas, admittedly, the immediate Messianic intensity of the heart, of the inner man in isolation, passes through misfortune, as suffering. To the spiritual restitutio in integrum, *which introduces immortality, corresponds a worldly restitution that leads to the eternity of downfall, and the rhythm of this eternally transient worldly existence, transient in its totality, in its spatial but also in its temporal totality, the rhythm of Messianic nature, is happiness.*

For nature is Messianic by reason of its eternal and total passing away.

To strive after such passing, even for those stages of man that are nature, is the task of world politics, whose method must be called nihilism.

—Walter Benjamin
Schriften (1955)

1 Celebrating the Virgin and Her City

What, then, is revealed in the quarrel between Remus and Remulus is the way in which the city of man is divided against itself, whereas, in the case of Cain and Abel, what we see is the enmity between the two cities, the city of man and City of God.
— St. Augustine

Life should be changed because the state of the world will be changed.... We shall not be what we have been, but we shall begin to be other.
—Joachim of Floris

Justice cannot exist where all the best things in life are held by the worst citizens; nor can anyone be happy where property is limited to a few, since those few are always uneasy and many are utterly wretched.
—St. Thomas More

WRITING AT THE TURN OF THE CENTURY his now classic autobiography (*The Education of Henry Adams,* 1900) where the Philippines is a place from which he was, in a manner of speaking, "glad to escape," Henry Adams marvelled at the dynamo in the Paris Great Exposition of 1900 as a "moral force," a "symbol of infinity." In that incandescent metropolis, Adams "had studied Karl Marx and his doctrines of history with profound attention, yet he could not apply them," leaving him perplexed, "his historical neck broken by the sudden irruption of forces totally new." He reflects that in America the dynamo of the classical and medieval past—Venus and Virgin—neither "had value as force—at most as sentiment." The author of *Mont-Saint-Michel and Chartres* (1913) muses further:

The Woman had once been supreme; in France she still seemed potent, not merely as sentiment, but as a force. Why was she unknown in America? ...She was goddess because of her force; she was the animated dynamo; she was reproduction—the greatest and most mysterious of all energies . . . this energy was unknown to the American mind. ...

All the steam in the world could not, like the Virgin, build Chartres.... Symbol or energy, the Virgin had acted as the greatest force the Western world ever felt, and had drawn men's activities to herself more strongly than any other power, natural or supernatural, had ever done.[1]

Eighty-three years later, Adams' compatriot Harvey Cox, theologian at Harvard University, upholds anti-Virginal secularization as "the unappreciated offspring of the prophets, including the prophet of Nazareth, who railed against religiously sanctioned injustice with as much fervor as any anticleric."[2] But since times have changed, Cox appreciates more than other postmodernist thinkers the persistence of the female image of the divine in a culture such as Mexico where Our Lady of Guadalupe, the Christian version of the Aztec fertility goddess, Tonantzin, becomes the site of a raging battle between the Church hierarchy and the masses of the faithful. Popular and learned consensus testifies that the Nuestra Señora de Guadalupe, "La Vida," continues to radiate a dynamic force replicated in liberation theology and in the fiestas of popular religion in Latin America and the Third World at which Henry Adams would have marvelled today even as he becomes anxiously sensitized to the tremors of an impending nuclear apocalypse. Without in any way adducing direct influence or indirect acquaintance, Nick Joaquin uncannily offers an inverted, more precisely, dialectical refraction of Henry Adams' historicist schizophrenia.

On first reckoning, Joaquin's world view is polarized into two apparently divergent but ultimately complementary tendencies. First, the mythologizing and intrinsically aestheticizing tendency to reconcile opposites and to explain complex historical events by a metaphysical and idealizing schema whose most densely charged chronotopic figure is the Virgin of the Rosary enshrined at Sto. Domingo church. Practically the entire thematic and symbolic strategy in Joaquin's fiction and drama gravitates around, and is permeated by, the figure of the Virgin Mother. This is the realm of utopian extrapolation. Second, the crudely mechanistic and technological determinism that informs such discourses as "Culture as History," "History As Culture," "Technology: The Philippine Revolution," and numerous magazine articles. Of course, this is a synoptic view made up for exigent analytic purposes, ignoring the chronology and circumstantial matrices of each text. Logically, if the proposition expressing the first tendency means what it says, then we can characterize the organizing principle, the controlling vision, of Joaquin's art at its best as a postmodernist reaffirmation of utopian desire, taking the term "utopian" here to signify the collective social project of humanizing and naturalizing Henry Adams' dynamo by establishing its organic linkage with the feminine dimension of the psyche and cosmic life; and at its worst, an apologia—that is what the inaugural key text in the Joaquin canon, "La Naval de Manila," essentially is—for patriarchal institutions and hierarchic power.

I submit that "Nick Joaquin" as the authorial simulacrum generated by an ensemble of texts embodies the multiple historic contradictions of contemporary Philippine society, reproducing these contradictions, inflecting and conjugating them in highly idiosyncratic ways, modifying and altering them, in the same process that the class divisions and the multilayered mode of production—that is, the social relations of production in the total Philippine formation—powerfully shape and overdetermine the ideas, forms, conventions, metaphors, and language structured in the body of texts ascribed to "Nick Joaquin."

Contextualized thus, "Nick Joaquin" is both an aesthetic problem to be posed and analyzed, and equally an ethicopolitical problematic reflecting our own national predicaments, sufferings, traumas, struggles, dreams and aspirations: what Filipinos are, have been and will be, insofar as beauty and freedom—following Schiller's insight—share a common destiny and are inseparably linked in praxis.

From his first important essay "La Naval de Manila" written in October 1943 to the most recent dramatic piece *The Beatas* dated 1975 and *Cave and Shadows* published in 1984, the central figure of the Virgin (and mother-daughter combinations) deciphered as the symbolic condensation of the utopian and unconscious stands out with all its contradictory implications and resonance. In Christian mythology, as Alan Watts and Mircea Eliade point out, *Mater Virgo* signifies "the Prima Materia prior to its division, or ploughing, into the multiplicity of created things." As Stella Maris (Star of the sea; *mare* = Mary), the Sealed Fountain, "the immaculate womb of this divine font," she is the water over which the Spirit moved in the beginning of time.[3] She takes on the identities of the Axle-Tree of the World, with the serpent at its roots and bearing alike the fruits of death and life (see "The Legend of the Virgin's Jewel"); the Rose and the Lily, flowers symbolic of the receptive aspect of man's spiritual transformation; as the Chalice or Grail which receives Christ's lifeblood; as moon-goddess; as Space, "the Womb in which the Logos comes to birth"—a process captured by the breathless periodic and hypotactic syntax of Joaquin's style; and in the thick, embedded phrasing of the conclusion of "La Naval de Manila."

So the Virgin then stands for matter, elemental substance (*matria*, matrix, *mater*); maternal womb of the universe, chaos, abyss of dark and formless matter cognized as feminine in contrast to Spirit symbolized by air and fire cognized as masculine. The Virgin is the original womb of creation, analogous to Maya in Hinduism and Buddhism; that "no-thing" which, when divided by the Logos, becomes separate things.[4] The theme of the imagination acting on matter (the body, earth, water) ramifies also into the necessity of sacrifice so as to give birth to the new, with the new "fallen" creation redeemed in turn by a repetition of the sacrifice—history as cultural ritual ingeniously rendered in *A Portrait of the Artist as Filipino*, in the two novels, *The Beatas*, and elsewhere:

Thus it is prophesied of Mary, "A sword shall pierce through thy own soul also," since in all the great traditions creation is always through a sacrifice; the multiplicity of things is the One dis-membered and divided. By yet another sacrifice the One is re-membered—"Do this in re-membrance (*anamnesis*) of Me"—for the original Unity is restored when the sacrifice is repeated, because the repetition is a recollection of what was done "in the beginning."[5]

In that brief description of the myth by Alan Watts is secreted Joaquin's conception of history illustrated in all his writings. Sacrifice, dismemberment and mutilation of what is whole, denoting the power of the Word or Logos, is what leads to the primal Mother's emergence, thus subordinating her (by "the Child on one arm") to the masculine Creator. History consequently appears as a manifestation of male power.

What has happened in actual history is the suppression of this thoroughgoing materialism, so dangerously heretical to the imperial post-Constantinian faith, by the promulgation of the dogma of the Immaculate Conception of the Virgin (distinguished from Eve the sinner) since she is "the Servant of the lord," her Son. Simone de Beauvoir comments on this fateful reversal: "For the first time in human history the mother kneels before her son; she freely accepts her inferiority. This is the supreme masculine victory, consummated in the cult of the Virgin—it is the rehabilitation of woman through the accomplishment of her defeat."[6] That treacherous circle—a virtual overthrow of the primacy of the body, matter, production—is marked by Joaquin's ethical dualism in "La Naval" between matter (tribal custom and taboo entailing "dreaminess," "our incapacity for decisive thought or action") and consciousness, in this case the medieval Christian military fanaticism in subduing heretics, Calvin, Islam.

Founded on the assumption that the pre-Spanish aboriginal inhabitants of the archipelago had no "history" for the simple reason that they had not benefited from the saving impact of Christianity, deprived of "this awakening of the self, this release and expansion of the consciousness," Joaquin's thesis posits that Spanish colonial domination is responsible for our national identity: "The *content* of our national destiny is ours to create, but the basic *form,* the *temper,* the *physiognomy,* Spain has created for us."[7] Note, however, that not only the form but also the significance and content are supplied by the traditional paradigm epitomized here by the exemplary cult of patron saints. How is this tradition formed? By the commemoration of events such as the Battle of Lepanto in 1571 and the Spanish naval victory of 1646 against the Dutch, both epochal successes attributed to the intervention or intercession of the Virgin. A sleight-of-hand maneuvering occurs here when those two events are juxtaposed so that by spatial contamination and shift, the Queen of the Most Holy Rosary traverses chronological distance and geography to save the "tiny Rome growing up by the Pasig" from "Calvin's shadow." The content of Philippine destiny is predicated on the Spanish military victories to safeguard the colony from other European powers, sacrifices marked by feasts such as La Naval, "which is purely ours," says Joaquin. While the text argues that Spain imbued the Filipino nation with self-consciousness, a sense of history and autonomy, that consciousness depends on its sacrifice to a perpetual repetition of an originary, archetypal event:"There is indeed no Philippine town or village, however humble, that does not feel peculiarly *itself*, as *belonging* to that spot of ground and no other, because of some patronal cult traditional to the locality, some holy image there venerated and investing the site with legend and association."[8] This mode of spatializing reflections dictated by the submerged or suspended materialism of the Virgin cult refutes Joaquin's thesis: "If Lepanto was its last act, our colonial history may be termed as oriental epilogue to the miracle-place of the West." Here rears the head of rampant "Orientalism" (Edward Said's term) that dogmatically affirms Western primacy by subordinating/marginalizing the Other: where are the natives who are supposedly creating the content of their national destiny?[9]

In describing the Image, Joaquin states that she "is arrayed as a royal lady at the court of the Felipes" unlike the dark Virgin of Guadalupe; her majestic queenly bearing, however, conflicts with the subsequent detail: "the face is individualized, is warmly human, and was surely chiseled by the Chinese catechumen." Surrounding this image, by metonymic exfoliation, is a wealth of childhood memories rendered in sensuous imagery evoking communal solidarity so that, on closer analysis, it is not the ethicopolitical and ideological stakes—the war between heathen fate and Christian freedom—that haunts the text but time and death itself, the "despair" coincident with self-consciousness, that very same isolated free will that threatens to shatter the unity of time and space. And when we recall Joaquin's fear of the "blood's memories of the communal tribe-house" encroaching and predetermining all action, his fear of "those submerged longings for the tight, fixed web of the tribal obedience" as contrasted with "the pain and effort of responsible and personal existence," then we see how the ironic twist of textual labor unleashes the political unconscious and releases the repressed in those intensely remembered tribal feasts and celebrations of the two Navals as an evocation of childhood innocence devoid of the "pain and effort of responsible and personal existence," more poignantly visible in the ecstatic surrender of a self-possessed Cartesian rational ego to the tumultuous mind-blowing music of the procession and the fiery blaze of vision, the conscious discrete self dissolving utterly in that amorphous oneiric space on which is inscribed the Prima Materia undercut here at the last moment by the idealizing phallic will: "Oh, beautiful and radiant as an apparition! — the Presence at Lepanto, Lady and Queen and Mother of Manila, the Virgin of the Fifteen Mysteries."

That the text of "La Naval" and its technique of montage splicing metaphor, synecdoche and metonymy distorts the more fluid and plastic reality of the historical past, homogenizing the Dionysian *materia* in an Apollonian structure (to adapt Nietzsche's terminology), and ironically subverts its thesis of unveiling the truth, is now more familiar to a contemporary audience rehearsed in the deconstructive theoretical play of Derrida, Foucault and other poststructuralist critics. In *The New Science*, Vico suggests that "men are naturally impelled to preserve the memories of the laws and institutions that bind them in their societies."[10] Opposed to Nietzsche's nomadic impulse, however, is Vico's insight into history as shaped and reproduced by human actions, not by intervention of a sacred transcendental power; actions which are repeated, filiative and genealogical. Such repetition coalescing reason with raw experience provides the means whereby humans represent themselves, disclosing in the act an objective, supraindividual rationality: "Men mean to gratify their bestial lust and abandon their offspring, and they inaugurate the chastity of marriage from which the families arise. The fathers mean to exercise without restraint their paternal power over their clients, and they subject them to the civil powers from which the cities arise."[11] This historical-materialist purposiveness, the dialectic of consciousness and mode of production, may be said to animate the tensions in all of Joaquin's fiction and also situate the ironic discrepancy of form and intention I have briefly alluded to in "La Naval" in its roots: the actual lived contradictions of class, gender, race, etc.

Unfortunately it is not Vico's problematic of repetition and of mind as historical memory capable of infinite articulation and change that has instigated Joaquin's excursions into pop anthropology but the reductive technicism or scientistic determinism of Marshall McLuhan, abetted by the obscurantist fatalism of Oswald Spengler. And this is the hyperbolic irony of all, considering Joaquin's quite correct insistence in rejecting the notion of "timeless" essences and his positive though somewhat ambiguous emphasis on existential becoming, on a dynamic and creative view of cultural appropriation, on metamorphosis, in his treatise "Culture as History."

Although now changing the rhetorical tactic of "La Naval" into a more empirical and outwardly scientific recasting of the basic argument that the Spanish introduction of tools and the Faustian spirit (strange epiphenomenon of sixteenth and seventeenth baroque!) in 1521 and 1565 forged the "basic outlines" of Filipino identity, Joaquin's essay "Culture as History" reduces "culture" into tools and technological sophistication which, rearticulated via McLuhan as "communication," makes possible not only the Asianization of the Filipino but also his maturation as citizen of the modern world. The birth of the Filipino is categorically dated to 1565 after which "we can be nothing but Filipino," and by Filipino is meant adobo, pan de sal, ati-atihan, Moriones, tropical gothic and baroque—in other words, an aggregate total or accumulation of practices empirically observed in specific times and places.[12]

With this massive accumulation of media—the wheel, plough, road, etc.—Joaquin finally locates the "sense of history" in the mediating institution of craft guilds or communities of technicians and artisans sharing the same knowledge, skills; such craft mastery, he speculates, "may have contributed to the formation of a national consciousness." So it is this "sense of social solidarity" that Joaquin postulates as the mediating agency or vehicle of our unification as a nation composed of various regional and ethnic groupings, allowing him in a subsequent essay, "History as Culture," to rehash the now fallacious contention that it was the elite or educated middle strata (*ilustrados*) and their ilk, who were singlehandedly responsible for creating a distinctly Filipino culture—an embarrassingly naive chauvinism anathema to the multiethnic and multiracial nationalist movement today involving Igorots, Moros, atheists, naturalized Filipinos, and others.

What remains disguised in Joaquin's idiosyncratic program of rearguard apologetics for the Christianization of the native, notwithstanding appreciations of the heathen elements syncretized in folk festivals zestfully described in "The Santo Niño in Philippine History," "A Theory on the Sinulog," and especially in *Almanac for Manileños*, is the fundamental episteme or problematic which, as I have suggested above, is prefigured by the symbolic richness of the Virgin cult.

Confronted with the profound temporality and alienation of modern existence, Joaquin realizes that the devaluation of the Goddess—technical knowledge, Logos, cannot but be masculinist will—is temporary; her disappearance is explained by Orthodox doctrine as a falling asleep (*dormitio*) and by Roman Catholic teaching as the Assumption of Mary—her elevation to heaven, bypassing death. She has temporarily relocated in another space, temporarily exiled if you will, but engaged in frequent incursions, showing forth in unexpected sites, speaking and communicating. This Marian figure of space lays the groundwork for conceiving a modality of time which has been ascribed (by Julia Kristeva and others) to a specifically female subjectivity: "repetition" as experienced in gestations, natural cycles of recurrence; and "eternity" or monumental duration, cosmic temporality. The two modalities conjoined trigger a hallucinatory *jouissance* that drowns linear consecutive clock time. Kristeva notes how the Virgin incarnates and sanctions this experience of cosmic, mystical time which in essence can only be textualized in space: "One is reminded of the various myths of resurrection which, in all religious beliefs, perpetuate the vestige of an anterior or concomitant maternal cult, right up to its most recent elaboration. Christianity, in which the body of the Virgin Mother does not die but moves from one spatiality to another within the same time via dormition (according to the Orthodox faith) or via assumption (the Catholic faith)."[13]

One can elucidate the narrative and parabolic function of Nenita Coogan's body and her mysterious death vis-à-vis the epiphany of the earth-goddess and her avatars in *Cave and Shadows,* and the mother-daughter polarity in *The Woman Who Had Two Navels* in the light of Marian temporality characterized by the experience of time metamorphosing into space. In a note to "The Art of Ancient Egypt," Joaquin betrays this antinomic consciousness when he mistakenly equates Egyptian art's urge to deny mortality by equating "the will to endure" with "history."[14]

The most elaborate virtuoso performance of Joaquin's diacritical sensibility where a precapitalist epistemology of space and time operates to program the style and structure of the text is *Almanac for Manileños*. Using the calendar convention of amalgamating discordant facts and incompatible topics for utilitarian purpose, Joaquin superimposes a cross-referential analogical unity on a vast encyclopedic catalogue of material through the device of astrology. Immediately the empirical and the supernatural are yoked together in a metaphysical conceit reminiscent of baroque poetics, each planetary or astral sign lending intelligibility to the montage of otherwise discrepant, incongruous, trivial or indifferent data. Thus, for the month of January, the commentary opens with a headnote detailing the physiognomy of people born under the horoscope sign—such headnotes serving as a figured bass, or dominant chord, to the composition. Time is filled with a succession of information: iconography of Janus, the primitive rites of passage, the chimera as oxymoronic emblem, the event of the Japanese occupation in January 1941, descriptions of downtown Manila in the past, the feast of the Nazarene in Quiapo followed by the feasts of the Sto. Niño in Tondo and elsewhere, a meditation on the etymology of place-names, a note on the 1872 Cavite uprising tied with a fiesta for La Virgen del Carmen, and finally a retrospective lament on the decline of Bilibid Viejo. Take another example, the month of May which begins (after the astrological headnote) with an account of the Battle of Manila Bay in May 1898, followed by notes on May Day festivals in England, May fiestas in various city districts, a note on the emerald, the legend of the Santacruzan, the fall of Corregidor, followed by Bonifacio's execution, a description of Sta. Ana and then of Marikina, of Chinese Mandarins in Manila, and finally a description of indigenous Maytime rituals centering on the earth-goddess and the Virgin cornucopia, anatomy, Borges' Library, Joycean palimpsest—the *Almanac* codifies for Joaquin the semiotics and grammar of the quintessential Filipino experience.

Unlike its genre, this almanac suspends the utilitarian and fetishizes the simultaneous. Addressed specifically to Manileños, it intends to synthesize past and present happenings under the hegemonic sign of the city, a city vaporized into impressions, auras, fashions, clichés and personified by folk heroes and celebrities, a metropolis (no longer Intramuros but sprawling

Metro Manila) that Joaquin celebrates less as locus of events than as a figure of the conjunction of linear/chronological time and cosmic/repetitive time—a symbol then of what for him is a project addressed to the Other: the always deferred sacramental constitution of Filipino subjectivity.

But what is fascinatingly unique and symptomatic in the contrivance of this project is the experimental handling of the almanac as a religious calendar of festivities crossed with that typically modernist invention, the newspaper and illustrated weekly with their unrelenting, rigorous flattening out of everything—the petty, the accidental, the numinous—into exchangeable counters. But in Joaquin's almanac, old news is always new; and the recent never gets obsolete as it oscillates in the general circulation of the ephemeral and the cosmic, all the antipodes and contraries fused in the simultaneity of a frozen mosaic. This experience of reading the almanac, subtly effecting a decentering of the subject, corresponds to Joaquin's notion of the world citizen in "Culture as History": "Shouldn't we rather recognize that each person is a sort of unconscious anthology of all the epochs of man; and that he may at times be moving simultaneously among different epochs?"[15]

Now, the model of the unintentionally oxymoronic and levelling effect of the newspaper exercises its appeal for Joaquin because it is the unprecedented textualization of the modern city in the age of industrial capitalism, a textualization comparable with the polysemous and analogical texture of Christian art and philosophy but only insofar as it can be subsumed within an ideology already surpassed by the logic of the expanded reproduction of capital. Can the Virgin and the Dynamo be wedded together in fruitful coexistence, as Joaquin strives to do in the *Almanac* and elsewhere? Can the Faustian spirit (Goethe's symbol of the ruthless hustler of capitalist property-values) which Joaquin idolizes as the legacy of 1565 (another bizarre hybridization!) be joined as the loving consort of the Great Mother Goddess hymned in the entries for May and October in the *Almanac*?

Such questions Joaquin has probably answered when, at the end of his discourse "The Santo Niño in Philippine History," he apostrophizes the Holy Spirit as "the heavenly dynamo." One extraordinarily illuminating approach to this pervasive antinomic temper of Joaquin's art and thought, which I have tried to formulate elsewhere as the inescapable predicament of the organic intellectual of the backward-looking but fiercely independent Filipino petty bourgeois class crushed by U.S. monopoly business but horrified by the resurgent masses of workers and peasants, can be derived from the incisive distinctions between the classical/feudal matrices of time and space and those of industrial capitalism proposed by Nicos Poulantzas in *State, Power, Socialism*.

Poulantzas explains that the spatial matrices of ancient and feudal societies share common features stemming from precapitalist relations of production and the social division of labor: continuous, homogeneous, symmetrical, reversible and open.

Instead of differentiation and hierarchy, the geometric topographical orientation reproduced in the political organization of the polis allows slave and master to share the same space:

The points at which power is exercised are replicas of the sovereign's body. In fact, it is this body which unifies space and installs public man within private man: it is a body with no place and no frontiers. All roads lead to Rome in the sense that Rome is at every point of the sovereign's moving around.... [What is outside, the barbarians, belongs to a non-site or no-land.]

Both the towns and feudal demesnes or fiefs were open and turned out, through a number of epicentres, towards that umbilical centre, Jerusalem. As Marx pointed out, the relations of production were such that religion played the dominant role in feudal social formations; it was directly present in the forms of the exercise of power and it patterned space by setting the seal of Christianity upon it.... As in Antiquity, people do not change their position: between the fiefs, large villages and towns, on the one hand, and Jerusalem and its diverse earthly incarnations on the other, between the Fall and Salvation, there is no break, fissure or distance. Frontiers and such intermediary points of demarcation as walls, forests and deserts refer not to a distance that has to be crossed in order to pass from one segment to another (one town to another), but to crossroads of a single route. The pilgrim or crusader—which is what every traveller is after a fashion—does not actually go to the holy places and Jerusalem, because these are already inscribed in his body. (This is also the case with Islam.) The body-politic of each sovereign incarnates the unity of this space as the body of Christ-the-King, and space is marked out by the paths of the Lord.[16]

In contrast, the spatial matrix of capitalism produces "the serial, fractured, parcelled, cellular and irreversible space which is peculiar to the Taylorist division of labor on the factory assembly line." Thus a territory like the Philippine archipelago can only become national by means of, and in consonance with, the power of the capitalist State apparatus.

Following Poulantzas' characterization of these two opposed spatial matrices, we can see that underlying the textual strategies of Joaquin's fiction and drama is the organizing category of the medieval/feudal spatial matrix colliding or interpenetrating with that of the capitalist spatial matrix, an occurrence typical of the unevenly developed Philippine formation. To put it another way, the figure of the Virgin as the harmonizing principle of the city is made to reconcile what is reversible and homogeneous with the successive fracturings, gaps, breaks, closures, frontiers and segmentations of modern urban experience.

In a previous article, "From Intramuros to the Liberated City: Salvaging the Aesthetics of the Polis" (included in my book *Crisis in the Philippines*),

I attempted a sketchy mapping of Joaquin's use of the city as thematic content and organizing technique based on the binary rhetorical antithesis of metonymy and metaphor, the paradigmatic and synchronic. Let me offer supplementary qualifications here. In *The Women Who Had Two Navels*, the experience of the city is dispersed, symmetrical, reversible, ultimately equated with the polymorphous feminine. The situation of Paco Texeira, the object of the *agon* between the Vidal women and the outsider, exemplifies this production of space: "By the time he met the señora de Vidal he had become deeply interested in Manila and was ready to be interested in any woman who most piquantly suggested that combination of primitive mysticism and slick modernity which he felt to be the special temper of the city and its people" (p.27). Opposed to elevated Hong Kong, the "Jerusalem" of Aguinaldo's exile and the site of Connie Vidal's hallucinatory redemption (her virginal "assumption"), the city opens out to the countryside which it incorporates as overlapping utopian prefiguration: "the mountains, and the woman sleeping in a silence mighty with myth and mystery—for she was the ancient goddess of the land (said the people) sleeping out the thousand years bondage: but when at least she awoke, it would be a Golden Age again for the land: no more suffering; no more toil; no rich and no poor." What the novel superbly enacts is the fabled dialectics of Christian "free will" and politicogeographical determinisms in a surface where all movement unfolds with reversible directions, so that the spiritual impasse and psychological blockages dissolve when the old Monzon experiences a rapturous homecoming—he has not really moved his place or position because history is inscribed in his body—where the city and the Virgin (now indigenized) occupy the horizon and fulfills time: "Here he was, home at last. Behind him were the mountains and the Sleeping Woman in the sky, and before him, like smoky flames in the sunset, the whole beautiful beloved city" (p. 223).

In the postwar years when Joaquin conceived and wrote his first novel, the national territory had just been formally separated from the U.S. empire but the weakness or false autonomy of the State as well as the dependent nature of the comprador-landlord-bureaucratic ruling bloc did not promote deterritorialization: the separation of the direct producer from his means of labor (peasantry; petty commodity and artisanal production), the persistence of personalistic bonds and kinship/familial ties, archaic religious practices. These material conditions, coupled with the 1949 victory of the Chinese workers and peasants which serves as the terminus *ad quem* of the 1899 Filipino-American War (Battle of Tirad Pass, etc.), underpin the expressive-realist structuring of the novel and its nostalgic clinging to the voice of the authoritative narrator still anchored to a stable, mythical world view.

By the eighties, when Joaquin completes his second novel *Cave and Shadows*, the peripheral underdeveloped formation has entered a crisis in which the great urban insurrections called "First Quarter Storm" of 1970 serve as prelude to the liberation of the city by the solidarity of individual solitudes (the people) and a new reterritorialization. Authoritarian manipulation of space and time now mocks feudal practices and fosters the duplicities of transnational domination. In ideology and program, the fascist dispensation shows all the traits that Poulantzas attributes to modern totalitarianism: "separation and division in order to unify; parcelling out in order to structure; atomization in order to encompass; segmentation in order to totalize; closure in order to homogenize; and individualization in order to obliterate differences and otherness." [17] What is at stake are certain liberal institutions and Enlightenment principles justifying laissez-faire enterprise now grown obsolescent with the avid transnational drive of profit accumulation and made precarious with the internal competition among the developed nations and the intensified rivalry between the U.S.-led bloc and the "socialist" sphere in the era of late capitalism.

With the collapse of the traditional liaisons and fraternizing between outsiders and insiders (between Paco and the Monzons, between Macho and the Vidals, and the adversarial ethos they represent)—a mutation dramatized in "Candido's Apocalypse" and "The Order of Melkizedek"—the traditional categories and norms suffer a cataclysmic upheaval so that the conceptual coordinates of reversibility, homogeneity, symmetry, continuity and repetitiveness lose relevance. The ideals of national self-determination and the possibility of real historical change, and the question of who is going to articulate them, now occupy center stage in the struggle of class and sectoral forces, of the national-popular will against the moribund power bloc and imperialist hegemony.

In this light, *Cave and Shadows* may be read as a belated response to the crisis in its structuring of time shifts and the choice of a detective-mystery thriller convention, contraposing the temporal-spatial matrices of the ancient and medieval order to the capitalist transformation of psyches, lifestyles, criteria of values and tastes, and traditions. The symptoms of the city's displacement are clear with the deterritorialization of the major protagonists: Jack Henson resides in Davao and returns to it after his ordeal and pilgrimage, Alfonso Gatmaitan is mayor of a suburban town where the cave is found, the Manzano mansion "collapses" with the breakup of the clan. These comprise so many telltale signs that the capitalist temporal matrix consubstantial with its social division of labor and relations of production is overthrowing the archaic and feudal, a transitional moment in which the conflict between the Manzanos and Gatmaitans (representing distinct social classes or fractions thereof) may be read as representations of the former, and the mythical-historical archive projecting the goddess in her various manifestations (Nenita Coogan and the Ginoong Ina as *dei ex machina*?) serve as a poetic figure for the latter. In parts 2, 4, 6 and 8, time moves backward and forward in a reversible and continuous sequence, so that whatever privileged moments occur in those flashbacks are absorbed in eternity (Christianity) or chance (archaic societies). Governed by a concept of time as eternal recurrence, the unfolding chronicle of the legendary fertility goddess contains no events in the strict sense, and moves in a circular direction; the past is always reproduced in the present, the essence is manifested in the here and now: "The present is included in the origins, chronology remaining a repetition of the genesis, if not actually a genealogical transfer." One can say that this novelistic drive to trace the origin of a sequence or progression testifies to a scheme to wrest an original omniscience belonging to God.

Once again, Poulantzas offers us a heuristic anatomy of feudal ideology applicable to our critical analysis of Joaquin's literary mode of production:

> Over and above the dependence of temporalities on the "natural time" peculiar to essentially agrarian societies (seasons, work in the fields, and so on), what matters is the temporal matrix underlying the agricultural, artisan, military or clerical times, that appear as so many singular times. While each of these involves certain datings, the various chronologies are not ordered throughout times that are divisible into equal segments; and nor do the various moments have a numerical frame of reference. These chronologies refer instead to a continuous time which, placed under the aegis of religion, appears as a time of eternity punctuated by second meanings, acts of piety, and belfry-chimes inserted into the rhythm of the mass. Rooted in this temporal matrix, a linear materiality of time does, of course, come forth as distinct from the cyclical materiality of Antiquity: history now has a beginning and end, located between the creation and the Last Judgment. But it is still a present time: beginning and end, *before* and *after* are fully *co-present* in the constant essence of the Divine. Whether it is a question of immutable truth or of progressively revealed truth, and whether individual salvation is predetermined or not, all that is ever involved is a repetition or bringing-up-to-date of the origins. Here where the irreversibility of time is a mere illusion, to reach for the end is always to regain the beginning.[18]

Simultaneity of before and after, past and future distilled in the present, is what exactly characterizes the *Almanac*'s textualization of time and the city, the reversibility of scenes in "Guardia de Honor," "May Day Eve," "Three Generations," *A Portrait of the Artist as Filipino*; the knowledge or enigma that crystallizes in Jack Henson's mind as he tries to pursue the origin of his dilemma; the entrance/exit to the labyrinth where Nenita Coogan's body or its simulacrum lies entombed, etc. Finally, the present and future rejoin the mythical past when the renegade Christian and the pagan priestess reenact their roles through their "degraded" surrogates Pocholo Gatmaitan and Ginoong Ina in *Cave and Shadows*.

When the city in this second novel is eclipsed by the deterritorializing process in which the revivalist impulse and nationalist activism begin to challenge the centralizing function of the church itself and its rituals, Joaquin is compelled to draw on the Virgin figure and her chthonic energies (expressed in the popular religion surrounding Ginoong Ina) to counter the atomized, fracturing and reifying forces of bureaucratic capitalism and its differential, cumulative, irreversible temporality. This compensating mechanism seeks to enforce a conception of history as something not made but commemorated, the present as reconcretization of the past; history as recollection or unfolding of genealogies, the past spreading like an echo into the present while it unceasingly foreshadows that future which will meet up with the beginning in an endless circulation. There is no history for Joaquin in the sense of progressive evolution, an inherently bourgeois perspective. Likewise, as Poulantzas states, "pre-capitalist territories have no historicity of their own, since political time is the time of the prince-body, who is capable of extension, contraction, and movement in a continuous and homogeneous space." For the prince-body, substitute the Virgin Mother and the earth as fields of inscription, of textualization and hermeneutics for Joaquin.

It seems that to preserve and sustain the archaic and feudal matrices of time and space in a period, especially after the Second World War, when the classic function of the city as "the form and symbol of an integrated social relationship," as the historian Lewis Mumford explains; where "the mind takes form" has become eroded, Joaquin, in *Cave and Shadows*, felt the need to reconstruct the subject-positions for Filipinos that he had outlined in his previous writings and, in Jack Henson's decentered or "castrated" position, broach the possibility of recovering a primordial but now lost symbolic site of community and authentic existence. I believe that Joaquin is in general conducting a futile salvaging operation, a rearguard battle against the powerful forces of the consumer capitalist market and its "specular" Faustian individualism that he sometimes extols. These forces, according to Mumford, effectively destroyed the time-space episteme or frame of reference incarnate in the medieval city: "The Protestant doctrine of justification by Faith and the doctrine of Divine Election came in with credit finance and the rise of the self-perpetuating urban patriciate: the visibly elect, the manipulators of intangible values. . . . The validity of the universal Church was denied; the reality of the group was denied; only the individual counted on earth as in heaven: nominalism or social atomism."[19]

Assuming that historical mutation of urban function, the Manila of *Cave and Shadows* can be interpreted as the space where phallocentric will has driven the feminine underground, exiled the Virgin into myth or the archives, and now desperately tries to manipulate the tortuous course of events. But the narrative undermines that order, subverts the sequential, arrow-flight time of the plot and the ratiocinative detective-knower, and eventually opens the masculinist logic of the proairetic code to the pressure of feminine modalities: repetition, cyclic rhythms, recurrence, cosmic sense of unboundedness, the vertigo of hallucination, dreams, rage and the shock of terror unleashing *jouissance*. Think, for instance, of the disorienting textual "madness" and dislocating carnival excess found in the description of Connie Vidal's car accident in chapter 4 of *The Woman Who Had Two Navels* (pp. 183-84), or the freakish weather and the fury of the elements in *Cave and Shadows*. The repressed returns avenging . . .

Caught in roughly the same inexorable antagonisms between the secularizing traffic of business and the archaic structures in our psyches, Charles Baudelaire, regarded by all as the greatest lyric poet of urban modernism, acutely grasped the desanctification process in the "moving chaos" of everyday life in the city. His response of cosmic irony (in *Paris Spleen,* for example), however, does not validate orthodox piety or a fashionable bohemian aestheticism. As Marshall Berman and others have demonstrated, Baudelaire perceived the possibility of heroism and discovery of pleasure in the modernization of public urban space, delineating primal scenes of poetic vision amid dangerous traffic whence works of art characterized by the modernist style of "undulations of reverie, the leaps and jolts of consciousness" are born.[20] Baudelaire's counterpastoral modernism, unlike Joaquin's, embraces the city as a locus of contradictions bereft of myths, into which the poet hurls himself to be renewed by its anarchic energies, by the sudden leaps and swerves of life in its labyrinth of kaleidoscopic streets and boulevards.

This is not to deny that Joaquin also exhibits a profound Baudelairean fascination for the city, for its mixture of beauty and despair, terror and ecstasy; but his interest focuses not on its perpetual novelty—the endless metamorphosis of market values in a commodity economy—but on what is repeated, reversible, continuous and symmetrical. The so-called baroque texture of Joaquin's language results from the deep inner contradiction in his art between the "Faustian" (a term misapplied to acts of free will) hero and the Virgin, between archaic-medieval and bourgeois orientations. While the closures of the earlier texts show a bias for a traditional orientation (first announced in "La Naval," "Popcorn and Gas Light" and reworked in recent anthropological excursions), I would stress that the resolutions in "The Order of Melkizedek" and *Cave and Shadows* betray an uneasy, troubled, bifurcated sensibility. Could it be that this mythopoeic almanac-maker has been affected by that exuberant outburst of the Filipino people in 1970 reclaiming the streets of "the ever loyal and noble city," an explosion that evokes scenes of the "festival" of the oppressed: the Paris Commune 1871, Petersburg 1917, Barcelona 1936, Paris 1968, and so on? This "festival" of the subalterns, the denizens on the edges and margins, the underclasses, erupted in Philippine history only once for Joaquin: in the 1896 revolution and the subsequent war against U.S. imperialist aggression. But in *Cave and*

Shadows, for the first time, the people-as-nation surfaces through the cracks and fissures of mythical and Establishment reality, a multitude of urban-rural solitudes that seem to presage a long-awaited regenerating apocalypse. In approximating Baudelaire's allegorical vision of "the heroism of modern life" in his essays and fiction, Joaquin assumes at last a genuinely prophetic stance which can be and ought to be integrated into a libertarian, ecumenical cultural politics. On the other hand, I think it remains a debatable issue whether or not Joaquin's exaltation of the Virgin's aura ("aura" connoting utopian plenitude and wholeness) can justly be appreciated only as a form of commemoration which Walter Benjamin defines as "the secularized version of the adoration of holy relics.... In commemoration there finds expression the increasing alienation of human beings, who take inventories of their past as of lifeless merchandise.... Relics come from the corpse, commemoration from the dead occurrences of the past which are euphemistically known as experience."[21] The succeeding chapters hope to contribute to a more dialectical analysis and interpretation of Joaquin's mimesis of that aura and commemoration in his short stories, poetry, plays and two novels.

2 Strategies of Compromising Truth and Power

"Three Generations"

OCCUPYING AN UNDENIABLE PRIDE OF PLACE as the first story in Joaquin's first collection *Prose and Poems* (1963), "Three Generations" disappears in the later and most recent compilation *Tropical Gothic* (1977). Whether this symptomatic but telling erasure or omission implies a revision of the canon or a subtle but obtrusive signal to recast and overhaul our orthodox judgments of Joaquin's putative traditionalism is a problem which this critique will hopefully engage in the larger process of formulating the specific problematic of Joaquin's art. This problematic inheres not so much in a set of thematic raw materials or a repertoire of narrative techniques as formalistically conceived by previous commentaries, but, as I have proposed in the introduction, in the production process whereby the text works on ideologically invested raw materials and generates a specifically aesthetic effect capable of being defined by sociohistorical coordinates and understood ultimately as political interventions in reality. What I aim to focus on is the production of the text, identifying it as a dialectic of content and form grasped here in terms quite different from the usual New Critical or neo-Aristotelian perspective.

We may begin this investigation by using "Three Generations," the story that marks the gap in the later collection, as a provisional model of how Joaquin's texts function as value-charged fabrications, something midway between a scientific knowledge of reality and ideological illusion— "false consciousness," as true indices of class position in life. Instead of a thematic interpretation or an *explication du texte*, we shall offer here a symptomatic reading or analysis of how literary production occurs in Joaquin's *oeuvre*.

In "Three Generations," Joaquin confronts the timely and urgent crisis of patriarchal authority, a crisis engendered by the erosion and collapse of the Roman Catholic Church as the hegemonic institution in feudal society after the 1896 revolution, the Filipino-American War (1899-1902), and the peculiarly syncretic but methodical establishment of capitalist economic institutions and bourgeois ideological apparatuses under American military and civil administrations since 1900. This demise of the Church is of course not explicitly referred to in the story, but it is significantly alluded to in the elder Monzon's acquiescence to his son's decision to "study for the priesthood," disrupting his pursuit of a legal profession. For the father, priesthood is like any other secular or worldly profession like law (it is unclear what the father's occupation is), hence no conflict arises here between the elder Monzon and his son. In fact, the elder Monzon confesses to his son, in one of those enigmatic moments of intimacy between these two exemplars of the generations/epochs, that he had wanted to share with his son "the experience of a vocation," whereby the sign of independence and maturity (somewhat qualified because it is the mother's want which presides in his choice) is elevated to the level of "vocation," a calling which defines a person's life and destiny—not just a job dictated by one's class position, by one's status as owner or nonowner of the means of production. The elder Monzon's world-outlook has been thoroughly secularized, it seems, by the impact of U.S. colonial rule and its ideological-political domination.

What challenges the supremacy of the father here, and with it the continued ascendancy of a male chauvinist standard of values in the extended family (a phenomenon also undermined by the commodity-oriented logic of dependent or semifeudal capitalism), is the pleasure principle, the will to carnal gratification, embodied by Monzon's father, Chitong's grandfather. Monzon's wife, Doña Sofia, poses the question in the opening scene: "Why will you not let him have his woman again, Celo? He does not have very long to live." What the text initially sets out to program—if we may use this term—is the conflict between two patriarchal wills: the secularized tendency to orderly irreversible transition acted out by Monzon, and what we might call the irrational will-to-power of the primordial father whose authority, imaged by the physical violence inflicted on his son and his women in a time when the father (as head of the household commanded property and status) is now undermined by time, by physical debility, primarily by loss of property: the clan dwelling, once "tremendous and eternal" in Monzon's eyes, had rotting foundations, leaking roofs, and disintegrating structure. Who will win in the end? This is the anecdotal temptation, the melodramatic lure which Joaquin insinuates as the naive reader follows the plot as bare skeleton of events.

By simply turning the pages, we can arrive at the solution to the crisis and the dilemma: the grandfather, through the grandson's intervention, enjoys his woman again—a trick or legerdemain of repetition. But that's surely a ploy, a false ending distracting us from the crucial confrontation between the father and son, two generations interlocked with the generation of the inaugurating patriarch, the feudal past. Monzon's physical violence fails to affirm the prohibition: the son violates the taboo and performs a dialectical overturning of the ethical dualism—good (spirit) versus evil (flesh)—and converts Monzon's violence into a symbolic epiphany.

We can argue this allegorizing translation of the story's meaning by suggesting that what Joaquin is demonstrating here is the superior metaphysics of Chitong: the reconciliation of matter and spirit, soul and body. Chitong confesses earlier to his father the motivation behind his "sudden conversion": To his father's query, "It was through the appeal of beautiful things that you found God?" he replies: "With the senses, yes. Certainly not with the mind; I am no thinker. Nor yet with the heart: I am not a saint. I guess that's why it took me so long to realize where I was heading." This neo-Platonic tradition of thought, developed further in the medieval speculations of St. Bernard and the mystics, allows physiological ecstasy a place in the trajectory of self-abnegating exercises. We discover this mystical participation of the spirit in the flesh/world antinomy, a recurrent thematic motif in all of Joaquin's writings. But that is not the fruit of textual production; that is one of the conceptual instruments used to explain why supposedly the boy Chitong feels strongly attracted to the grandfather and thus allows him his indulgence—indulgence not really of the flesh but of the will.

What escapes this traditional thematic and allegorizing analysis is precisely how the text works on these materials: Chitong's notion of spiritual purification through the senses, Monzon's emotional bitterness and jealousy toward his son, his ideas of morality, etc. And, above all, the paradox that in this dramatic clash between wills, between opposed notions of spirituality (medieval versus petty bourgeois), it is the maternal principle, the figure of the woman as incarnation of Desire, which supervenes as the real or authentic project of the text.

Appropriating the legacy of modernistic psychologizing narratives (Joyce, Faulkner, D.H. Lawrence), Joaquin seeks to elucidate the crisis of a whole socioeconomic formation by concentrating on the internal disintegration of the will (particularly the contemporary father's) in a colonial society and its redemption by, first, the catharsis of self-knowledge and, second, by a species of liberal tolerance or resignation to the "weakness of the flesh." Modulating the omniscient to a limited, third-person point of view, Joaquin deflects our attention from the overarching superstructures of class and ideology and directs it to contemplate, nay, eavesdrop at the labyrinthine vertigoes of inwardness within Monzon primarily, and his son secondarily.

By a psychologizing narrative mode, I mean to indicate that Joaquin diagnoses the conflicts and tensions of a historically determinate formation in terms of agonistic vicissitudes of consciousness. This, of course, is a reductionist strategy inherent in metaphysical thinking. But in spite of this, and chiefly because of it, the text succeeds in illuminating vividly the limited impact of capitalist rationalism and its capacity to accommodate feudal survivals in a peculiarly overdetermined synthesis. Let us chart the staging of the internal drama in Monzon with his aborted attempt to communicate with his son in the Dominican church. Unable to pray, he is overwhelmed by "a sharp, hot, rushing, jealous bitterness towards that devout young man praying so earnestly"—his son who, ironically, has not found that earnest peace from utter submission to God so profoundly envied by his father. He then recalls his past, trying to discover in it the roots of his anguish:

> His own youth had been very unhappy, yes; but whose fault was it that he had suffered so much? The old man had really been no more heavy of hand and temper than most fathers of that time. He knew that. Those times gave to the head of a family absolute dominion over his women and children. He could not remember that any of his brothers had found the system particularly oppressive. They bowed to the paternal whip as long as they had to; then broke away to marry and breed and establish families over whom they had in turn set themselves up as lords almighty. (p. 5)

"Those times" possessed specific mores and customs which justified the patriarchal excesses, Monzon reflects, neutralizing even his sympathy for his exhausted, oppressed mother whose spiritualizing force has penetrated and seized him to the point of generating that internal psychic division tearing him apart:

> She had singled him out from among all her sons to bear and fulfill her few childish dreams and ambitions; and in her last, long, lingering illness, this faith in him had shone in her eyes and trembled in her hands whenever he came near her, and it had frightened and terrified him. For, even then, he was beginning to realize that, though he might set himself against all those things for which his father stood as symbol, he himself, would never quite completely escape them. Go where he might, he would still be carrying the old man's flesh along; and that flesh smoldered darkly with fires that all a lifetime was too short to quench. (pp. 5-6)

Note that the power of the flesh is reaching us through thought, through the articulations of consciousness that also serve as the mediating agency of repression: the ban against concubinage, the upholding of monogamy in the evolving nuclear family. The same voice of "conscience" warns Monzon if he submits to the temptations of the flesh: "You would be as miserable in your surrender to your body as you have been in your struggle against it. Besides, it is too late." Thus, burdened by the legacy of feudal patriarchy but deprived of its material underpinnings, Monzon lives a perpetual struggle as he maintains his social status as authority-laden father in a time demanding puritanical restraints.

Ironically, it is a lack of this persisting agony, this inward turmoil, which paralyzes the father that the son Chitong bewails. He confesses to his mother that he needs a formidable and dangerous antagonist so that his love of God could be tested and proved. Misinterpreting his father's motives, in fact misrecognizing the father's familial role, the son bewails his cowardice and attributes to the father— "He knows everything"—an all-knowing power which points to the fatal rupture of clan unity in which socioeconomic upheavals are unequivocally registered.

Before the final scenes where the three generations converge in the Monzon house, the narrative tries to establish a momentary community of minds between father and son, an attempt to heal the split which Joaquin wants us to think is an outcome of moral/spiritual struggles but which the text itself shows as the cumulative effect of a whole social system whose evolution through internal contradictions impacts on father-mother-children relationships. What the dialogue in the car shows is the last chance for solidarity between men, between father and son, as a secret—the failed vocation of priesthood for Monzon inscribed by the maternal impulse—is shared between them:

For a moment, the wall that stood always between them disappeared, and they could touch each other. I am an unclean man, the elder Monzon was thinking, but what was depravity in me and my fathers becomes, in my son, a way to God.

And the young man thought: I am something, after all, I am this old man's desire that he has fleshed alive. It sprang from him, began in him; that which now I will myself to be. (p. 8)

Ironies multiply even as resolutions seem to be magically conjured by each character. Opposites collide, depravity metamorphosing into sacramental will and thus setting the stage whereby we understand that Monzon's striking his son is nothing but a confirmation of those thoughts. In any case, thought wins in the end.

Such a conclusion seems premature. For what the narrative insinuates over and beyond the authorial commentary and interior monologues is the pervasive and ineluctable presence of a primal narcissistic drive that conceals itself behind discrete egos. Note the ambience of the car scene where father and son, in the twilight fragrance exuded by rain and earth, behave like "lovers." But this narcissistic self-gratification yields to its opposite, self-annihilation, as Chitong faces the old man:

But Chitong came forward and kissed the old man on the brow. The boy felt himself fascinated by those intensely hating eyes. He, also, was rather afraid of this old man; but with a difference. Even as a boy, he had felt the force of those eyes, lips, hands; but his grandfather had still been, then, in the plenitude of strength. But now, when he lay helpless, his legs paralyzed, the flesh gone loose about the bones, the face grown pale and shriveled, did he communicate all the more unbearably that pride, that exaltation in simple brute power.

The boy felt himself becoming a single wave of obedience towards the old man. His lips lingered upon that moist brow as though they would drink in the old man's very brains. The feel of the wet flesh was an almost sensual delight, something new and terrifying to him and, at the same time, painful; almost as if the kiss were also a kind of death. It was a multitudinous moment for the boy. When he straightened up he found himself trembling. And at the same time, he wanted to run away—to some quiet corner, to pray. (p. 10)

Sensual delight, pain, terror, panic, loss of consciousness: all these sensations and feelings coalesce in Chitong, cancelling any distinct privative ego and compelling him to prayer. The will to self-dissolution, paradoxically, surfaces here and is confirmed in Chitong's thought of Tía Nena, the patriarch's daughter: "She was in his power; and like himself, Chitong thought bitterly, she was the kind for whom life is possible only in the immolation of self to something mightier outside it." This "something mightier" is not actually the grandfather nor his father's authority, but Chitong's impulse to finally make a decision to counter his father's will, a decision which signals his release: "It was the first time in his life he had made a decision. He felt released." Independence and maturity are wrested in defiance of the father, so Joaquin seems to indicate here, in the form of the son's exercise of the will to choose.

But the content of that decision precipitates the exposure of the mystical rationale, the notion of the senses as agency for spiritual enlightenment, as the rockbottom ideological grounding for filiative patriarchy. The central irony is that the son's gesture of liberating himself from the superegoistic shadow of the father, a formalistic morality maintained in appearance only, coincides with the victory of the patriarch's desire and the body's impotence. To be free, the present must vindicate the past, its ineluctable origin.

And so, when we arrive at the confrontation scene between father and son, we know that behind the self-righteous efforts of Monzon to regulate the household allocation of pains and pleasures, it is the pleasure drive that sabotages his pretense at a utilitarian/bourgeois morality which earlier has already assigned to "depravity" a positive role. We cannot but remark on the flabby and unconvincing rationalization or explanation behind the instant self-knowledge foisted upon us by the narrator:

Monzon, horrified, heard the boy's cry through every inch of his body. He had never before laid hands on the boy. The impulse to strike had come so suddenly, he tortured his mind for an explanation. He had not wanted to hurt the boy, no. He had, the moment before, desired the girl evil, but it was not she, either, who had prompted his fist. Was it the old man, then? Was it his father he had struck?

No. No, it was himself: that self of his, inherited, long fought, which had, the moment before, looked on the girl with strange fury. It was that self of his, which perpetuated the old man, against whom he had lifted his fist, but it was his son who had received the blow—and the blow was a confession of his whole life. (p. 15)

What is it that the self knows? That desire cannot be repressed for long? That the pleasure drive can infiltrate the most unlikely agent and accomplish its devious wish? That repression of the physical can wreak havoc on the Symbolic order, delivering the father's sin to the son? What is clear at this juncture is that both males represent the same thing: the ego's claim to adjudicate over what is wrong and right, what is sinful and what is not. But the text exhibits the contingency of this claim, its futility as rational consciousness or thought, precisely because it is asserted at the expense of the Other: the woman as wife, mother, daughter, concubine, lover.

To discern the way the narrative distances Joaquin's obscurantist metaphysic of self-illumination and enables us to apprehend its limitations, it is necessary to shift our attention away from the plotted events and focus on the margins. Exactly how are women depicted through and beyond the consciousness of the male characters?

Male supremacist thinking of course characterizes the reading of women in this narrative, particularly the notion that girls become women only in the arms of their lovers, that they find fulfillment in the sexual pleasure afforded them by men. Yet this thinking, for all its patent ideological and apologetic function, fails to entirely suppress the woman's differential presence. Note Monzon's balking at his wife's recalcitrance:

For all the years they had lived together, he was still startled by a certain nakedness in his wife's mind; in the mind of all women, for that matter. You took them for what they appeared: shy, reticent, bred by nuns, but after marriage, though they continued to look demure, there was always in their attitude toward sex, an amused irony, even a deliberate coarseness; such as he could never allow himself, even in his own mind or with other men. (p. 4)

The "amused irony" seems like a tolerance of the fact that men have called the shots in the world, that their legal ownership of property has extended to the female body and female labor power, etc. On the other hand, it is a subtler hint that men's dominance hinges on the women's continuing to allow or tolerate such inequality. Doña Sofia is seen again, from this same chauvinist perspective, when she enfolds her son: "She stooped and gathered him to her breast. She was terribly frightened. She was suddenly only a woman. Men were entirely different and alien creatures. Yes, even this one, whom she had borne in her own body. This one, also." Only a woman? Men as alien creatures?

There are two instances in the text which undercut severely the evasive and reductive thrust of the last quotation and which will substantiate my thesis that "Three Generations," instead of being on the surface a representation of intergenerational war, dramatizes within the clan the male chauvinist revolt against the female, specifically the sexual identity of woman as mother and lover, which indeed constitutes the symptom of the crisis of the patriarchal dispensation. The first occurs in Monzon's evocation of his parents in the church:

> Monzon had wept as a boy for his mother; but later on he had found out that she was only too thankful, worn out as she was with toil and child-bearing, for the company and assistance of these other women. If she fought the old man at all, it was in defense of her children, and especially of himself (for she had been quick to notice that he would not be so easy to break).
>
> She had singled him out from among all her sons to bear and fulfill her few childish dreams and ambitions; and in her last, long, lingering illness, this faith in him had shone in her eyes and trembled in her hands whenever he came near her, and it had frightened and terrified him. (pp. 5-6)

What stands out here, through the father/male's sensibility, is the mother's fortitude and endurance, the solidarity among women workers or producers, and their nurturing/reproductive function (the reproduction of the social totality). With the father effaced, it is the mother's libidinal investment in the son which transcends the oedipal barrier, guaranteeing and preserving that inwardness which insures the communication between father and son in the car scene, and purges the father's wrath against the concubine.

The second instance manifesting the resistance of the woman against sexist *diktat* occurs at the sala when Monzon returns frustrated:

> When he saw the girl, he flushed darkly and he felt again the multitude of pins pricking his flesh. He dropped his eyes at once, but the girl's image persisted before him: the fierce eyes, the small, round mouth, the long, thin, girlish neck. She had drawn her shawl away and he had seen where her breasts began and how they rose and fell with her breath.
>
> He had a sudden delirious craving to unloose his belt and whip her again, to make her suffer, to tear her flesh into shreds, to mutilate that supple, defiant, sweet, animal body of hers. His hands shook and his desire became an anger towards his son who had brought this voluptuous being so near. (pp. 14-15)

The girl's presence evokes his childhood awe and fear, but more insistently his ambivalence, his intimate identification with brute male power and its sheer inability to control the woman (the sexual drive) through the bonds of the monogamous family—although for Chitong, the wrathful but impotent father becomes a figure of the Old Testament lawgiver. In that oscillation between desire and anger lies the clue to the fatalistic resignation of Monzon to his self-perpetuation of the founding father: his subsistence in the imaginary realm (Lacan), the self-enclosed world in which objects obey the phantasmal urges of the unbounded infantile ego.

I do not mean to suggest that Monzon has degenerated into an infant whose imperial narcissism transforms his son into a mirror-image of himself, and himself as the latest embodiment of his father—a gratuitous repetition. What the text unfolds is the tremendous castrating power of the grandfather, whose physical deterioration cannot prevent his lawgiver's image from exercising its hold on Monzon and his son. When Chitong refuses to heed his father's law, that is, thwarts his castrating dictate, he enables the grandfather to act through him and subverts the father's authority, his puritanical resolution to demarcate the boundaries of pleasure in accord with social decorum. But here the grandfather symbolizes no longer masculine potency but the fragility of the flesh and the woman's (Desire's) conquest of the body. Listen to the voice of celebration: "No," she was saying, "I shall never leave you again. I am not going away again. No one shall take me away from you again."

The quest for spiritual unity in both father and son announced at the beginning of the narrative can either lead to death (the grandfather's future) or to absolute surrender to God (Chitong's yielding to his father's violence, the grandfather's tormented cries). Both possibilities hide what is foregrounded in our analysis, namely, the mother/lover—the role of wife is annulled because of its subordinate status—and the woman's presence occluded here by the authorial commentary but brought to light by this deconstructive reading. And what the figure of woman symbolizes here is the negation of patriarchal will, rationalizing thought which neutralizes the body, and the affirmation of Desire evinced in the materiality of the flesh, food, language, work, childbearing, social practice in general. For if Monzon "perpetuated" his father's will, not his mother's wish, why would he refuse to satisfy his father's need? In fact, it is the Mother's "faith in" Monzon which explains the punishment inflicted on the patriarch, even though Monzon deludes himself into imagining that his "carrying the old man's flesh along" pushes him to doubt and vacillation. On the contrary, it is his unadmitted and unconscious denial of the flesh which makes him an accomplice of his father's will to power. And it is paradoxically his son's yielding to the woman (not the grandfather) which earns him release from self-division and induces Monzon's misleading epiphany of himself as the old man's incarnation. If we separate the grandfather's will as the insignia of male supremacy from his desire for pleasure, then we can propose that Monzon signifies the surrender of this will to his son who stands here for the cancellation of that will in the name of need. And the collective or generic name of this need, in this context, happens to be Woman: Mother/Lover.

When Joaquin rendered "Three Generations" (written, we conjecture, before the Second World War, perhaps in the early forties) into dramatic form, most of the authorial commentary and practically all of the articulated thoughts in Monzon's head were distributed to the wife Sofia, the son Chitong, and also to Nena. *Fathers and Sons,* subtitled "A Melodrama in Three Reels," written in September-October 1975, strikingly diverges from the story on several counts, chiefly: the fuller visual/acting illustration of the grandfather Zacarias Monzon whose socioeconomic background as peasant-turned-carretela king is translated into words and gestures; the potrayal of the concubine as updated a-go-go dancer Bessie with her gospel of love (versus sex); and the rehabilitation of Chitong as a born-again messenger/avatar of what now constitutes the informing principle of the play: everyman's vocation of charity.

It is this last element, Chitong's sudden acquisition of the insight that charity should determine will, that drives home the imperative of tolerance. Chitong's peremptory tone is suspiciously the playwright's own anxious didacticism exceeding the bounds of character:

Father, will you hear me? I just want to point out one thing. Father, *listen* to me! Character is not something we inherit. It is something we create. If we cannot blame our fathers for what we are, neither should we blame ourselves for that new person. Oh yes, there are fathers and grandfathers and who knows what ancestors crowding within us—but all of them are just *ghosts,* Father—impotent, powerless ghosts, unless we *allow* them to create us in their image. That was a primitive age that said the sins of the fathers would be visited on the children unto the third and fourth generations. Charity began when God said...when God himself said: "no more shall anyone say that, because the fathers ate sour grapes, the children's teeth are set on edge." (pp. 148-49).

From this validation of will conditioned by charity, Chitong goes on to redeem the sinfulness of the flesh, thus valorizing the existence of prostitutes as a necessary function (Bessie assents to this when she agrees with the Joaquinian vision of femininity as donated by men and that femininity's destiny to assuage masculine distress: "And now I know my job") for individual redemption:

And if the soul is provided with sustenance for its last journey, why not the body as well? This poor body that has served us so faithfully: when the time comes to dismiss and discard it ... when it has to go out into the cold and the dark ... alone and afraid ... how can we deny it its own pitiful viaticum: a last communion of the flesh?

By so moving the thematic gravity of the narrative from Monzon's divided consciousness (his existential dilemma in the play is subdued, made somewhat comic because completely externalized, depriving him of that echoing chamber of the interior monologue) to the family encounter, we find Chitong, and especially the wife Sofia and the unmarried Nena, attract the tensions and pressures formerly gravitating around the Monzon father-son polarity. This is the outcome of the theater's material practice exorcising the "ghost" of narratological conscience and attributing ideas and values to speaking performers/bodies.

Instead of interpreting and assessing the structure of *Fathers and Sons* as a theatrical event—I concentrate on Joaquin's dramaturgy in another chapter zeroing in on *A Portrait of the Artist as Filipino* and *The Beatas* from a semiotic angle, a superfluous task since the thematic problems are basically those treated in the remarks made above—I would like to point to the ingenious but telltale introduction of the "long, long, long table" which, according to Zacarias Monzon, his son considers as emblematic of his greed for food, power, and women. Ambiguously coinciding with the audience and thus implicating the public/conventional standards of the mid-seventies where bureaucratic-military corruption has exacerbated the rampant, barbaric iniquities endemic throughout, the long table is ordered destroyed by the son. Monzon deliberately identifies the table with the Philippine dependent formation from the Commonwealth administration of Quezon and Osmeña to the present, characterized by intensifying class divisions between peasants and landlords, capitalists and workers.

It may be that since Monzon now represents the petty bourgeois stratum, more strictly, that stratum which has uneasily allied itself with the compradòr capitalists and landlords of Forbes Park, he is hostile to the fact of hierarchy and monopoly itself. This much is evident from his expressed decision that the table be scrapped so that "nobody else must ever sit again at the head of this table." On the other hand, it may be simply a rejection of the tribal/patriarchal/feudal order for an arrangement where juridical and formal equality in a constitutional framework can harmonize class and gender rivalries—nothing changes in the women's position here, in fact Joaquin advances an ethic of propriety for all ranks including prostitution and all escapist withdrawals. The father's death and the consolidation of the monogamous/nuclear family under Monzon's aegis marks a transitional phase of our uneven and overdetermined social development, although the unexpected emergence of "constitutional authoritarianism" signifies that Joaquin's expectations may be premature or utopian.

Suffice it to conclude here that *Fathers and Sons* demystifies through the materialist demands of theatrical enactment the essentialist and idealist premises of the story "Three Generations." On the other hand, the static roles of women as reflectors and ministering hands/bodies apologized for by Chitong/Joaquin's all encompassing charity, and the unquestioned supremacy of the father Marcelo Monzon (no longer head of the clan with the loss of property), head of household, reinforces the outmoded ideology of the narrative already riven through by the shattering and intractable insinuations of Desire. The final spectacle of the laborers destroying the table, however, may be viewed as Joaquin's concession to the threatening advent of an apocalypse much more complex, intimate, and radical than the overthrow of the clan patriarch by the private household father. What is more dangerous to both artists and audience is the resolutely unified and resourcefully decisive action of the laborers, in contrast to the privatist and reified individualism that not only vitiates the philosophical and emotional sincerity of the protagonists but also the universalizing, contemplative and conciliatory intent of the artist.

"May Day Eve"

It would seem that for Joaquin the Muse of history assumes the lineaments of a "dark and fatal creature," beautifully seductive but parasitic on its victims–a haunting Medusa of memory. This is how Agueda strikes the aged Don Badoy Montiya, how time acquires psychic figuration for the protagonist. But it is the irrepressible memory of this woman that immobilizes the flow of experience, short-circuits it, restores the dead and the obsolete, and captures the subject in the imprisoning and unrepresentable inertia of pathos. Time is betrayed as an illusion, history a cyclic myth.

While the story at first glance concerns itself with May Day rituals, in particular the night of divination in which men/women can see their future husbands/wives in a mirror, using the case histories of Agueda and Don Badoy and their children, it really engages the crucial question of what influence the European rationalist enlightenment and critical disruptions of dogmatism stemming from the French Revolution exerted on that isolated Spanish colony in Asia removed thousands of miles from the republican upheavals in the peninsula. The year is 1847, eve of the insurrections in France, Germany, Austria and Italy, unfolding in the wake of the rise of Chartism and the emergence of socialist political organizations; a year before the publication of the *Communist Manifesto*. In Spain, the reign of Maria Cristina is characterized by a series of uprisings, military coups d'etat, new constitutions, and dictatorships. Agueda's chiding of her superstitious sisters– "This is the year 1847. There are no devils anymore!"—highlights the peculiar conjuncture of a culture sustained by archaic rituals mixed with a romantic sensibility whose individualistic impulse rejects tradition and communal faith but succumbs to the fetish of eternal youth, the mirage of eternal recurrence.

All the allusions to historical data—Don Badoy's serioflippant response to his grandson: "Oh, ho, my young Voltaire! And what if I tell you that I myself have seen a witch?"—are merely tokens or counters to anchor the make-believe or fictional milieu, a concession to the conventions of realism. In reality, the narrative seems to convey how, from 1847 to 1890, changes have transpired only in the physical aging of the body in harmony with the routine passage of punctual, mundane time:

But, alas, the heart forgets; the heart is distracted; and Maytime passes; summer ends; the storms break over the rot-ripe orchards and the heart grows old . . . the memory perishes...and there came a time when Don Badoy Montiya walked home through a May Day midnight without remembering, without even caring to remember; being merely concerned in feeling his way across the street with his cane; his eyes having grown quite dim and his legs uncertain—for he was old; he was over sixty. (p. 105)

The eloquent asyndetonic style combined with parataxis and a series of metonymic qualifications not only produces an effect of proverbial finality but also tries to persuade us that the punctual/serial procession of events does not really exist except when remembered by a subject; and it is the act of remembering that validates the import of what is done and said. On the face of Don Badoy's involvement with an epochal break in the continuity of Spanish domination, namely, the Katipunan "conspiracy," the text can only articulate it in a fuzzy impressionism: "his mind still resounding with the speeches and his patriot heart still exultant." "The mass upheaval" signified by "a secret meeting of conspirators" (the 1896 Revolution and the future it bears) is not just a minor accident in Don Badoy's life; in fact, it has prevented him from becoming aware of the mirror and the ghostly face in it, an awareness of those objects earlier triggering the mechanism of memory into a wild leap back into the immutable past when "he was a gay young buck again, lately come from Europe." Quickly, the avalanche of words leads to a vortex of nostalgia for the past, unchanging youth, death.

History, then, is a mirage or a whirligig of illusions that can be frozen in three tableaux: first, the Anastasia-Agueda scene when the young Agueda, peering into the mirror, beholds a "dead mask" that "bloomed into her living face"; second, Doña Agueda's exchange with her daughter (located between 1847 and 1896); and, finally, Don Badoy's confession to his grandson. By a montage technique of juxtaposition of these scenes and the use of time shifts, the text tries to reveal the truth/falsity of ritual—the whole superstructure of custom and tradition associated with May Day Eve, the carnival of the heathen.

If the mirror of divination reflects the truth of the present for the spectator, not the future, the story reflects the truth of the past measured by the present, by contemporary readers. And the truth of the past points to the destructiveness of May Day Eve as the saturnalia of the repressed.

What Joaquin has invented in this instance is a model of imaginary space where Otherness is experienced as a pure relationship between consciousness and its images/reflections, whereby the ego fights or loves the Other, occupying positions indifferently, unable to escape from this circuit into the symbolic order, the realm of history. Both characters—Agueda, Don Badoy—operate in the realm of the Imaginary (in Lacan's definition) nourished and sanctioned by a system where male privilege/domination prevails. The woman is conceived ambivalently, as victim and antagonist: "Oh, he would have his revenge, he would make her pay, that little harlot!... But—Judas—what eyes she had! And what a pretty color she turned when angry!" But the male is not possessed by any perception of the woman as a differentiated, concrete, alterable person; she serves only as a pretext or catalyst for something else, namely, the hypostasis of a temporal stage in life—youth—and, for Joaquin, the Spanish ascendancy in its May Day ripeness. Consider this telling passage with its histrionic tone and operatic atmosphere:

> He sang aloud in the dark room and suddenly realized that he had fallen madly in love with her. He ached intensely to see her again—at once!—to touch her hand and her hair; to hear her harsh voice. He ran to the window and flung open the casements and the beauty of the night struck him back like a blow. It was May, it was summer, and he was young—young!—and deliriously in love. Such a happiness welled up within him, the tears spurted from his eyes.
>
> But he did not forgive her–no! He would still make her pay, he would still have his revenge, he thought viciously, and kissed his wounded fingers. But what a night it had been! "I will never forget this night!" he thought aloud in an awed voice, standing by the window in the dark room, the tears in his eyes and the wind in his hair and his bleeding knuckles pressed to his mouth. (pp. 22-23)

Even when Don Badoy, in 1890, looks back and sums up his married life with disarming candor to his grandson— "she bewitched me and she tortured me. She ate my heart and drank my blood," said the old man bitterly—his portrayal of his wife as unquenchable vampire (the devouring Kali archetype) is unrelentingly fused with the obverse image:

> "She was beautiful! She was the most beautiful creature I have ever seen! Her eyes were somewhat like yours but her hair was like black waters and her golden shoulders were bare. My God, she was enchanting! But I should have known–I should have known even then–the dark and fatal creature she was!" (p. 25)

This conception of the female accords with romantic tradition—from Goethe and Byron to Hawthorne and Poe—and can be appropriated within the animistic, heteroglotic universe of May Day Eve and Christian mythology (Eve, Delilah, Salome, etc). But what the author's mythicizing strategy can not hide, what ruptures the doubling of the past into the present and prompts an unwinding of the circular vision, is the woman's unqualified perception of the diabolic—this time speaking through the medium of the boy's innocence: "Well, you saw this witch in it. And Mama once told me that Grandma once told her that Grandma once saw the devil in this mirror." Through the mother, the grandmother speaks; and through the grandson, the mother expresses in language what her face presented earlier, when Doña Agueda looked at the same mirror and saw her old face: "A hard, bitter, vengeful face, framed in graying hair, and so sadly altered, so sadly different from that other face like a white mask . . ." (p. 20). What is the woman's protest all about? It cannot be just a simple condemnation of Don Badoy's vindictive and wayward conduct, nor the anticipated "hysterical" refusal of decrepitude.

Joaquin's protean and incandescent narrative art exhibits its limits here, unable or averse to probing into the woman's predicament, primed and synchronized only to defuse the explosive charge of the woman's insight into the awkward, riddling patter of the grandson, and finally disperse it into the vertigo of Don Badoy's disrupted memory.

We are supposed to marvel at the eloquence of memory attempting, by virtue of its libidinal investment in a vivid chiaroscuro of images, to redeem Doña Agueda's fate. Don Badoy is made to perform the role of elegist descanting not just on beauty's ephemeral quality or passion's brevity but on the liberating freedom of death and its memorializing virtue:

Don Badoy started. For a moment he had forgotten that she was dead, that she had perished—the poor Agueda; that they were at peace at last, the two of them, and her tired body at rest; her broken body set free at last from the brutal pranks of the earth—from the trap of a May night; from the snare of summer; from the terrible silver nets of the moon. She had been a mere heap of white hair and bones in the end: a whimpering withered consumptive, lashing out with her cruel tongue; her eyes like live coals; her face like ashes . . . Now, nothing!—nothing save a name on a stone; save a stone in a graveyard—nothing! nothing at all! was left of the young girl who had flamed so vividly in a mirror one wild May Day midnight, long, long ago. (p. 25)

What posture does Don Badoy take in the end? We are led back to the beginning, the text evoking a seeming permanence of environment and a seeming inalterability of ritual, enveloping the lived experiences in the palimpsest of "medieval shadows" and the cyclic recurrence of the seasons: *kairos* relapsing into *chronos*.

By slicing the homogeneous continuity of experience, valorizing those moments of youthful flirtation and of recall by choosing the male sensibility as the screen/filter through which we form a judgment on life, femininity, love, time, etc., the text excludes any other mode of knowledge except through mystifying ritual/superstition and a manner of remembering that apprehends nothing but banalities and platitudes.

Could it be that this is exactly what the text intends to produce?

Despite the hypnotic bracketing of the three episodes by a tactic of cumulative repetition, timeless landscape of "tiled roofs" and "evil old moon" and "murderous wind" encapsulating the old man's grief and diminishing its existential pathos, the structure of the narrative illustrates the rhetorical ruse of repetition and difference. While May Day Eve and its specular game of prophesying the future preserves the intensity of hope, dream, fantasy—a virtual explosion of Desire—it also, in Agueda's case, deludes women into marital bondage; and, in Don Badoy's case, into fixation on an absence—the instant of plenitude, of original fulfillment. But this instant is a ludic phantasmagoria, as Don Badoy discovers, defying his own education in Voltairean skepticism. Strangely enough but metaphorically revealing, Don Badoy recoils when his grandson delivers to him verbally a reflection of his wife, the mother/grandmother, who in turn identifies him as the "devil in the mirror."

Despite the repression of the woman's testament that the mirror both conceals and reveals, that tradition/faith—and its code of repetition—can mesmerize thought, the narrative apparatus pursues the mode of mediating discovery through the interrogation of Agueda's daughter and Don Badoy's grandson–the proofs of difference–and poses the question which the author could not answer. And this question, "Was it of the scare that Grandma died?" innocently reverberating at the end, tied with the image of the fetishized Agueda as "a whimpering withered consumptive, lashing out with her cruel tongue; her eyes like live coals," vigorously testifies to the blanks, fissures, holes which the audacious exuberance of language fails to fill up or gloss over.

In the long opening paragraph, we note the obsessive motivation to overcome social norms by a resort to the magical: "How carefree were men but how awful to be a girl and what a horrid, horrid world it was." Trapped still in the casuistic universe of devils and witches, the subjects here—Agueda and Don Badoy—are unable to escape the enchanted circle of taboos and prohibitions. The narrative does not allow them such a possibility, but it permits us to perceive the irony between the text's valorizing of repetition, of ritual/ tradition, as a mode of self-knowledge and its disclosure that it necessarily destroys the centered subject whose memory is needed to generate meanings and ascribe responsibilities.

In most of Joaquin's works, memory and recollection function as the means toward the constitution of the subject and the recovery of the self-sufficient origin prefigured in a primitive cult of archaic rite (the "tadtarin," hallucinatory visions, etc.) or the visitations of a tutelary numen. Hence the technique of juxtaposing temporally disjunct episodes whereby the present or future comments on the past and the past critiques the present usually as a degradation of some original virtue or initial harmony. The most dangerous fault or sin, then, is the failure of memory and the slippage into the circumstantial abyss. Don Badoy suffers this for a moment when he is swept up by the contingent speeches (still a recall!) of the patriot-conspirators, until he is revived into cognitive enlightenment, into the stasis of Bergsonian duration, upon catching the face in the fabled mirror.

Analogous to the recurrent impulse to inwardness in "Three Generation," "Guardia de Honor," and other stories, the rendering of Don Badoy's consciousness in "May Day Eve" is meant to persuade us that external events possess no intelligibility unless appropriated and organized by the protagonist's memory. It turns out that this capacity of recall serves also as the instrument of terror. For it is not Agueda who tortured, ate and drank

Don Badoy's blood; the truth is the reverse. Operating with the latent energies of shamanistic idealism, the text however foregrounds its putative anchorage in the sociohistorical context (Don Badoy's rationalism exists in a subterranean sphere) and refutes it with the materiality of truth as successful communication and heterodox message: "And Mama once told me that Grandma once told her that Grandma once saw . . ."

In sum, the hero of "May Day Eve" is time spatialized, the spirit of communal territory or milieu always-already charted by the avenging Mothers/Furies preempting and aborting the emergence of the property-owning individual, the "free" agent of the capitalist marketplace.

"The Summer Solstice"

One of the most contentious fields in cultural politics today involves the question of the social construction of gender, woman's position, sexuality in general vis-à-vis the rectification of the base/superstructure dichotomy. While empirical research in anthropology has displaced the issue of matriarchy for the more substantial questions of a dispersed power and the sexual-social division of labor modifying the hypothesis advanced by Engels' classic *Origin of the Family, Private Property, and the State* (1884), one consensus is that in the prehistoric stages of hunting-gathering and horticulture, egalitarian social relations accorded the sexes decision-making powers commensurate with their share in expending socially necessary labor.

In primitive communal society where private property of the means of production and labor was absent, where class therefore did not exist, the division of labor was reciprocal, not biased according to biological sex. The economic, kinship-based organization of society did not allow a monopoly of power in the form of the State to accrue to either sex. With the onset of private property of land, tools, slaves, etc., and monogamous coupling within the framework of nascent class division, women lost their equal status. Kathleen Gough suggests that women's childbearing and childrearing roles—the sexual division of labor—and the cultural elaboration of physical differences in strength, led to women's subordination. For Eleanor Leacock, women's oppression rests on the "transformation of their socially necessary labor into private service through the separation of the family from the clan."[22] In brief, the change in property relations owing to the transformation of the mode of production underlies the formation of gender and the exploitation of women as a subordinate caste.

Contraposed to this materialist perspective, Joaquin's text revolving around the Tadtarin festival aims to resuscitate the myth of matriarchy as the occluded but irrepressible antithesis of male-dominated society (c. 1850), exorcising patriarchal guilt by a symbolic sacrifice and chastisement.

The celebration of the Tadtarin rite serves as the occasion to stage the revenge of women and the recovery of a buried unconscious displaced and projected onto the male, here in the person of Don Paeng:

The cult of the Tadtarin is celebrated on three days: the feast of St. John and the two preceding days. On the first night, a young girl heads the procession; on the second, a mature woman; and on the third, a very old woman who dies and comes to life again. In these processions, as in those of Pakil and Obando, everyone dances. (p. 117)

This cult resembles the magicoreligious fertility ceremonies in primitive agricultural societies designed to insure abundance of harvest and birth of children. Through various rites (dances, prayers, incantations, sacred dramas), the tribe seeks to control otherwise unpredictable forces of nature to guarantee the fecundity of earth and the regeneration of organic life.

In pagan myth, nature is usually personified as the Mother Goddess symbolizing the fertility of the earth and the periodic renewal of life. This is inscribed in the narrative of the Goddess's search for her lost (dead) child or lover (Isis/Osiris, Ishtar/Tammuz, Demeter/Persephone); the stages of birth, death and rebirth outlined in myth and enacted in mystery religions correspond to the regenerative powers of the earth (Adonis, Attis, Osiris, Christ). But the central protagonist in these myths is the Mother in various cultural guises: Cybèle, Ishtar, Isis, Hera/Aphrodite/Demeter, Ceres, and, through a syncretic process, the Virgin Mary.

One notes that in the Indian Kali, the Mother manifests dual aspects: the beneficent/maleficent, a synthesis movingly rendered in Thomas Mann's *The Transposed Heads.* In India, too, the belief exists that in deflowering a virgin with the *lingam* (stone phallus symbolizing Shiva), fertility is insured.

Within the framework of the operation of sympathetic magic, we find such tribal performances as the scattering of the reproductive organs of animals in the fields, the display of phallic symbols, ritual prostitution, the kindling of fires emblematic of the sun, etc., together with sacrifices aimed at releasing the powers embodied in living animals/humans. Vestiges of these rituals exist, such as the Maypole dance in Europe, a spring rite glorifying the procreative male organ, and the Tadtarin feast of St. John the Baptist in the Paco district of Manila in midnineteenth-century Philippines.

For Joaquin, the Tadtarin bears witness to the persisting charisma of fertility goddesses/female deities of aboriginal times who were all overthrown by evangelizing Christianity but who continued to survive a clandestine life owing to the spontaneous irruption of primitive elements in Catholic liturgy and their hypnotic appeal to the largely female congregation. In any case, the Tadtarin represents the pre-Christian, organic-communal form of society founded on the inexhaustible fertility of the earth and of the natural body, both of which are defined as female.

Unlike Joaquin's typical habit of manipulating time loops and yoking ambiguous contrarieties and parallels, the narrative method here pursues the mimesis of a quest—Don Paeng hunting (the male as paleolithic hunter!) his fugitive wife in the maze of the Tadtarin orgy—culminating in defeat/submission of the hunter to his quarry. Such inversion is meant to demonstrate the superficiality and thinness of official Catholic discipline informing the conduct of the ilustrado class. By subjecting the virtuous and genteel Don Paeng of the ordeal of pursuing his wife by threading through the Dionysian/Bacchic frenzy of the Tadtarin participants and thus "castrating" him in the process, the plot seeks to prove the power of the instinctive and irrational, the supremacy of Desire over masculine reason, the patiarchal logos.

Before the humbling of the chivalric husband, however, the wife Doña Lupeng needs to be recast so that her thoughts of woman's original primacy would govern her own feelings and actions. Doña Lupeng rehearses in her mind the argument that male domination ultimately derives from the woman's active/passive submission:

> And she wondered peevishly what the braggarts were being so cocky about? For this arrogance, this pride, this bluff male health of theirs was (she told herself) founded on the impregnable virtue of generations of good women. The boobies were so sure of themselves because they had always been sure of their wives. "All the sisters being virtuous, all the brothers are brave," thought Doña Lupeng, with a bitterness that rather surprised her. Women had built it up: this poise of the male. Ah, and women could destroy it, too! She recalled, vindictively, this morning's scene at the stables: Amada naked and screaming in bed while from the doorway her lord and master looked on in meek silence. And was it not the mystery of a woman in her flowers that had restored the tongue of that old Hebrew prophet? (p. 112)

She begins to realize that she has been entertaining "obscene" thoughts, appalled at the "discovery of such depths of wickedness in herself." When the young Guido, his head stuffed with Byronic bravura, Napoleon and the French Revolution, "dragged himself forward on the ground and solemnly kissed the tips of her shoes, " Doña Lupeng "stared down in sudden horror, transfixed—and he felt her violent shudder."

But for this dutiful and prudent woman to shed off the trappings of Victorian hyprocisy and sentimentality, she needed to dare join the procession, unloose the trammels of conformist habit and yield to the temptation of ego-annihilation. As the Tadtarin enacted the passage into self-dissolution, Doña Lupeng "was watching greedily, taut and breathless, her head thrust forward and her eyes bulging, the teeth bared in the slack mouth, and the sweat gleaming on her face." After the resurrection of the Tadtarin and the frenzy of dancing, she "was shaking with fascination; tears trembled on her lashes," finally wrenching herself free from her husband's hold:

> She flung her hands to her hair and whirled and her hair came undone. Then, planting her arms akimbo, she began to trip a nimble measure, an instinctive folk-movement. She tossed her head back and her arched throat bloomed whitely. Her eyes brimmed with moonlight, and her mouth with laughter. (p. 119)

Coincident with this transformation of Doña Lupeng, her immersion in the collective ecstasy whereby she forfeits her categorical status as subordinate wife, is the dethronement and chastisement of Don Paeng's ego:

> Terror possessed him and he struck out savagely with both fists, with all his strength—but they closed in as savagely: solid walls of flesh that crushed upon him and pinned his arms helpless, while unseen hands struck and struck his face, and ravaged his hair and clothes, and clawed at his flesh, as—kicked and buffeted, his eyes blind and his torn mouth salty with blood—he was pushed down, down to his knees, and half-shoved, half-dragged to the doorway and rolled out to the street. He picked himself up at once and walked away with a dignity that forbade the crowd gathered outside to laugh or to pity. (p. 120)

Taunted by his wife later on that he should admit that his self-respect hinges on his respect of his wife, caught in the logic of the Imaginary where the ego identifies the Other as an extension of his body, Don Paeng could not recover his erstwhile haughty and domineering stance: "Her eyes were upon him and the shameful fear that had unmanned him in the dark chapel possessed him again. His legs had turned to water; it was a monstrous agony to remain standing." It is not the wife's boldness but the traumatic impasse in the Tadtarin chapel that emasculates the husband, vindicating the autonomous force of the women in their bacchic solidarity. But is this experience enough to abolish the sexual division of labor and the class oppression of Doña Lupeng, her servant Amada, and all women? What does the text unfold?

The concluding scene of Doña Lupeng successfully extracting a confession that the male's pride depends on the woman's subservience dispenses with the myth at one stroke and restores to Doña Lupeng her "civilized" or christianized mind in order to relish its superiority over the instinctive, the animal and primitive into which maleness is now subsumed, in contrast to the intense rhetoric of women's priority and their self-activized free play quoted earlier, and the powerful rendering of the Tadtarin orgy which disintegrates the separate individualities of those caught in it. For all its vivid gothic *frisson* and the seductive trope of the moon (the female) and the synesthesia of eroticized particulars, the concluding passage shows us the ascendant will of Doña Lupeng to command, with the foot fetish suggesting her ritual recuperation of the phallus—the long lost object—and Don Paeng metamorphosing into the female/slave worshipper:

He was exhausted at last: he sank heavily to his knees, breathing hard and streaming with sweat, his fine body curiously diminished now in its ravaged apparel.

"I adore you, Lupe," he said tonelessly.

She strained forward avidly. *"What?* What did you say?" she screamed.

And he, in his dead voice: "That I adore you. That I adore you. That I worship you. That the air you breathe and the ground you tread is holy to me. That I am your dog, your slave. . . ."

But it was still not enough. Her fists were still clenched, and she cried: *"Then come, crawl on the floor, and kiss my feet!"*

Without a moment's hesitation, he sprawled down flat and, working his arms and legs, gaspingly clawed his way across the floor, like a great agonized lizard, the woman steadily backing away as he approached, her eyes watching him avidly, her nostrils dilating, till behind her loomed the open window, the huge glittering moon, the rapid flashes of lightning. She stopped, panting, and leaned against the sill. He lay exhausted at her feet, his face flat on the floor.

She raised her skirts and contemptuously thrust out a naked foot. He lifted his dripping face and touched his bruised lips to her toes; lifted his hands and grasped the white foot and kissed it savagely—kissed the step, the sole, the frail ankle—while she bit her lips and clutched in pain at the window sill, her body distended and wracked by horrible shivers, her head flung back and her loose hair streaming out the window— streaming fluid and black in the white night where the huge moon glowed like a sun and the pure heat burned with the immense intense fever of noon. (pp. 121-22)

By metonymic substitution in the last images and the metaphoric linkage of sun and moon, it is clear that Doña Lupeng has occupied the actantial position of the male impregnator, giver/donor of the Law. It might be apposite here to note that such a reversal approximates the manner in which the medieval courtly code glorified and marginalized woman in the abstract (Bachofen's notion of motherhood as Nature comes to mind), shrouding the idealized Female with reverence compounded of awe and fear, whereby this symbolic distance, instead of connoting high status or privileged position accorded to women, mystifies or normalizes the ongoing exploitation of women as a fatally dependent species-gender in the hierarchy of a male-dominated world.

"Guardia de Honor"

What the reader discerns in "Three Generations" and "May Day Eve" as mere stylistic or rhetorical devices of time shifts designed to evoke intertextual epiphanies, devices that constitute the reconciling mechanism of Joaquin's narrative apparatus, makes its appearance in this story as the frame or armature for a complex, dialectical interrogation of "lived time" or temporality in its existential dimension.

Analogous to the role of May Day Eve rituals, or the Tadtarin feast in "The Summer Solstice," the October celebration of La Naval in Manila—whose historic and religious significance is elaborated in Joaquin's hermeneutic/ apologetic essay of 1943, "La Naval de Manila"—acts as the parenthesis, the enveloping event that provides the continuity threading six generations, from Natalia Godoy's to Josie's, with Natalia's single emerald earring serving as index and symbol to the preservation of tradition and the intrinsic values of fidelity and communal/family solidarity. Within these punctual brackets, the text unfolds an interpenetration of time segments, episodes from two periods— Natalia's and Josie's—to show the similarities and differences in behavior of the two women, and with them the degeneration of the secular present vis-à-vis the vital harmony and plenitude of meaning in the sacramental past of old Manila.

We can propose at the outset that Joaquin seeks to vindicate the paramount virtue of tradition—for him, a teleological selection of elements in the past tied to religious ritual and its syncretic assimilation of folk customs—as that which transvalues the routine anonymity of time and elevates it to public or "narrative" time based on a concept of Being-with-Others. Through the "cunning" of the text, however, this endeavor to reinstate the past as virtual present in fiction, the past as origin and self-presence, is at all times severely undercut by our recall of Josie's refusal to heed her mother's wish, or rather (the same thing) Josie's decision to sell the earring, pursue her lover to Hong Kong and dissolve her mother's trust—a gesture of self-definition which paradoxically inhibits her to do what she really wants. We are left at the end with a rhetorical celebration of the founding act whose termination we have glimpsed in the future, which the text's duplicity has surreptitiously infiltrated beforehand.

As hinted by the concept of Being-with-Others, we may employ here a Heideggerian problematic to elucidate the structuring of episodes in the narrative. One might quickly summarize here how Heidegger has analyzed temporality as the plural unity of future- past-present, a unitary constitution oriented toward the future, from which historicality arises. Historicality comes about through narrative, through the human activity of recollecting, modulating the experience of "within-time-ness" to repetition through memory. Whereas the existential category defining man is care *(Sorge)* or concern, as "being-toward-death" in which the future is closed in the untransferrable singularity/privacy of each person's death, the function of memory as embodied in narrative is to reverse the basic orientation of care, enacting "a retrieval of our basic potentialities inherited from our past in the form of personal fate and collective destiny." Paul Ricoeur suggests that narrative in fact functions primarily to establish human action at the level of genuine historicity through repetition, making events more than unique or singular occurrence. [23] Plot in this sense establishes human action in memory which repeats and retrieves the potential lodged in the past in anticipation of a project: either individual fate or collective destiny.

From this unavoidably synoptic precis of Heideggerian phenomenology, we can grasp the logic of the narrative strategy as a return to origin through repetition, whereby retrospection and anticipation coalesce reciprocally. The text has to inescapably foreground the story of Natalia Godoy, making it the prism or screen through which is refracted the fragmenting of Josie's family and the reification of social life. In the same breath, it is the eroding and explosive potential of this future which the enveloping frame of the past contains that imposes a judgment of irony: the impotence of the past to affect the present, to change or influence its course. Between the fatality in the story and the freedom in the discourse, we grasp the kernel of the historic contradiction that Joaquin's ideology of Christian freedom cannot but reveal: a parallelism between the fetishism of commodities expressed by Josie and her brothers, and the fetishism of the emerald earring as the symbol of transcendental intervention, both irrational or extrarational, capable of being comprehended only in the context of the tortuous historical transformations overdetermining Philippine society.

Notwithstanding this existentialist schema, it is possible to articulate the formation of a double bind, an aporia, constructed by the text even as it tries to belabor its materials, in which Being-toward-death is precisely displaced by Being-with-Others (tradition and community) on condition that it shatters kinship, blood ties, ritualized togetherness. This is already intimated by the thematic coordinates of free will/predestination, and its permutation of individual will versus family custom. Undercutting these oppositions, we face *jouissance*: the figure of motherhood implicated in the liberation of desire and its confounding of narrative progression, of plotted linear direction.

The craft of the text displays the process whereby the subversion of its own authority is staged. In the opening scene which already anticipates the eruption of accident, unpredictable mutations—"And time creates unexpected destinations, history raises figs from thistles"—which later on is reconceptualized under the rubric of the Virgin's miraculous intercession, we observe the father cancelled by Natalia's choice of Mario, her lover/beloved, instead of the "good" and "gentle" Esteban. While marriage proceeds under the Law sanctioned by the symbolic order (the physical father functions as a stand-in), love signifies an excess, a surplus, which requires encapsulation in a fixed emblem, the emerald/gift of the father. The father's perception epitomizes the technique of simulation-dissimulation played out in the text:

"Father—?"
At that word the door that had slammed shut opened again; but it was not his baby, not his little girl, that he saw, but a towering, faintly familiar person, a mature woman, before the radiant nakedness of whose passion he felt shy and formal. (p. 124)

Before he disappears from the text, becoming the absent or dead father which allows the quest for substitution—the textuality of Desire—to proceed, he conflates Elisa, the aging Aunt and Natalia, and insures a space for the Law's upholder Andong Ferrero to replace him as the guarantor of a wholeness that comprehends gratuitous dicontinuity and breaks attributable to the play of psychic drives.

The story then overlaps with a scene from the present, with Natalia and her mother, which establishes through the metonymic device of the single earring the vitality of tradition. For Josie's mother, the jewels "are sacred: the tokens of a vow," becoming then a metaphor of trust that links mother and daughter as the matrilineal keepers/custodians of a sacramental practice which validates and legitimizes the arbitrary transactions of the secular world. Such transactions include "feelings" and the freedom to sin without which order and law could not exist. The mother then gives a resumé of the miracle/accident where two deaths occur—deaths which constitute the Otherness of the past and occasion the birth of memory. The text then cinematically dissolves the voice of Josie's mother and cuts in Natalia, this time with Josie—a linkage of past and present, a conjunction which annihilates the past and renders everything into the immediacy of the self-sufficient present. Whereas Josie's mother could only invoke the past to justify the logic of the present, here a dialectical movement is concretized.

At first glance, it seems that Josie and Natalia are an antithetical pair, a disjunctive conjunction. Josie's reality is premised on a notion of time as mere succession, punctuated by incidents without any organic progression, dominated by the commodity-fetishism of the capitalist world where the precious family jewels possess only market value, a counter or abstract cipher of exchangeable labor time. Obviously, Joaquin wants to make Josie the helpless and pathetic victim of capitalism, reduced to a fatalistic acceptance of circumstances, paralyzed by the sheer repetitiveness (duplication of forms in consumer advertising, for example) of time in which what is happening has already happened:

[Natalia replies]: "I feel as if you were *wringing* me out of those jewels, Josie!"

"And I *am*!" cried Josie between her teeth, "—wringing and squeezing and straining you out of them; and not only you but mommy also, and everything else they mean. Nothing must be left except a price tag!"

"But why should you want to do that?"

"Because I have to, because I must. I have gone in too deep; there is no turning back now, and no use struggling: the pressure is terrific! But when was life ever a question of one's wanting or not wanting? Life is just one pressure after another. Whatever one does one was always bound to do, like it or not."

"Oh, nonsense. One can always stop, or do something else."

"If I did something else, it would still be Josie. If I stopped, Josie would still go on. What is impossible is not to be Josie." (p 129)

Where the exchange between Josie and her mother is a one-way delivery of a modified story/legend belying the claims of trust and respect of freedom, the Josie-Natalia dialogue posits a difference only to underline an unintended similarity. Josie poses the problem: "But how can you stop something that has happened already? The premonition felt by Natalia through the voices she hears in the mirror of what is going to happen, an intuition of the future crystallized by Josie's ghostly presence, enables her to be traversed by, first, her stubbornness and, second, her erotic impulsiveness which surfaces in the concluding episode.

Meanwhile, Natalia remains in the past that vividly animates into her present, a dream that metamorphoses into an indeterminate and unconditioned zone of wish-fulfillment—the upsurge of the repressed:

But that other today was only a dream.... As she thought how all those things that were *herself* still lay in the distant future a fierce relief consumed her—not the terror she had felt as Natalia's eyes looked through her "as though I did not exist"—but a relief intense and immediate, a bliss of liberation. No more pressures; no more tensions; and ages and ages, yet, before she would awake and anguish, before this cluttered room would be stripped to provide her a streamlined setting: the modishly bare, coyly hygienic chamber where her flesh would writhe and her young tears flow. But the reality now and "Creep slowly, Time," she prayed: "creep slowly, slowly" was this harp, these pedestals, these rocking chairs, these huge beds; and she moved among them, a detached ghost; unconcerned, uninvolved, absolved— (p. 132)

If we regard this as an escape into the past, a wish-fulfilling withdrawal into a scene of plenitude, the oneiric but not timeless dimension analogous to the circularity of the imaginary travel in the paradigmatic fables cited by Ricoeur, then it affirms the value of tradition and community as definer of individuality. At the same time, this regression allows Josie to detach herself from the present and observe from a distance her brothers' cynical and callous attitude. This scene of discovery which Josie happens upon, replicating the eavesdropping stance of Natalia earlier, contains within it the brothers' fortuitous eavesdropping on the conversation between Josie and her mother, which discloses to Josie the course of the future. So the future materializes in the images apprehended in Natalia's mirror, the past becoming an alienation device for exposing the deceptive facade of the present.

If Josie's relapse, an imaginary transit, into the past or the phantasmatic realm which recuperates the past, affords her a vision of the future, then her fate is sealed: she will do what she is bound to do. What then of the fabled notion of freedom enunciated by her mother? Or the gesture of free will enacted by Natalia? What is still to come has now congealed into homogenizing narrative, so that the dramatization of what's occurring can be conveyed only as retrospective accounting, a chronological recall. Note that it is the brothers, tied to a reifying and fragmented mercantile society, who give us a third-person access to a scene hidden from our view. Even as the brothers joke of their suspicions and mock moralizing, their hostility at women sharpened to the point of obscene accusations, Josie in a faint has retreated into the unconscious and the mother, upon discovering Josie's farewell note, slides into the void. With the future observed in the past by Josie, a future only moments away from her present, a future closed and bounded by the familial killing of the mother, we can see the tricks played by the metonymic shuffling of discrete episodes based on the argument that the past stabilizes, unifies, or lends an unequivocal center to the heterogeneous contingencies of life.

From this pivotal junction marked by the sacrificial or symbolic killing of the mother, the text interweaves four scenes: first, Josie's attempt to rectify the mother's first version of Natalia's accident based on her belief that Natalia "defied the fates, she made things happen!" The mother contributes a version of the legend incorporating the dialogue between Natalia and Josie, an intertextual performance emblematic of temporality as a fusion of retention/attending/expectation, and historicality as repetition. The second scene dramatizes the legend, emphasizing Natalia's defiant independence—"I shall ride with whom I please, sir!" She refuses Mario, her lover's plea to ride with him, and asserts her freedom to do what she likes, taunting him to dare stop her. The text depicts her psyche seized with the paroxysm of Desire: "We are riding with you, Esteban! We are riding with you!' she shouted shivering, glittering, with fury and hatred and love." Note the rhythm of passion here mimed by the asyndetonic sequence of phrases culminating in the catastrophe, the collapse into instinctual depths for Natalia and the void of death for Esteban and Aunt Elisa.

The next scene builds on the inevitability of what has been enacted by the text itself, impelling Josie to wonder at the futility of Natalia's effort to control the unwinding of events. And so paradoxically, Josie breaks the chain of tradition, finally confessing her deceit and communicating at last with her mother. But it is the duplicity of the mother's message we encounter here, her offer of freedom premised on the wily and treacherous masks adopted by good and evil, a freedom conditioned by trust and predicated on the authority of the mother as the primordial founder/savior:

"Oh stop, mother, stop! Don't speak! Don't speak!"
"I placed those emeralds in your hands," wearily continued Doña Pepita, "because I wanted you to be free to choose. I know the crucial temptation that afflicts you, and I wish to help you, to save you, Josefa, by showing how deeply I still trust you—for you know what those emeralds mean to me. Whatever you choose to do now, you will choose deliberately, with full consciousness; knowing what you will do to me and to
"Oh, it's no use–no use at all! It just happens! IT'S HAPPENING RIGHT NOW!" (p. 139)

What Josie suffers is the past (the future transformed into a past when she overheard her brothers) catching up with her nemesis-like, a future-become-past beyond alteration, a recognition that abolishes consciousness for the moment in order to unfold a totally unbounded semiotic horizon into which Josie, governed by the same impulse of passion exhibited by Natalia, plunges.

There are two obliterations of consciousness rehearsed in this penultimate scene, Josie's fainting and her mother's death, before we receive the concluding commentary and reflection by the survivors, Natalia and Andong Ferrero. That penultimate scene, then, is meant to substitute for the gap between the catastrophe and the pregnancy of Natalia, a lacuna where the unrepresentable miracle happens. And the text fills in this lacuna with Josie's leap into the abyss and her decisive act of rupture conditioned by her own experience of the past—hence, tradition permits its own violation—and the intense individualistic fragmentation of the present. The narrator tries to gloss over this latter fact attested to by the brothers' conduct with Doña Pepita's sermon about the Christian responsibility to choose and the awareness that everyone enjoys this freedom of choice, hedged in by warnings not to disappoint others (the mother, the brothers) nor challenge male authority.

According to Doña Pepita's story, Natalia "cried that at the very moment of disaster she had called on the Virgin of the Rosary, and the Virgin had snatched her away." When Natalia recalls that incident, she tells her husband: "But whenever I thought of that afternoon it was your face I saw—and I felt your arms lifting me up again from the ruins." And the explanation for this foresight is that of "a lover's premonition."

With the demise of the biological father, the lover Mario reappears, this time as a man caught by "God the cunning hunter," "a holy man." The symbolic father emerges here in the wake of three deaths in the figure of the cunning hunter who pursues his prey through the circuitous passages of time.

Within a milieu circumscribed and dominated by patriarchal authority, the phenomenon of care, the existential anguish of *Dasein* which dictates the orientation toward the future, is sublimated into the sphere of memory where everything falls into place. What supplants it is the phenomenon of Being-with-Others, the communal dimension of historicality, identified here with the festival of La Naval and the ritualized performance of the originary event repeated every generation. Joaquin's aim seems embodied in the epilogue where the skeptical Andong relents to Natalia's wish/vow, the father-to-be formulating the solution to the problem of communication between predecessors, contemporaries and successors:

"But I shall have a daughter too," said Natalia, offering him on her palm the earring shaped like a chandelier." And I have vowed to the Virgin of the Rosary," she continued as she clasped the jewel to her ear, "that my daughter, too, shall march as a guardia in her procession."

"—wearing this one earring?"

"And may she never, never lose it!" whispered Natalia Ferrero, her eyes suddenly bright with tears as she stood arrayed in her emeralds: a bowed old woman now, heavy with child—but feeling herself for a moment the young Natalia Godoy again, dancing in this room that afternoon her father gave her these emeralds, the afternoon she first told him she loved . . .

And yes! she should wear that earring as a trophy, as a trophy of battle—thought Andong Ferrero, seeing in the tranced figure bowed before him—heavy with the past, heavy with the future—a Guard of Honour indeed, a warrior scarred but unconquered—for the Fates had won nothing from her save an earring. Tonight she would walk hieratic among hieratic women—women equally scarred and equally jewelled: priestesses bearing the tribe's talisman, the clan's hearthfire. And because of her lost jewel (a jewel dissolving now into myth and the earth's mist), the moss would be greener on the walls; the leaves brighter on the trees; the fine air more silver; and the heart's pang of happiness more poignant, more complex, when, at the city's core, the city's Virgin rode radiant against this cold wind singing with bells.

October in Manila! (pp. 140-41)

Why are the women "equally scarred"? Perhaps the text can respond with that enigmatic answer Natalia gave when asked what her lover's premonition was: "When no one asks, I know. When someone asks, I find I have forgotten." At the moment Natalia wards off Mario, she still possesses that share of authority imparted by the father, the emerald becoming the phallic emblem of the Law; death and the loss of one earring brought about by the irate and wrathful male Mario may be read as the enactment of castration, just as the loss of the emerald with Josie's departure connotes a privation that cannot be remedied unless the realm of the Imaginary where narcissistic doubling is emptied, hollowed by a lack which will trigger off the progression of time and the installation of the phallus as the signifier of that loss. But it is precisely in granting that the order of tradition and sacramentalized community can sustain itself only through the destruction of the phantasmal world of identifications (Natalia as mirror-image of Josie, etc.) and its replacement by the symbolic Law founded on "castration" and the hierarchical subordination of woman that we see the profound antinomy underlying Joaquin's tribute to the mutilated females, to Natalia with "her lost jewel," to the myth of transcendence which reconciles opposites by miracle and surrenders freedom to the game of providential chance.

Rhetorically, the vision of the future in Andong Ferrero's mind enunciates itself in the subjunctive mood, in the mode of wish and hope, annihilating Natalia's individuality by its absorption into the category of priestess, and inflecting the whole discourse into a dithyrambic eulogy to the October ambience presided over by the Virgin of the Rosary. It is a vision surprisingly reductive and one-dimensional, given the elaboration of a metaphysic of freedom vis-à-vis the predetermining power of grace incarnated in the text of narrativity itself. Yet in that sense and judgment of incommensurability is precisely where the demystifying virtue of "Guardia de Honor" resides.

"The Mass of St. Sylvester"

How can the Filipino artistic consciousness such as Joaquin's, committed to a vision of society and culture as synthesizing archetypes of transhistorical events, envisage the reality of disrupting violence and discontinuity experienced in war? I submit that for Joaquin's project of reconstituting the integrity of the Western (Christian) inheritance in the sphere of the imagination, the Second World War offered a pivotal test and a challenge: a test of whether the synthesis of the past and the present can be achieved, a challenge of exhuming and salvaging from the past the vestigial elements of a viable future.

In the structure of this narrative, we see how the narrator serves as the focal bridge between the legendary past—the ordeal and transfiguration of Mateo the Maestro who lived in the eighteenth century—and the ruins of the present. Looking backward through the medium of collective/folk memory, the voice of the narrator recuperates the virtue of cyclic order invested both in the miraculous death and resurrection of Mateo, and in its concomitant textual repetition. This retrospective technique eclipses the sterile void of the present. Looking forward, the narrator strives to fill in the void by another act of remembrance, this time embodied in the spare, paratactic style of the GI soldier-turned-tourist whose testimony confirms and also undercuts the phantasmal, reconstituting vision of St. Sylvester's mass.

Joaquin positions the narrator at the ambiguous conjuncture in our history when the old is dying but the future still languishes in the womb of the fluid amorphous present; hence his choice of St. Sylvester, the Christian version of the Roman god Janus, the Mass as the Christianized saturnalia, and the city of Manila as the locus of this magical attempt through art to establish unity in time and space, the centered or fully conscious subject, after the war's holocaust.

In Roman religion, Janus, patron of doors and of beginnings, acted as the custodian of the universe in presiding over the death of the old year and the beginning of the new. His figure with two bearded heads placed back to back and looking in two directions was installed at the gates of temples, and also in the Roman Forum's threshold which was closed in time of peace but open in time of war. His function was assumed in Christianity by St. Sylvester (pope during the reign of Emperor Constantine I) whose feast falls on 31 December—a transition that itself emblematizes the durable stratum of myth which underlies the incessant aleatory shifts of the historical process.

By placing the celebration of St. Sylvester's feast in the cathedral city of Manila, the narrative identifies the eschatocosmological function of the myth of New Year, the abolition of past time and the repetition of the Creation, with an elaborate flourishing culture centered in Manila: the colonial Hispanic world of conspicuous pomp and institutionalized ritual. It is this feast that guarantees the preservation of order and power, and sanctifies patriarchal hierarchy: note the meticulous and detailed description of the ceremonial rite, the officials and participants, the sequence, etc.

What the mass enacts is a fundamental theme of mythical thought: the eternal repetition of the cosmogonic act (the creation of the world) which, by transfiguring every New Year into the inauguration of an era, allows the return of the dead to life, and sustains the hope of the faithful in the resurrection of the body. In choosing this New Year inaugural rite, Joaquin establishes the allegorical framework for reconciling the meaningful, carnivalesque plenitude of the past (instanced by the exuberant procession, rich garments, the sensory density of texture in the depiction of the feast in contrast to the laconic rendering of this same event by the Brooklyn veteran Francis Xavier Zhdolajczyk (circa 1945) and the barren, unknowing, stunned present.

At the same time, what undermines and disrupts this framework, revealing the limits of authorial ideology, is the internal narrative spinning the legend of Mateo the Maestro.

The legend of this magus, rendered here with the fantastic and baroque realism typical of Joaquin's rehabilitation of folk materials, is meant to illustrate the limits of human aspiration and the power of the Church (or its superstructure of beliefs) to chastise secular/rational thought. But in spite of the narrator's vigorous, heretical attempt to revivify the legend, Mateo the Maestro fades more quickly and easily into myth.

In the figure of Mateo the Maestro, the narrator synthesizes falsehood and "truth," the prefeudal animistic world of the natives prior to the Spanish conquest, and the Renaissance type of the Faustian scientist. Memory yields to fabulation: the repressed (violent destruction of pagan temples, artifacts, etc.) returns as the magician-experimenter (Nostradamus, Roger Bacon) threatening to supplant mystery with practical secular knowledge:

Because no one could remember him young he was believed to be hundreds of years old, surviving (some said) from the days before the Conquista, when, being a priest of the ancient cults, he wielded great power, wearing his hair long and affecting the clothes and the ways of women, but had hidden away from the Castilians in various animal disguises to plot a restoration of the old gods—those fierce and fearful old gods now living in exile on the mountaintops....

The truth, however, was that Mateo the Maestro was not yet eighty years old and could not be remembered as a young man because he had spent his youth in incessant wanderings all over the country, thus acquiring his mastery of the arts, his command of a dozen tongues, and his profound knowledge of herb-healing and witchcraft. (p. 144)

Mateo has "consulted the dark deities in exile," the overthrown pagan cults, who advised the stratagem of profaning the grave of a holy man to steal his eyes and graft them into his eye sockets, so that he could witness the mass and gain immortality. The mass proves indeed "unbearable to human senses"; Mateo mutilates his flesh to stay awake only to be turned into stone. His sacrifice of his body earns him the privilege of repeating the cycle of the New Year renewal, this time as part of St. Sylvester's entourage. Pagan belief and Renaissance enlightenment are swallowed into myth which feeds on the materiality of the present: the senses, the narrator's voice, the synchronic and diachronic impulsions of writing.

What I would like to call attention to aside from this abortive ploy at reconciling past and present in which the Brooklyn outsider (the pragmatic Yankee liberator) recapitulates Mateo's observation but without the excruciating ordeal and with the camera lens replacing the "eyeballs ravished from the dead" is the fact that the narrator, like Mateo (though without magian inclination), is "obsessed" by the horror of change, evanescence, death, and yearns for continuity:

And just as soon as the Liberation Forces opened the Walled City to the public, I went to see what war had left us of our heritage from four centuries. Nothing had been left—except the oldest and most priceless jewel of all: St. Augustine's. The Puerta Postigo still stands, but most of the city walls have been leveled to the ground and the cathedral is a field of rubble. Into what city (I wondered) would St. Sylvester now make his annual entry? In what cathedral would he say his Mass? The retablo of the Pastoral Adoration has been smashed into pieces and dispersed into dust. Does that release Mateo the Maestro from his enchantment—or must he still, on New Year's eve, reassemble a living body from stone fragments to fulfill his penance of a thousand years? (p. 172)

These questions beget their own answers in the "epistle" of a latter-day "missionary" with his antiutilitarian ambience: Francis Xavier Zhdolajczyk who lives in Barnum Street, Brooklyn.

The GI's vision, though a verbally threadbare and touristic account, is intended to confirm the miracle of renewal, the continuity of legend and tradition amid the phenomenal surface changes in the physical environment. Its chief purpose is to authenticate the restorative primordial rite. Candid and unprepossessing, the tone and style of the solicited letter effects the camera trick it promised to do: it transfixes in this representative of the anonymous urban inhabitant, citizen of a pragmatic and technological culture, the numinous instant where the flux of time and eternity converge—the utopian moment of textuality.

Although this testimony of the modernist sensibility registers also the total ambiguity of the experience, culminating in its awed gaze at endless ruins, it occurs, however, in the context of the GI's mood of homesickness and longing to return to his point of departure, coinciding with the text's quest for origins in a single, endlessly repeated founding act which manifests itself variously, relative to the permanently altered perspective of humans.

While the narrator adopts a stance of innocent wonder, of puzzled and anxious nostalgia, the text has already performed its demiurgic function: it has reenacted the mass itself in full detail, even as it asserts that it is "unbearable to human senses." It has done so in the absence of the physical supports: the cathedral and city walls. The text has become the site of transcendence, the emblem of immortality, in its capacity to infinitely recreate the mass by virtue of the dynamics of its signifying practice. The narrator as magus/witness escapes the curse because he functions as a vehicle of popular legends and folk myths, and as transmitting medium for Francis Xavier Zhdolajczyk's communication from abroad. Thus the text combines both functions, transposing the narrator's faith and Mateo's Faustian will to knowledge into the American GI's yearning to return home to his family, to a milieu where faith and knowledge have coalesced into a drive for the new for complete and absolute rupture with the past; where St. Sylvester's mass can be appreciated only as a commodified object, the consumable image in a photograph.

So then in that suggested analogy, the text discovers its own truth. Just as Mateo is petrified the GI is caught in a trance, duplicating the narrator's enchanted and at the same time disenchanted gaze. For the GI's letdown, the anticlimactic dénouement, has been presaged in the beginning, hinting that the destruction of Manila and the mutability of worldly things are all subsumed and foreknown by the inaugural mass:

But when the clocks strike one o'clock, the bells instantly fall mute, the thundering music breaks off, the heavenly companies vanish—and in the cathedral, so lately glorious with lights and banners and solemn ceremonies, there is suddenly only the silence, only the chilly darkness of the empty naves; and at the altar, the single light burning before the Body of God. (p. 169)

Contraposed to the repetitiveness of myth, the cyclic unfolding of the narrative voice, is the climactic incarnation: the ruins and rubble. Lodged in the womb of the text itself is the exfoliating difference which explodes any illusion of serial continuity and unequivocal meaning. Outside the text, the mass evaporates.

Perhaps this incarnation is already realized in the text when Mateo's stone figure is restored to life: "His flesh unfreezes, his blood liquefies, his bones unlock, and he descends from the retablo to join the procession." He participates in the renewal of time, only to be penalized again into stone. The city has been reduced to formless stones, the raw materials worked on by human energy and will; the resurrection of the past, the repetition of the mass, can occur without any physical/material support, the conclusion seems to urge; that is, it can occur in the realm of pure imagination. Aestheticism triumphs. And yet, after this mass, we confront only the ruins and rubble—"the chilly darkness of the empty naves" and the darkness-enshrouded "Body of God." Could this be Joaquin's exemplum of an inescapable antinomy, the genuinely undecidable, an abysmal and vertiginous aporia?

"After the Picnic"

In exploring the intricate play of gender positions and the multiple, enigmatic embodiments of the psyche in Joaquin's art, it is easy to succumb to the temptation of applying the formulistic depth-psychology of Jung. The schema of the Mother Archetype delineated by Jung in his essay "Psychological Aspects of the Mother Archetype" can define for us the character of Fe Chavez as a phenomenon combining both the hypertrophy of the maternal instinct and the overdevelopment of Eros. In the first, the unconscious Eros in Fe manifests itself as a will to power over her father Dr. Chavez and over the weak-willed Pepe Valero. In the second, the intensification of Eros leads to what Jung calls "an unconscious incestuous relationship with the father." There are traces of both these aspects, but in the final scene Fe's identification with her mother (now dead for the last ten years) who was proud to her last breath in having shaped, nay, created the heroic masculinity of her husband, vanishes. The spell is broken: the father, having yielded to the temptation of desire, releases the daughter but finds himself the more arrested and bound to the mother/wife. Fe turns out to be only a simulacrum/projection of his psyche.

Such a reading can satisfy those who are already convinced of the a priori status of the archetype, but it is obvious how mechanically reductive this approach is, lacking the mediations of the text, the disseminated nuances and connotations infiltrating and saturating the narrative fabric. A similar error of haphazard generalization would ensue with the application of Jung's fascinatingly suggestive axiom: "The structure is something given, the precondition that is found to be present in every case. And this is the *mother*, the matrix—the form into which all experience is poured. The *father*, on the other hand, represents the dynamism of the archetype, for the archetype consists of both—form and energy."[24]

What defies the static and simplified symmetry of Jung's axiom is the narrative rendering of disintegrated or decentered personalities in which father and mother elements, the passive and active, the rational and erotic, mix and interact to generate not the rounded character in the sense E. M. Forster defined it but lines of forces, dynamic configurations of tendencies and relationships that can only be exemplified but never conceptually pinned down.

Take, for example, the intriguing figure of Chedeng Dacanay, the "Profesora," who offers a provocative challenge to the doctor. Described as "the only daughter in a family of cultured but ineffectual males," Chedeng develops ambivalent attitudes to males based on her role as the family income-producer:

She loved them and supported them even while she despised them. She did as she pleased; they stood in fear of her. She enjoyed being their bully; she would have liked to be their pet. A part of her craved for tenderness, envying those feminine women who make such docile wives; but another part of her bitterly spurned such women, was proudly independent, cynical and hard. (p. 33)

Chedeng perceives men as childish and infantile, anxiously wanting to be mothered, so that she has contempt for them. But mindful of the public mask, the assertion of her independent will, the narrator diagnoses what is repressed or submerged:

And yet, for quite a number, she had to suppress a very real and biting desire. For how can you give yourself to men you cannot help despising? Probably, the poor fools thought her frigid! She knew only too well how shameless the essential woman within her was, how voluptuous. If she went clad in armour, was it not for fear of being betrayed by the little panics of the flesh? (p. 33)

She has anticipated the male supremacist assumptions of Dr. Chavez, but she has determined to deny him "the rights of possession," the privilege which he enjoyed with his wife "to twist and torture and pound the soft woman and the hard woman that she was to fit into his cruel and perverse definition of a wife." Although she wants him, as she admits, she would not surrender: "I will not confound my will with his." This conforms with her view expressed earlier about marriage: "I will not make myself the mere mimicking shadow of the most perfect man in the world."

In contrast, Fe Chavez voices an attitude reflecting her mother's: Love is predicated on respect based on unquestioning belief that the man is in control, knows where he is going, so that the woman "feels herself impelled to follow him, to make his road her road...." Chedeng chides the implied advice of "looking up" to the man, a corollary of Dr. Chavez's notion that "A wife was one flesh with her husband." We are told that Fe has taken the place of the mother in complete devotion to satisfying the needs of the father, including that of listener to and worshipper of his legendary exploits in the 1896 Revolution. Virtually absorbed in such maternal care, a quasi-incestuous tie which her suitor Pepe Valero sees as slavery or self-renunciation, Fe identifies herself with her father to the point that she feels broken and shamelessly defeated when she realizes her father's symbolic yielding to Chedeng and, in effect, to the forces of modernity and chaos.

An antithetical pair, Fe and Chedeng illustrate the twin poles around which the thematic material gravitates: the subservient daughter emulating the traditional model of a woman as protector and nurturer, the energizing shadow or anima behind the male; the "liberated" woman who assets her will to the point where the power of Eros smolders and heats up, terrorizing the males, hence Dr. Chavez's premonition: "A paid harlot, he had long found out, could, after all, take nothing away from a man except his chastity. But this woman, if you gave in to her, would not leave you enough to hide your nakedness with, and then would taunt you for it." But Dr. Chavez is driven beyond prudence or rational self-preservation to shave off his moustache—a symbolic gesture of accepting Chedeng's wish as command—and answer a deep-seated craving to possess "this Chedeng Dacanay, this long-desired and long-resisted piano teacher, this woman of perilous contradictions, with her flesh so softly ripe and her eyes so hard, her body so languorous of build and so sharp and alert in motion" (p. 28).

Why is Dr. Chavez, whose unified or integrated psyche Fe extols to Pepe—"Either you like him wholly as he is or you do not like him at all. He is all of a piece"–so drawn to "this woman of perilous contradictions"? The text is dumb. The doctor explains it in his mind: "But now, this woman had come. Son-of-a-harlot—he was in for it again!" We can hazard a guess: an allegorical displacement occurs when, with the defeat of the Filipino revolutionaries and the consignment of their energies to the temporizing and reformist program of the Quezon-Osmeña *ilustrados* throughout the whole period of U.S. colonial domination, Dr. Chavez and his generation privatizes what was then a historically necessary if romanticized struggle. Note how the Filipino rebels incorporated within their thinking and sensibility the Spanish/medieval ideology, not the Renaissance humanist sentiments nor the radical ideas of the French Revolution, conceiving the anticolonial war as a resistance against the mother, a love-hate affair of adolescence inscribed in the memories of those who fought and died:

Fe Chavez rode with him to battle and found throbbing in her heart the harsh conflict of a hate that was also a love, of an anger that was also a tenderness, of a fear that was also a respect, because the proud, dark, tragic nation whom these men rose to meet as a foe, they also rose to salute as a mother.

Is the doctor then all of a piece, though lonely and alienated? It is Fe who registers "the outbursts of a man increasingly ill at ease in the world, of a man stranded and lost among an alien people, with whom he had in common neither speech nor sympathies, neither ideas nor gods" (p. 38).

Fe disappears from the concluding scene, merging with the ancestral house, but invoked as the ultimate authority—the phallic mother—without whom chaos supervenes.[25] Hence Dr. Chavez's last utterance here is a plea to preserve his identity reposing intact in the Other, the maternal daughter Fe—"Fe, where are you? I did not go to her, Fe! I never went at all! I swear it! Do you hear me, hey? Where are you?" We know the answer: Fe is there, the metaphor of a society and culture defined by a revolutionary purpose, by a collective will to resist. Such a determination to assert one's independence is mirrored in Chedeng Dacanay, the antithesis of Pepe's irresolute and inchoate self; but Chedeng's public or manifest stance conceals the profound splitting she experiences both physically and emotionally, a disintegration that is the modern woman's fate. She looms as a figure of transition from one order to another in the throes of being born:

There was a noise going on in her ears, a maddening sound of things falling, as though walls and pillars of stone were crumbling down upon her. She thought: I have never suffered like this before, but I would go through this the rest of my life rather than surrender. She was vaguely alarmed to note how, even at such a moment, there was a self of her that stood apart thus, watching and commenting, while another self was being so grievously tormented. (p. 37)

Knowing that love would make her tolerate and make up for the man's weakness, would make her extinguish her own consciousness of being separate, Chedeng subsists in the realm of the Imaginary, where transitivism characterizes the psyche's response to the world.[26] Her predicament is the mirror-image of Dr. Chavez; both are victims of the colonial fragmentation ruining that picnic called the Commonwealth era. And while Joaquin may want us to join with Pepe's horrified escape from the claustrophobic anxiety and incestuous isolation of the Chavez family, this invitation does not really distract—in fact, it serves to focus attention more on that failure of the text to heal the cleavage between Fe's conception of her father's integrity and her self-enclosed subjectivity bound to a past fixed in memory, unable to realize itself in the present, and the father's quest to relive that past or restore it by addressing another, Chedeng, and possessing his vanished identity in that site of the other woman whose refusal in itself signifies the cunning of desire.

In a sense, the contradictions we perceive between the futility of a nostalgic affirmation of a sexist code glorified by its association with the 1896 Revolution, and the painful, ambiguous ordeal of individualism instanced separately in Chedeng Dacanay and in Pepe Valero, stand out clearly—contradictions which Dr. Chavez's return does not efface. This is what we confront "after the picnic," after that interregnum of fantasy and make-believe in the existence of free-floating monads called egos: the power of desire to seize bodies and wills in that ineluctable gap when needs remain unsatisfied by the response to the demands for love, so that what comes out in the balance is a fetish of an image, the protective and quietly suffering dead mother. Coeval with the father's resurrection of the past in his narration to his daughter enchanted by it all, the mother looms as the signifier of difference, the primordial lack or absence which the text tries to fill up but instead paradoxically magnifies. For Dr. Chavez, embodiment of the Name-of-the-Father and therefore of the Law/taboo against incest, himself witnesses to the infinite distance that separates the static aura of the revolutionary sacrifice which supposedly begot "a new nation" and the defeat of that project by U.S. imperialism which has substituted itself as the new Law, the new Name-of-the-Father, rendering Dr. Chavez impotent and unable to make peace with the representatives of this new dispensation, Chedeng and Pepe. Both father and daughter (described as a homogeneous pair) are fatally caught up in maintaining a myth which occludes but cannot prevent the disruptions of history, and their predicament can only be resolved by that absent but everywhere diffused Law or Prohibition against incest, to which the whole text alludes: the reality of American colonial domination.

"A Pilgrim Yankee's Progress"

Unique among Joaquin's narratives for its choice of introducing an ostensibly American protagonist embroiled in a slight affair of misunderstanding which becomes a parable of cultural relativism, "A Pilgrim Yankee's Progress" illustrates the limits of thought and intention removed from the context of history. Except for the inclusion of an American witness to the miraculous event in "The Mass of St. Sylvester," this is the only occasion in Joaquin's fiction where an attempt to grapple frontally with the U.S. presence is made.

Curiously, however, the representative of American society and culture here, Andrew Newman, displays a classic if stereotyped Puritanism complete with scrupulous ethical earnestness and totally unpragmatic tactlessness. It is quite difficult to believe that Newman would behave in a nasty way upon visiting the Camachos whose patriarchs (both Doña Concha's father and her husband are employees of the American firm) are closely associated with Andrew Newman's grandfather. Newman's hidden romantic impulse may explain this inability to heed the particular demands or expectations of his host. But it becomes clear that his paying homage to a dead uncle killed by Filipino insurgents in the Filipino-American War of 1899-1902, and his courtesy call at the Camachos, form part of what I would call the imperialist syndrome couched here in the ethos of Puritanical idealism. Talking to Pepang in the cemetery—the dead or the past lies completely at the mercy of the living—Newman interprets the motivation for the American military-political-cultural invasion of the Philippines during what he calls "that comic-opera war," the Spanish-American War of 1898: "But for a million boys like him, it was an escape at last, a release from the boredom and the tyranny of the small towns." The war then provided the relief and escape from U.S. commercial-business society where straightjacketed small towns languished as a result of the expansion of the industrialized cities. Newman of course does not comprehend this phenomenon. Aside from escape, another motive surfaces as more compelling: "Might helps make America become a part of the world instead of being a world to itself. That all those astonished American boys that sailed out to discover the Orient afresh might discover it for good, and that the blood they spilled here might help fix the Orient in the American imagination."

The key to the tragicomic irony and paradoxical resolution of the plot inheres in the last phrase: "fix the Orient in the American imagination." The "fix" we discover concerns, first, Newman's fixation on a fanatical moralism that indicts capitalist corruption—"We're afflicted with something like that curse on Midas: We corrupt what we touch"—but rests content with an easy confession to his mother whose function here, her absence/silence, underscores the ambiguity of the text. Second, the Camachos who supposedly fill in the blank called "Orient," for all their gracious and selfless hospitality (based on an utterly colonial mentality evinced by gratitude for the "liberators," etc.), exhibit a slavish or self-negating attitude to the antiimaginative gesture of unspoken apology offered by Newman.

What needs closer analysis is how the colonial, self-deprecating attitude of the Camacho couple is shrouded by a feeling of egotism, as witnessed in Edong's scorn for the "*absurdum* of Yanqui innocence": "But what welcome, what affection in this world is entirely disinterested? . . . Certainly the rest of the world had long learned to take for granted that no prayer is pure piety, no kiss pure affection, no alms pure benevolence, and that even the noblest act of sacrifice is selfish somewhere." But this argument is opposed by their existential renewal, by one disinterested impulse behind their entertaining Newman: "Because they had become thoughtful through suffering and were feeling profoundly human for the first time in their lives." This is contained within a kind of pragmatic realism on the native's part, a realism which itself stems from psychic distortions spelled out later on when Pepang maneuvers the second encounter with Newman to prevent his offering any apology—a species of ingratiation, leading to Newman's rejection of the

Camacho couple's accommodation to their own illusion.

Are we then confronted with the clash between Newman's earnest desire to be taken as an honest individual validated for his pure intention of appreciating the "Orient" and the Camachos' ethical-moral agonizing, torn between a fascination with American "candor" (or what they think of as candor) and their guilt in not acting with serious self-denial?

To resolve this conflict, the narrative employs the figure of Doña Concha, sixty-year-old mother of Edong, who incorporates the past in her memory of the first sight of Americans appareled in her colorful blouses and skirts—an image of the brutal conqueror neutralized by the spontaneous energies of the feminine: "Those gorgeously colored and gorgeously appareled giants were, indubitably, the strangers they had so craved a terrified glimpse of . . . in her mind, she was busy rigging him up in the drooping laces and the vivid balloon skirts of her girlhood." This causes her to misconstrue Newman's visit: "For young Newman had clearly come in a spirit of gay malice, as one comes to enjoy a highly unsuccessful pageant put on by one's foes," hence her suspending convention for this invented persona. She is proven wrong: Newman accuses them as "rats." To which she responds by a meditation on the uncompromising egotism of innocence:

She had had experience of innocence and knew how stubbornly it refuses to bargain, to compromise, or (when the rest of us wink and bear it) to be cheated of a grain. And in her heart she knew it to be right. Impossible, yes, its dream of perfect charity; impossible the people who measured reality by the dream. Impossible but not mistaken, though the reality of human relationships be a shameful traffic in profits. The realists took what they could get; the dreamers, demanding the true measure or nothing, usually got nothing. That was better than the spoiled commodity the "realists" always ended up with—the dropped crumbs of love that so quickly became ashes in the mouth....To be loved for oneself—that was what the speechlessness of babies demanded of the grown-up heart. And surely she had seen everything when a big full-grown man demanded to be accepted as one accepts a child! (pp. 102-3)

Doña Concha opts for innocence, for dreamers, as against realists. This reckoning precedes and supplements the explanation for the first contretemps in Newman's letter to his mother where he posits the incommensurability of cultures, the fatal ethnocentrism each one labors with, and the ubiquitous self-blame entailed by one's assumption of being right. Newman's letters serve to deconstruct Doña Concha's thesis of innocence as a homogeneous condition, for we see how bifurcated and decentered Newman's consciousness is, endlessly undercut by the doubt which springs from immediacy, the upholding of appearances and the moment as the truth: "I messed up everything with all my damnable suspicions, dratted cuss that I am. And it's such a hopeless circle, Mom. First you botch all relations with other people by being so difficult and wary, then you worry yourself to death wondering if you hurt somebody."

Newman's letters of self-interrogation and evaluation of the preceding incident generated by the incident itself exemplifies how the text achieves a self-awareness which exposes the inadequacy of Doña Concha's belief in the intelligible meaning of events and the insufficiency of her role here as a kind of central intelligence imposing order and significance to the narrative scheme. The text exploits these letters—effects of incidents—to generate in turn another incident which will fulfill the requirements of discourse and also subvert its call for coherence.

When Newman returns after four months, things are not in the same place as before because precisely what has happened impacts on the Camachos (both of whom experience the cycle of penitence, shame, disgust and self-hate) and impels them to (in Doña Concha's words) cancel the past by ignoring it. Doña Concha urges the Camachos to accept Newman's apology on the ground that by standing fast on conventions, he would draw the right conclusions. Whether Newman knows those conventions, is an unbroached topic; but Doña Concha, suffused with her memory of the fierce conquerors draped in women's apparel, operates with a comic distance that permits her to allow that "perhaps he [Newman] possesses a conscience. Perhaps he understands the dignity of penitence and of the desire to be forgiven." Unable to persuade the Camachos, she refuses to see the American; and this refusal, plus the subsequent fiasco of the couple's plan and their resumption of "normal" bickering, begets the final rationalizing which tries to make sense of what has transpired:

And if to be mad was now to be normal, thought Doña Concha, sitting down and resuming her beads, then it was futile indeed to preach moderation, and too late for moderate cures. The pattern of society, mutilated by war as it was, had better be pulled loose altogether. How now invoke the ties that bind men when all human intercourse was an infection? A plague was abroad and a plague calls for quarantine. Herded together, men rotted each other; apart, their own loneliness might heal and purify them. It was time again, thought Doña Concha, for the cell of the ascetic and the cave of the anchorite. Time again for harsh hermits to lead the populace out of the cities and to disperse them among the wastes of the desert. Thus had the world saved itself once from the violence of its own disgust with itself. Disciplined and rejuvenated by solitude, tears, fasting, silence and wrestling with devils, it had emerged to discover, with awkward awe and astonishment, the green of the leaves and the joy of human companionship. Had emerged to discover and to adore Salvation as a Woman (whether virgin or mother), and, enthroned in her arms, Deity as a Child. How long before the world would be fit again to make that discovery? wondered Doña Concha, hearing another glass break, downstairs, and Pepang shrieking. It would take a long time, she feared, considering that the world had fallen so low there were no more women these days. No more women and no more children, grimly concluded Doña Concha, rising and going off to fetch ammonia and mercurochrome. (pp. 110-11)

As if to fulfill her eschatological musings, Doña Concha's discourse in turn begets the image of the ascetic and solitary hermit Newman, the lone individual—we don't see him at all as part of the Liberation Day celebrations observed by Edong in the Manila streets—whose one-way colloquy with the absent mother is the text's mimesis of Doña Concha's notion of the solitary prophet adoring salvation as a Woman (Newman's mother). In effect, Newman is the Deity as Child whose epistolary reflections critique Yankee imperialist chauvinism amid his stubborn self-righteousness—a weird combination indeed:

You never know (he wrote) just what to expect people to do at a certain moment until the moment occurs and they don't do it. I think it funny now to have brought along candy and flowers but only because I have realized that, after how I acted the other time, if I ever dared to show up again they would naturally (if they were really innocent) and promptly have done certain things—like slapping my face, breaking my neck, and throwing me out the window. When they came down instead with grins a mile wide and started trying to get me all hot and confused by giving me the 50-caliber talk-stuff and winking at each other all the time—why, I started smelling that rat again, all the way from Denmark.

It's a strange thing all right, to be an American. But maybe it's just as strange and difficult to be other people. Trouble is we Americans act as if we owned a patent on strangeness. We do any number of things that must annoy and flabbergast other people and we do them as if it were our duty to annoy and flabbergast others. But we don't like to find other people's actions annoying or flabbergasting in any way. We take for granted that anybody that's civilized at all and smart acts like an American. It will surely take a lot of time, goodwill and labor before no people are strange to other peoples and nobody's a foreigner anywhere. We Americans don't exactly hasten the process by being so awe-struck by the strangeness of us.

Notice here that Newman's education, the import of his pilgrimage, assumes the traditional *Bildungsroman* pattern of intent or purpose being contradicted by the twist of circumstance. Yet he learns nothing except that others are alien to your habits of thinking: he presumed the Camachos would be angry, remembering the nasty treatment he showed them, but this presumption fails to take into account the Others' existential plight. This is of course his blindness, a defect not compensated by his condemnation of the "American" as a national type. To shift his disappointment to a lack of American tolerance or liberalism, is to avoid allowing empathy with the Other even as he repudiates chauvinism and self-righteous indignation in the same breath. Finally, Newman believes that the Others were trying honestly and sincerely to communicate, to empathize, although the Camachos' efforts, as I pointed out above, operates from wrong assumptions too. Newman attributes the failure of communication to his impatience: "As usual, I had sullenly turned off the lights too soon."

Newman's letter, a model of heterogeneous and dispersed writing, explodes the assured and prescriptive tone of Doña Concha's commentary on the malaise of the times. One can conjecture that Newman is really addressing Doña Concha, who by discursive logic becomes the mother surrogate; it is her affirmation of the Madonna (mother and child) and of innocence which presupposes Newman's agency, his actantial function, as a negation of culture and society as such founded on egotistic reason and self-hating individualism. But if Newman is the Child-Deity, he is also sealed off in a solipsistic universe established by the mother's absence/presence, incapable of interpreting cultural signifiers correctly because he is hopelessly detached from what Lacan calls "the Real," which is history. What the text underlines here is that moral intent alone, whether Newman's or Doña Concha, proves unavailing in the face of class violence and imperialist terror. Pepang's haunting memory of her house's explosion and the screaming of her children who perished in the war while momentarily displaced by the hedonistic impulse of that time, obtrudes as a recalcitrant objection to the totalizing gospel of Doña Concha and the flawed liberalism of the Puritan conscience.

Beyond or amid the din of the Camachos quarreling and the private thoughts of Doña Concha and the confessional letter of Newman is more than a half-century of U.S. colonialism and neocolonialism, from the barbaric counterinsurgency campaigns of the American military in what the scholar Bernard Fall calls "the bloodiest colonial war ever fought by a white power in Asia," to the Cold War suppression of the Huks and the present, which has been summarily encapsulated in Edong's metaphor of the War as the magnification of everything corrupt—"the criminal greeds and cynical grafts." It is this silence of the text on what underlies the Newman-Camacho affair which counterpoints and exacerbates the heteroglossia of utterances, the layers of contradictions and antinomies conflated in this parodic pilgrimage.

"It Was Later Than We Thought"

No other historical or sociopsychological event in all of Joaquin's textual practice looms so cataclysmic in impact, so incalculably fraught with nihilistic and sinister implications as the Second World War, the holocaust of the Japanese occupation of Manila and its subsequent total destruction—in particular, the scorched-earth tactics inflicted on Intramuros by U.S. bombs and artillery during that ambiguous transitional moment called "liberation" ushering the Philippines into the postmodern era. Because it physically disintegrated the cultural artifacts of the past and coaxed onto the surface far more insidious treachery and base survival instincts than the U.S. invasion of 1898 and the savage onslaughts which followed, the interimperialist rivalry we know as the Second World War proved more disruptive and recalcitrant to the synthesizing powers of Joaquin's imagination. It was the intractable historic difference that the rhetoric of metaphysics could not flatten or reduce to equivalence. Not because Joaquin did not understand that it was an interimperialist fight for markets and sources of raw materials. Not because he failed to understand that both the Japanese and Americans would not respect the sanctity of Intramuros and the integrity of persons—Joaquin provides ample evidence of this awareness in his *Free Press* journalistic period, and in other historiographical forays. It is because the fundamental moral conception of good and evil which informs his judgment of history prevents him from fully grasping the complex nature of social forces in conflict by locking him into a cosmic, abstract conception of change so vigorously attested to here in the fiercely casuistic commentary of Angel Cabrera, dramatized in the seriofarcical exchanges between Tony Banzon and his wife Chayong, and filtered in the public/private discourse of Lulu Cabrera. What qualifies and somewhat redeems this insistent axiological bifurcation of the world is the subdued, almost drowned-out voice of Father Noe Cabrera and his invocation of the utopian force of Blake's revolutionary vision of building Jerusalem on earth in his sermon during the novena to the Immaculate Conception, 7 December 1941.

To that pivotal day on the eve of what in Joaquin's calendar would be the singular apocalypse of the century, the narrative directs us in a passage from Angel Cabrera's journal—Cabrera's thoughts occupy a preponderant role and are invested with a qualitatively zealous, obsessive tone. He bewails the curse of progress which has afflicted Babel and its latter-day descendants, a curse whose immediate symptom is the form of the narrative itself—a seemingly random, heterogeneous accumulation of ad hoc thoughts, data, etc.; seemingly arbitrary extracts from letters, diaries, sermons, journals, and magazine column which span the range from the intimate confessional mode of the letters and diaries to the reflexive mode of Cabrera's journal to the public modes of forensic or epideictic speech in Father Noe's sermons, and the mock-private exhibitionism of Lulu Cabrera's column in the *Merchandiser*, a label signifying precisely the crisis-ridden world of commodity-exchange which unknowingly is the real theme of this story, albeit the ostensible target of Angel's jeremiad: "And not a soul in all that roaring whirlpool of confusion—not a soul in all that vile welter of lust, lies, greed and pride and corruption—not a soul in all the damned miles of Babel-town to realize that it was cursed, cursed, and cursed." By so bluntly and starkly thematizing the design of the text itself, the excerpt condemns itself as one more shrill "truly Babelian" sound, just like Tony Banzon's mawkish complaint of guilt and pathetic vacillation which succeeds it, or

Father Noe's eloquent sermon which precedes it.

Could this be then the text's self-deconstructing strategy inscribed in the very texture of seriality hollowed by the ultimate already-absent but present effect of a cause, history itself?

It is not the portentous advent of the war that preoccupies the narrative desire-producing machine, an unprecedented violence which would shatter illusions and restore the disillusioned to their senses, but rather the anarchy and decadence of modern urban society, its hypocritical worship of Intellect and Progress (to echo Angel Cabrera's journal entry of 28 October 1941) which the Second World War symptomatically represents. The text's antitechnological stance—a typically romantic or Lawrencian harangue—condemns the milieu's spurious cosmopolitanism whose Babelian deceitfulness (the text itself) is captured by Angel Cabrera's impressions of an election rally in Manila, 4 November 1941; and by Lulu Cabrera's impression of a "Red, White and Blue Ball" (5 December 1941). In both these instances one can glimpse, underneath the kaleidoscopic texture of sensory distractions and surface enigma, the bankruptcy of a moribund colonial system, the failure of U.S. imperialist hegemony to maintain coherence and teleological meaningfulness. The text itself registers the surface manifestations of the crisis of colonial-liberal democracy where culture serves only to vainly distract Chayong Banzon from her marital problems (see her impressions of a literary conference in Manila, 12 November 1941) and an excuse for Angel Cabrera's speculation on the need for transcendental essences, "some vantage point" (see his entry, 12 November 1941). And for the collapse of the hierarchic and essentializing politicoeconomic structure, one can note the anti-Babelian and deliberate juxtaposition of "pools of wine eddying round piles of ordure" and the highfalutin slogans of "Dynamic National Uplift" during the Commonwealth election rally recorded by Angel Cabrera on 4 November 1941. The Yeatsian prophecy—"the centre cannot hold, mere anarchy is loosed upon the world"—echoes through the half-orchestrated syncopations of the voices traumatized in/by the text.

What is strikingly obvious here at this point is the way the carnivalesque alternation of voices seemingly emitted at random, the playful whirligig of notations, the veritable polyphony of idiom and styles—all these acrobatics of discourse, the mimicking of variegated intonations, the dialogical fugue are meant to produce a simulacrum of order, albeit the order of confusion and anarchy evolving toward apocalyptic judgment: the unitary goal, the harmonizing purpose, the absolute telos. This observation directly contradicts our earlier allegation that the artist's synthesizing power has broken down here on the face of an impending social and moral catastrophe. It seems as if war, this irrational unleashing of repressed energies and desires, would finally shame the hubris of reason. But if so, then such an argument would only prove that the cunning of the text can escape or avoid its thematic fate, and conversely that the theme of linguistic (or ideological) strife—perhaps the materialization of competitive, predatory capitalism in the mercantile stage—can only be mimetically captured by its dialectical opposite. In any case, what we perceive is the metamorphosis of war as the vindication of a providential genius or spirit which presided over the now archaic centralized feudal dispensation, war as the restoration of justice, i.e., the founding father's vengeance. (I refuse to confine this text merely to the level of a language game or aesthetic ruse along the lines that a mechanical structuralist explication would decree.)

For, indeed, there are substantial issues, thematic concerns foregrounded by the text itself, which cannot be resolved by mere formalistic description of synchronic paradigms and diachronic repetitions. And the thematizing of the form itself testifies to the urgency of the issues not the least of which is the spectacle of a conventional narrative apparatus (classic expressive realism) strained, tortured, and ravaged by the very absence (and thus obsessive presence) of any object of desire, an absence whose only adequate figure in this anxious and jazzed-up medley of voices in quest of a harmonizing chord would be the breakup of marriages and the dissolution of the traditional family in its role as prime ideological suture.

We can also trace the vicissitudes of this absence or symptomatic presence in the sickness and final withdrawal of the father from the world and the retreat/confinement of the harassed, nonconforming Bitoy at Camp X. Between the father and the children, a breakdown of communication supervenes; ruptures multiply between Tony Banzon and his wife, and between them and their circle of relatives and friends. Amid the mutual accusations and recriminations, Tony asserts his determination to "stay out of the world," playing in an illusory "china-universe" to which Chayong responds:

> Break your shell, Tony; break your shell and come out to this world.... I never made a doll out of you. I found you the lone toy-dweller of the lone toy-house in a lone toy-world and I stayed as long as I could stand it. But it's not safe any longer—this china-universe of yours. There's going to be an earthquake soon and I don't care to be smothered under your fragments, or the fragments of your house, or the fragments of your world. (p. 68)

This allusion to the destruction of an imaginary shelter is both literal (the collapse of a watchtower in Samar, the recurrent blackouts, etc.) and metaphoric (the dissolution of marriages, family, etc.). Underlying these images of instability and breakdown is the moral fanaticism of Angel Cabrera and its corollary in the erratic, frenzied response of Tony (telegram and letters from 21 November to 2 December). For Tony, the "toys and dolls" of his world (as Eden Rios and his other women) can only be paltry substitutes and replacements for that eclipsed and forever vanishing object of desire ("liberty," individual freedom)—the space of time ritualized in the sacred city—which could no longer be located in bodies, wealth, status; and which has now evaporated into the phantasmagoric realm of chance, accident, caprice, indecisiveness, whence his refusal "to face the world."

With the positioning of the Symbolic Order at stake and the place of the castrating patriarch vacated, and the putative husband in hiding, the mother and her daughters assert themselves and dominate the scene, the mother consoling her son Bitoy and Lulu paying homage to the past: "Trouble is: he's a gentleman, and none of us could be. We're this ugly and vulgar world he hates so much, and here it is, eating right at table with him!" What this preemptive assertion of the feminine implies, among others, is the transcendence of eschatology and the surpassing of the ethical dualism in Angel and Lulu by a genuinely dialectical vision embodied in Father Noe's voice. It is a revealing tactic for the narrative to deploy the "Father's" voice and its confessional thrust mediated through the sister Chayong whose reflections in turn indicate the repudiation of a purely individualistic, liberal atomistic orientation:

No, I'm not concerned about culpability. Maybe it's your fault, maybe mine, maybe not ours at all. We picked a ghastly age to be married in, Tony-boy; an age where "nothing is clear, nothing defined—not the relation of man to God, nor of man to Society, nor of man to woman. Wherefore, in the streets, a war of classes; in the home, a war of the sexes; and within the flesh, a soul that is its own battleground and its own fierce foe." (p. 63)

This totalizing outlook, an analogical and manichean vision, can be amplified in his advice to Bitoy, his brother, not to torment himself too much: "You are not culpable. It is not your faith that is little: it is the faithlessness of the world that is great. For, modern notions notwithstanding, religion can be no one man's private affair. What the rest of the world believes—or fails to—conditions his capacity for either affirmation or denial. In an age of faith everyone is devout, even the most depraved; in an age of heresy everyone is a heretic, even the most orthodox; and in an age of unbelief, everyone is a skeptic, even the saints...." But the invocation of the spirit of the times (*Zeitgeist*) cannot explain the discontinuities, ruptures, transgressions.

Although the space devoted to Father Noe is proportionately less than those accorded to Tony and Angel, his voice here performs the strategic function of sublimation and transvaluation, or at least he enacts the function of victimization and purification. His rhetoric incorporates Angel Cabrera's distrust of Progress and anxious search for a "vantage point" ("Above this madness of waters, this eternal flux of salt waters, does no rock rise unconfounded: unmoved, unmoving, and unmovable; for ever assailed and for ever victorious?"). By assimilating all the anxieties and doubts pervading the consciousness of the other characters, Father Noe may be conceived here as the central reconciling intelligence. He resolves (or gives the illusion of resolving) the historic contradictions by a dialectical mysticism—the Holy Child "is of nowhere in particular and everywhere in general"—infused with a sense of species solidarity ("We are responsible for the slackers too.") and a determined theodicy that discerns a submerged rationale in every event: marrying and having babies "was saying yes to the God who authored creation and found it good."

While rejecting individual culpability, Father Noe assigns collective culpability to sinful humanity. But he maneuvers beyond a Calvinistic despair (strongly resonant in Angel Cabrera's last journal entry) by an orthodox Christian humanism whose genealogy with pre-Counter-Reformation, renaissance world view Joaquin would make explicit in other works. His allusion to Blake and the utopian motivation of supernatural/radical humanism suggests for us what would be Joaquin's ultimate approach to the problem of the Second World War and its paralyzing deferred action (Freud's *Nachträglich* effect), an approach elaborated in the play *The Portrait of an Artist as Filipino* and the novel *The Woman Who Had Two Navels*, namely, a militant secular activism presided by the constantly renovating myth or trope of the Immaculate Conception:

The Building of Jerusalem! Is not this the task to which we are called and to which we should be dedicated? The ground on which we must build: it is defiled; we must make it holy. The air in which we must build: it is shackled: we must set it free. Why are there today so many refugees in the towers of ivory? Is it not because we have made a vast sty of the earth? And why are there among us so many sitters upon fences? Is it not because we have cluttered the world with fences?

So must we travail to bring forth Heaven's empire upon earth even as *she* travailed the feast of whose conception we celebrate tomorrow; from whose flesh was hewn the corner-stone upon which we are to build; and like whose flesh, even the New Jerusalem must arise: *out of all our imperfections, yet itself perfection.* (pp. 74-75)

The context and reference are clear, yet we cannot help extrapolate from this prophetic invocation the reason why, instead of concluding positively and triumphantly with Father Noe's sermon, the text instead privileges Lulu Cabrera's message: an ambiguous celebration of sacrifice.

However, the ambiguity cuts both ways as a purgative or cathartic stage in the process of incarnating the providential, or matrifocal unity underlying punctual chaos. We perceive that her impulse of wish-fulfillment, her fanciful conversion of the Babel city to "a sleeping palace in the fairy tale" evokes the same utopian motivation, a coalescence of negation and affirmation, which informs Father Noe's final comment, a cancelling of the individualistic anarchy of a market-dominated commodity world fragmented into atomized wills and privatized consciousness. Significantly, this "father" (a stand-in signifier for the annulled patriarch) affirms an imaginary community founded on an ordered hierarchy of values centered on the Virgin Mother. Lulu Cabrera no longer writes about her family; her distance to events affords her a sense of humor, and her "Advice to Girls in These Parlous Times" discloses feminine gusto, a deterritorialized drive which, in serving as the vehicle of the erotic death wish, impels defiance of the risks of pain, suffering, war, chaos. There is no easy formula of optimism and guaranteed salvation unless one contends for a strictly doctrinal hermeneutic of the text.

We thus end our reading confronted by ironic and satiric verbal play, a spoof at the conventional morality of aggressors, the interpretation of blackouts as magical reinstalling of a fantasy realm where desire awaits its enchanted but forever suspended, delayed fulfillment, where the whole world becomes invested with the irrepressible energies of the unconscious. But again, this theme entails a political project: Father Noe's faith reveals the limits of individual hedonism which, lacking any collective force to compensate for its inadequacies, demands the advent of a more rigorous materialist critique of that psychic distress which Marx, in his "Contribution to the Critique of Hegel's Philosophy" (1884), calls "the expression of real distress," "the sigh of the oppressed creature, the heart of a heartless world, . . . the spirit of a spiritless situation."

3 From the Terror of History to the Return/Doubling of the Repressed

"The Legend of the Virgin's Jewel"
"The Legend of the Dying Wanton"
"Doña Jeronima"

HURLED INTO A WORLD where life is "nasty, brutish and short" already far removed from the patrocentric cosmology of Hobbes, the artists of late twentieth-century global capitalism inhabiting the periphery are often tempted to envision an original past of secure and blissful organic community—Rizal's "Lost Eden" perhaps, or an even more remote millenarian nexus of individual psyche and collective totem which informs the *episteme* of utopian-anarchist sects throughout the underdeveloped margins of the Third World today. For the radical avant-garde, say Ursula LeGuin and Stanislaw Lem, the utopian genre of science fiction affords the space for recuperating archaic elements of the naturally heterogeneous in fictional planets made credible by the device of "cognitive estrangement." Earlier, before the definitive crisis of imperial capital, D.H. Lawrence tentatively explored the possibilities of reconstituting a new contract between individual and society through a willed revival of pre-Columbian Aztec myths by transitional protagonists dramatized in *The Plumed Serpent*. Such efforts have yielded ambiguous practices capable of decentering or undermining the received consensus of beliefs guaranteed by realist and postrealist texts, but they only underline the difficulties of the liberal imagination educated into suspecting and rejecting all genres, forms, conventions in the name of the "free individual."

Joaquin's approach to the impending dissolution of the bourgeois ego unstuck by the atomistic fragmentation of the semifeudal formation under U.S. colonial bondage proceeds by a detour: the resuscitation of legends or quasi-parabolic tales of individual dissolution and the founding of society through sacrifice. Such legends are narrative exempla designed to contain the irrational surd in form and content; their strategies of containment presuppose our complicity in witnessing and testifying to the numinous, the originating rupture, by identification with both narrator and protagonist.

Is Joaquin then simply refurbishing the realistic mode and revitalizing it by demonstrating its efficacy when used to transmit fantastic, abnormal or eccentric material, thus capturing our belief through empathy? What indeed are the conditions of the texts' possibility, the enabling rules of these myth-making, Desire-fabricating machines?

The first paragraph of "The Legend of the Virgin's Jewel" approximates the veridical Chekhovian announcement of character plunged in action:

The first time Brother Fernando noticed the bowl of milk he had been too busy to wonder. He was new to the country, having but lately arrived from Spain in this year of our Lord 1620, and too engrossed in his duties as brother-sacristan of the convent of Santo Domingo of Manila to worry about a bowl of milk left at the foot of a tree. (p. 42)

The juxtaposition of the institutionalized ritual attached to convents and the spectacle of pagan offering before "a massive Laocoon of a tree" (this allusion to the punishment of Laocoon, as I will note later, becomes a trope for the negation of the patriarch), reinforced by details on the dependence of the convent on "a flock of goats pastured outside the City," sets the stage for the Spanish friar's encounter with heathen/diabolic propitiatory practice, his initial curiosity and repulsion, and the delirium the spectacle induces in him. The thematic conflict between Christian faith and an incomprehensible pagan devotion, an opposition already domesticated and resolved in Philippine culture through the syncretic absorption of the latter into the former, is what Joaquin foregrounds in order to conceal what we can bluntly state as the annulment of the Oedipus complex by the successful castration of the father (here symbolized by the decapitation of the serpent, the wresting of the phallic jewel and its eventual offering to the Virgin Mother) and the terrible price it exacts, the loss of ego-identity. This allegorical formulation of the subtext, however, is qualified by the fact that Brother Fernando's experiential horizon (the combat and ordeal) is traversed by "tortured dreams" and feverish delirium, thus setting the groundwork for the reader's acceptance of the macabre violence delivered in baroque prose style within the framework of a believable pathological context.

Brother Fernando's psychology as constructed by the narrative establishes the rationale for the slaying of the tutelary chthonic monster, the keeper-guardian of the prized offering: "He was insatiable and, having exhausted the secular, now turned to the spiritual domain for newer sensations and profounder adventures." This confidence springs from the ideological apparatus sustaining the Spanish colonizer (friar or soldier): "Spain was mistress of the world, and all the earth was Spanish earth." The combination of imperial power as feminine and the earth as subsumed within it (both metaphoric and metonymic) anticipates, of course, the animation of the Virgin as mother/bride. But more important, the attribution of primacy to the earth already subordinates the serpent as the mythical representative of subterranean deities; moreover, under the aegis of the feminine psyche symbolized by the moon (eclipsed however by the jewel construed as phallus), the serpent's power is already diminished before the actual encounter. But these mythical analogues and tropes deflect from the text's real project: the founding of community through the emergence of the phallic mother.

It is through Brother Fernando's withdrawal into thoughts on "the popular devotion" to the Virgin in Spain—before the Spanish victory over the Dutch in 1646, the Virgin was still eclipsed—and the invocation of the communal particularization of the Virgin as presiding goddess of the local hearth that enables him to repossess himself after the process of self-disintegration watching "the nameless, ageless, meaningless horror outside." So this exiled and uprooted Spanish subject does not really find himself a "native" of the place; his alienation or decentering can only be remedied by a retreat into a sacred precinct, the chapel of the convent: "But tonight the world of Christendom, the world of his childhood and of his fathers, was represented by this poor Virgin, this colonial Virgin, clad in simple robes and wearing a simple crown. She was history and tradition. She was familiar. Primeval terrors dissolved before her smile"(p. 44). And yet, despite this retreat into his homeland and birthplace, Brother Fernando fails to exorcise the seductive terror of that "primal scene," the descent of the serpent from the tree, its voluptuous motions and its sucking of the proffered milk. Note the erotic cathexis underlined in this sentence: "Brother Fernando watched in horror and fascination, unconsciously working his tongue in rhythm to the sucking of the serpent." The verbally induced fetishism of the jewel as a dazzling transfiguring flame, already prepared by the observer's hunger for exotic pleasures and outlandish sensations, strikes us then as an emblem of excluded and condemned nature (mother, earth) which needs to be tamed, bound, captured, just as the "old man" who offers the bowl of milk has been rendered anonymous and accidental, a prefiguration of the castrating deed Brother Fernando will perform. But before his assumption of the role of adventurer-hero, the text inserts his hallucination or dream of the Virgin of Zaragoza ("patroness of Columbus, symbol of the race"), in which the Virgin—her veil was around his neck—appears to him, the surrogate-mother consoling him, reminding him of his childhood days in Alcala: "Then he said, with much formality, how it pained him to the heart, Señora, to see her thus, clad so simply, who had seen her most nobly crowned and arrayed in her shrine at Zaragoza." I t is this desire to endow the mother with the prized object, a possession that will distinguish her and consecrate the milieu to her, that drives him to kill the serpent who appeared with an "embroidered coat... luxurious enough for a king"—the heathen tutelary god displaced by the Virgin Mother.

The priest-hero who enacts the ordeal of killing the native deity, which we may also read as the castration of the patriarchal numen (Joaquin later repudiates this patriarchal ascription in favor of a matriarchal descent) associated with the pagan tribes, offers the jewel to Mary whom he also addresses as "my lady" and "my mother," a double eroticizing gesture not attenuated by the reference of "the Child [who] slept in her arms." This Madonna figure who "had emerged from the dusk of her altar" inscribed in the delirium of the seventeenth-century mystical hedonist thus inaugurates the founding of the community, a completely ironic refusal of, or disguise for, the patriarchal violence of Legaspi and Salcedo. But the text, in its foreshadowing devices and construction of the psychic predisposition of the protagonist, rationalizes the violence as proof of intense religious dedication and normalizes the violation of the incest-taboo as part of the (warrior-priest) colonizer's celebration of the Virgin Mother.

This is then a "legendary" or genealogical unfolding of a conquest, the negation of rupture (separation from the mother/land), through an act of symbolic castration whereby the individual ego fades in the maternal embrace. Instead of the Father's will (the Law) materializing, it is the son's offering of "the Law" to the Mother and thus the Father's absence that the text enacts, implying that the conquest of the non-Christian world demands this compensatory revenge against the imperialist plunder of the colonies for gold and silver. Earth (sublimated here in the localized fertility goddess made acceptable under the Virgin Mother's guise) takes revenge, a fact that is simultaneously refused (the priest-son faints) and acknowledged.

Framed within this heroic quest, the psychological verisimilitude of a homesick anxious priest-soldier unweaned yet from the maternal fold of imperial Spain, the guilt of murder—the brutal rape and looting of cultures anchored to the soil—is propitiated by the workings of a "natural" love (between son and mother) which heals the rupture of birth and separation. Thus the aesthetic ruse of the legend yields its effect by a subtle encapsulation of the scandalous—the historic crimes—in the fantasy of the generic secular romance propagated in evangelical mass-consumed literature.

What "The Legend of the Virgin's Jewel" merely alludes to as the universalization of the Virgin Mother's responsiveness to her sons at the precise moment when the boundary between the sacred and secular is drawn, is further elaborated in "The Legend of the Dying Wanton" whose task is to herald (the time setting is 1613, antedating the first legend) the effective and ubiquitous intervention of the Dominican madonna, the "Santo Rosario," in justifying and consolidating Spanish ascendancy and the terror of its reign. Such terror is defused and sublimated through the cunning of the narrative genius which incarnates the reconciling and synthesizing power of art, a genius concealed behind the wiles of the sensuous and marvelous.

In this baroque stylistic performance where extremes collide and dialectical mutations shift with deceptive spontaneity, Joaquin invents the scene of sacrifice—the prolonged agony of Currito Lopez and his death—as the plausible authenticating site for the irruption of the miraculous: the Madonna's descent earned through suffering, pain and contrition. In the long passage before his discovery by the soldier-friend Salgado, the text stages the fusion of aesthetic sensuality and mystical ecstasy, the worldly pleasures to which the public self is tied and the asceticism of the private conscience, made possible by the coming of the Virgin Mother and child: "that utterly agonized, utterly enraptured moment of being almost but not yet one with the beauty that was a total music, and with the music that was a total wisdom, and with the wisdom that was God—." But the human voice intervenes, and the union with the Absolute is prevented, precisely because here, as in all of Joaquin's rendering of moral or political crisis, the feminine (the semiotic corpus of drives, the unconscious) must reassert its decisive legislative and executive authority.

In lieu of the libidinally charged spectacle of combat in the first legend, here the protracted moment of dying (thirteen days compressed in a few paragraphs) deploys, in Kristeva's phrases, "the expenditure of semiotic violence . . . which mimes the movement of the symbolic economy," reproducing the signifiers associated with the semiotic chora.[27] What we confront in the exuberant recollections of Currito, a virtual Dionysian celebration of the Spanish renaissance, is the "deluge of the signifier" which inundates the symbolic order—the paratactic syntax and the dominance of the metonymic/synecdochic mode implement this havoc of the logical—and cancels the manichean dualism ("this commingling in a single nature of vice and piety") in a rigorously controlled hallucination.

This whole dithyrambic performance of unfolding the life of a schizoid sensibility while the torment of bodily decay erodes its material foundation may be construed as an extended trope of the imperial psyche constituted by contradictory tendencies and drives. From the passage beginning with "So, the poor Currito lay on the flooded ground" to his final breath "dying thus indeed: his lips parted, as if the last breath were a cry of wonder," the text charts the passage from voluptuous hedonism to realistic disgust ("For an evil world had formed him; poverty had formed him"), then to chivalric pride and stoicism, then to comic detachment and finally to self-chastisement and humility. His vision of the Virgin as the stern critical Sophia (Wisdom as female) he rejects, generating fear and despair to the point where he acquires distance from himself and perceives the conventionality of his role ("a mystic Tenorio") until, in this nadir of resignation, he clairvoyantly apprehends the engulfing chorus of prayers—a cosmic panorama of interceding voices incorporating his mother in Malaga and Doña Ana de Vera—which would eventually crystallize in the figure of the Madonna and the child Jesus. These contradictions are finally sublated in the ideological theme of suffering as propaedeutic agency for insight and revelation.

Joaquin's performance here seeks to depict the individual/psychic process—a sustained interior monologue orchestrated in consonance with the procedures of classical rhetoric whose minutiae I will not catalogue here—ostensibly as a microcosm of the Spanish/Christian temperament and its vicissitudes leading to salvation, its programmatic telos. But underlying this anecdotal didactic purpose and the hyperbolic realism of the episodes it organizes is the much more deeply embedded structuring rationale of the form itself which I have already touched on above. Instead of paraphrasing the form of the content, we need to analyze the content of the form which ultimately permits the signifying process to engender the specific discourse of knowledge/power.

To stabilize the centrifugal if rationally directed flux of Currito's experience and mediate the raw immediacy of sensation, the narrative employs the figure of Doña Ana de Vera whose civilizing mission supposedly tempers the barbarism of the conquistadors:

Señor Vera had tried to dissuade his mother from coming along—she was over fifty and rather fragile of health — but Doña Ana had mockingly feared he would degenerate into a savage in three days if she were not there to keep house for him. So, across two oceans and half the world she had come, one of the many spirited women who, hard on the heels of the conquistadores, sallied forth with kettle and skillet, with fan and mantilla, devoutly resolved that even in the heathen wilderness the rites of the altar and of the hearth should be performed with as much elegance as at the Court itself. (p.48)

The spontaneous friendship that develops between the luciferic Currito and the saintly Doña Ana, and her substitute role (at the moment of giving her blessing, she foreknows his death), provide the framework that would invest Currito's dying with a signifying intent: "Long after he was gone she still knelt before the altar, praying the Virgin to recall her promise that no one devoted to her and her rosary would suffer a death so sudden as to make impossible a last act of sincere contrition." Following the implicit rules of this genre, this prayer is answered by the hallucinated miracle and its "realistic" proof in the muddy robes of the Madonna and the scraped, muddy boots of the Child which exceeds, as floating signifiers, the commonsense explanation thought up by the practical Doña Ana. It is through the mediating consciousness of Doña Ana, guardian of hearth and altar, that the transaction between the solitary uprooted psyche and the institutional symbolic order is negotiated. For what ultimately Doña Ana represents is the solidarity, the unhypostatized collective self established by faith. In contrast to the putative total indifference of Christ, the narrative voice counsels: "For such is human solidarity that where any of us lack others may supply and the virtue of a single member nourishes the entire body." The organic metaphor of the body politic, together with the equivalence of virtues and properties, betrays the generative formula of this text. The paradigm of substitution (Doña Ana = Currito's mother = Madonna) intersects with the schema of diachrony (the chronology of Currito's departure, shipwreck, delirium, and so forth) to produce the illusion of documentary truth relying on our own trust in everyday conventional (the woman as domestic caretaker) and hierarchical routine (the prior as authority). As an ironic conclusion, despite the dangerous erotic potential of the body (physically repudiated here) and the mother in Currito's unconscious, the mother and Madonna are safely allocated their proper niches in the institutional fabric of seventeenth-century Spanish hegemony.

The formal coherence and thematic intelligibility of this text can only be comprehended then by exploring the possibilities of the drives—the desire for the castrated mother—and their limitation (the Madonna as the self-sufficient image), supplemented by the more insidious and fundamental exclusion hinted by this statement after the shipwreck: "A few men had saved themselves by swimming ashore, Currito among them and some other Spaniards, but the rest were natives who had been impressed to the service and who now turned against their cruel masters, pushing the Spaniards off the cliffs and hurling great rocks at them until they were all dead or dying, whereupon the natives fled to the wilderness" (p. 50). But the cruelty of the masters is nothing compared to the treachery of the heathen natives, nothing contrasted to their immense capacity for repentance and forgiveness!

Perhaps the instigator of these texts sensed the gravity of these exclusions and judgments so that in his next strategic act of proving the limits of the human, "Doña Jeronima," the repressed returns with unwanton vengeance.

And what is this enigmatic, incommensurable repressed if not what makes possible the shaping of legend and the creation of the signifying process: the collective practice of the people? Unlike the first two genealogical exercises, this pursuit of the inaugural matrix required not just a shipwreck and combat but a cycle of tests, discoveries, reversals—permutations of thematic motifs inscribed in all the narratives—that would resolve the logical antinomies and metaphysical paradoxes into folk-myth. Veritably Joaquin's version of Hegel's itinerary of the "unhappy consciousness" delineated in *The Phenomenology of Mind*, "Doña Jeronima" epitomizes the Althusserian notion of the distantiation of ideology (Christian platonism) through textual estrangement and the disclosure of gaps, fissures, absences in the narrative texture that tries to naturalize the artificial.[28]

Rewriting in allegorical terms the nomadic oscillation of the moral and philosophical positions represented by the Archbishop and Jeronima, we obtain the tension between spiritual and physical claims, love and justice, the temporal and transcendental views, concentrated in the disparity between the young man's vow of eternal love for Jeronima and the seductions of secular power to which the Archbishop, after the King had dispossessed him of his father's estate, succumbs. The institutional mask of the Archbishop prevails:

> "But hear me, my lord bishop: [says Jeronima in the first confrontation scene] would not a vow made to such a goddess supersede a vow made to a mere mortal?"
> "The gods are law," replied the Archbishop, "and if they themselves will not keep faith, why should mankind? Therefore is every vow between man and man sacred, not to be overthrown by a second vow, though this be made to hell or to heaven." (p. 64)

Underline here the contract between the male parties, the primacy of gods over the goddess. Ironically, the Archbishop's judgment undercuts himself—he is the saboteur of the sacred vow. For him, however, justice cannot be grasped (Jeronima aptly consigns the ring to the Heraclitean river) because of the mutability of the body and the sheer impermanence of worldly experience.

Like Currito Lopez and Brother Fernando, the Archbishop is a child of the interregnum crisis marked by the inflationary bankruptcy of the Spanish court, the ruin of domestic agriculture, and its growing indebtedness to the financial resources of Holland and England, her Protestant enemies. Here is how the text seeks to condition our tolerance of the Archbishop's baroque, even mannerist sensibility:

> In this Manila of the seventeenth century, folk but a father away from paganism, but a baptism away from the Conquista, were (like their more sophisticated brethren in Europe) already exploring mystical ground, already knew of the dark night whereof St. John of the Cross speaks, already craved a total illumination, probing their souls alone, in self-imposed solitude, or together, in experimental communities, with an anguish that was yet an ecstasy, being (though mostly simple and unlettered folk) informed by the high style of their century: changelings that, in the prime of life or beauty or fortune, abruptly fled the carnival and shut the world out, impelled to a quest for something firmer by a fever in the soul. (p. 61)

The existential metaphors for this ideological reflex of the sociohistorical crisis are the shipwreck and involuntary privation on the island (the irony of his popular prestige hiding his sense of vanity and fraudulence) and the obsessive "quest for reality," the interior "heart of stillness" which, the

Archbishop comes to realize, cannot be attained except through its opposite: the immersion in the marketplace, living through "the disguises of a man in the process of becoming."

This anguished craving for the permanent within the kaleidoscopic flux of appearances imaged by the river, this deeply felt sense of lack or precariousness is provided an objective correlative in the emergence of Jeronima, the quester for "justice," whose untarnished beauty symbolizes precisely the stasis or timelessness the Archbishop is haunted by. It is not just youth, infinite appetite and pleasure he wants to recover, despite his confession of being satiated by carnal concupiscence and power-lust; he wants the restoration of the Imaginary, the embrace of the phallic Mother, where self-identity expressed as "infinity," "justice," etc., affirms itself in the enduring motility, dynamism and multiplicity of matter.

As the Archbishop's past is evoked by the hypostatized beauty of Jeronima and her demand for proof of his fidelity and honor (feudal ideals subordinating the woman to monogamy), the text triggers a dialectical operation that would exhibit the antimonic double-bind paralyzing thought, a phase in which every idea is at once both true and false: "The fleer from illusion was himself an illusion." Reflecting on his past, the Archbishop's neoplatonic impulse is subverted by the insidious semiotics of Desire:

What he feared was not the failure of flesh but of faith. Which was the reality: the temporal or the spiritual realm? What if the world's masks, images, ghosts, were not the illusions they were despised as being? Might not the senses and their transient pleasures be the one permanence after all in a flux of thought and creed? Had he been reading the lesson in reverse? What if the itches of the flesh, its greeds and ambitions, were the true fire that gave off as mere smoke and vapour the sciences of the mind and the metaphysics of the spirit?

He thought in dismay of the woman in the veil, kept hard and fresh by her passions. He recalled his image in youth of the world as a vague heap of bodies forming one huge hump of venery. Yet this vile hump it was that spewed gods and goddesses, arts and cultures, and the other spiritualities that waxed and waned on it, while itself remained constant. Mortal man was not mortal save in the things of the spirit, which sensual man survived. This or that body died; but flesh, and the heats of the flesh, outliving its gods, persisted and endured forever: the bush that burned unconsumed.(p. 69)

Here the symbolic order, culture based on sacrifice and castration, is what occasions and vindicates an uncompromising dialectical materialism—as thesis and organizing principle in Joaquin's art—that his aesthetic religiosity has been relentlessly trying to repress.

Proof of the coincidence of opposites comes with Jeronima's mimesis of the Archbishop's agnostic skepticism in the scene where, with the Archbishop afflicted by the delirium of temporality (the river, "the haemorrhage of the unstaunched wound of his life"), she confesses that she has been motivated by pride, vanity, the fixation on an egotistic absolute:

"The gods are law, you said; but were they only that, then pettier would they be than men, who know how to wed rule and truth, and to mix maxim with mercy. For to read only the letter of the law, as I did, is not justice but spitefulness. Therefore do I beg your forgiveness, my lord bishop, who prized you as a thing to be possessed, in the name of justice, and not as a soul to love, in the name of charity."

Here the code of property and the practice of possession are subverted in the name of an acceptance of the law of change and the rejection of life:

"I am weary of my beauty, that is the parent of my pride; and this flesh I wear hurts me worse than a hairshirt. Now do I think no curse more terrible than to be young and fair forever. Who shall deliver me from the bondage of this life?"

Here the characters seem to coalesce, more precisely their positions are doubled, exposing the futile circularity and tautology of Neoplatonism (mutual forgiveness). The Archbishop's predicament is recapitulated in a passage before Jeronima vanishes as an individual and assumes mythical status, a passage that reasserts the vision of dialectical materialism:

He knew this quiet was but a respite. Presently he must descend again into the stream, this time for ever, and learn if for ever be indeed hell, or heaven—or purgatory? The soul appalled by the vanity of the world and the transience of flesh swung to the other extreme and, in turn dizzied by thought of infinity, rebounded to a cynical acceptance of flesh as the first, the final, the only truth. He had, thought the Archbishop, swung up and swung back, and now waited for, without pressing toward, a further revelation. Whatever that might be, it would not be alien but of himself, something he had willed, caused, created by being this man with these passions—not light dropped from above but light grown below: the light from the burning bush when smoke and vapour had cleared. (p. 76)

Before the text can finally wrestle and subdue the irrepressible demiurgic potential of matter and the vitality of the female, Jeronima must be put on trial by the folk. At first identified as a fertility force in harmony with the rhythm of nature, she is later condemned as a witch/harlot at the instigation of the friar (the counterreformatory inquisition may be glimpsed here). In a face-to-face interrogation, the Archbishop sees again his double, the chastised and tortured flesh duplicating his at the beginning for which he was acclaimed an Elijah: this repetition engenders the crucial difference which we find dramatically instanced in the last scene where the Archbishop and his servant eavesdrop and behold Jeronima's ritual, an expiation and punishment, a cancellation of her identity as moral-psychological presence and her reduction to myth. However, the opacity of the woman's figure resists any unequivocal interpretation, as attested to by the servant's inconsistency and the Archbishop's perception of a mirage:

Prostrating herself on a slab of stone, she began to pray; and such a keening rent the stillness it seemed that here wailed the whole world's conscience in contrition. The moon rose high, and still higher, and the night chill sharpened, but still the prostrate woman prayed, moaning and groaning, lifting imploring hands to heaven, like some mythic victim of the gods chained to a rock. But at last silence seized her, and more than silence; and the watchers on the rock above saw her as though dragged up by the hair, and dragged up to her knees, her arms opening, and dragged up to her feet, her arms opened wide and her veiled face wrenched toward heaven by a bliss that shook the air. The tremor lasted but a moment, and she fell, as though dropped, on her knees, where she stayed a while, swaying and shivering, her face in her hands. Then she rose and disappeared into the darkness of the cave. (p. 80)

The rhetoric of the narrative executes retribution on the woman who once presumed to demarcate the Archbishop's wisdom and also bind the male *virtù* in the chains of romantic love. But this romanticist anachronism contaminates the scene when the Archbishop sees his own youthful ghost repeat its submission to the woman in the cave, an ironic and deferred epiphany which contradicts the violent punishment of Jeronima and directs us back to the impossibility of refusing the protean, sensuous, inexhaustible energies of worldly life:

Children accepted the earth with frank pleasure, and lost innocence only in the grief of knowing themselves exiles from elsewhere. Was the quest, then, a relearning of this frank pleasure—and of reverence for the despised flesh, astonishment for the scorned world? Was it this quest which, extending beyond this life, made flesh and its fevers, even if they be for ever and ever, not hell but, at worst, a purgatory, a school for lovers? "I never loved you!" the woman had cried; and never indeed had she, who needed more than youth's season or life's term to learn the prizing of the body, not as a minute to possess, in the rush of time, but as a being to love, in the light of eternity. Was this not the awful fate that lovers did not know they embraced when they cried *For ever and ever*? But their vows would stand—"lest chaos befall the world." (p. 79)

Desperately the Archbishop here struggles to resolve the classic polarity of flesh and spirit by short-circuiting it in a Renaissance Enlightenment that seems to have eluded seventeenth-century Spain and medieval Manila. But is he successful?

What the text exhibits in the end is the closure of secular romance, the resurrection of the pagan nymph in the cave (temporarily eclipsed by Cross and Conquistador) articulated with Doña Jeronima's presence as the "new *diwata*," a vindication of unconscious matter and natural desire over the patriarchal Law (whose emblem is the Archbishop's ring drowned in the Heraclitean river). If the text may be said to be insistently self-deconstructing, the paradigmatic locus of reversal, that is because Joaquin's art is fatally crisscrossed by the unsurpassable historic contradictions of our time which are persistently registered in the ruptures and ambivalences of his work.

We shall soon see how, in Joaquin's recent novel *Cave and Shadows*, the prophetic and charisma-radiant figure of the *diwata* returns blasting the continuum of history and at last redeeming nature in her messianic triumph.[29]

Candido's Apocalypse

Without contraries is no progression.—William Blake

How would contemporary society look like if the deceitful trappings of convention, ritual, networks of institutional differentiation systematized in what Foucault calls discourses of "power/knowledge" were stripped off in one grand demystifying gesture? How would life look like, in particular, to Filipino adolescents in the early sixties; or to those who would programmatically insist on a relentless demystification and exposure of what the activists of Kabataang Makabayan and the Movement for the Advancement of Nationalism then called the rotten, iniquitous "semifeudal and semicolonial" system?

Having chronicled with journalistic élan and empathy the vicissitudes of a consumer-oriented youthful generation born in the Cold War fifties and coming of age in the years of Recto's crusade, Sartrean existentialism, import substitution, IMF devaluations, and the advent of the Nixon Doctrine at the peak of the Vietnam War, Joaquin sets out here to mount his own individual campaign to denounce the thoroughgoing capitalist commodification of urban middle-class life in the Philippines (split-level homes in suburban "Villages," Beatles, gadgets, technology) with this fable of growing up and accommodation. Unlike the traditional apologue of initiation and development, however, this text does not deconstruct the illusions of youth but tends to displace or transvalue these illusions into the prevailing essentialist myths of organic society centered on the patriarchal family and a renaissance humanism which, given the context of the rapid erosion of faith in cosmopolitan enclaves like Manila, form part of Joaquin's project to revise Christian beliefs and adjust them to a modernizing, pragmatic culture. With this modernizing theology proper to the milieu of "the secular city" (Harvey Cox) and the attempt to recuperate for a twentieth-century ethics the Church's motivating force of charity (*agape*) dominant over romantic/narcissistic eros, this narrative undermines its original intent and reinstates the problematic of the unitary, autonomous, reflexive subject which constitutes the pretext for the quasi-Nietzschean reductionism in the first place.

We shall see how Joaquin tried to evade and/or anticipate this aporia of his thinking in "The Order of Melkizedek" by evoking the Unconscious and its archaic connotations, thus triggering once more the unceasing dispersion of meanings between the polarities of the Imaginary Realm and the Symbolic Order and unsettling the uneasy, temporary compromise arrived at in "Candido's Apocalypse" (more on the former text later).

From Bobby Heredia's ordeal in the anxious passage from seventeen to eighteen, less a punctual transition than a psychic slippage from the moment of separation when he hated "being called Bobby" and invents his phantasmal double Candido (note his derivation from the Catholic folk calendar; *Candido, martir*) to his resumption of the filial role sandwiched by mother and father in the end at which the alienated martyr Candido raises "an eyebrow at the togetherness," one cannot help perceiving here an irreversible closure of defeat. Momentarily reversed in the return of Menchu from New York and the thirties, evoking the nostalgic recollections by Bobby's parents of an ordered nameable past—a plenitude of known idioms, styles, mannerisms and clichés (jazz, Mickey Rooney, etc.) time as linear progression-maturation and as return to familial/class identification supervenes. The grandmother—her house is the locus of an organic, filial order and security—intervenes at the last moment in the hospital only to mediate the reabsorption of the errant youth into the space of what the text names as "balance": "One would have to strike a balance between loving people too much and judging them too hard" (p. 55). However, this balance which Marcuse calls "repressive desublimation" is undercut by a qualification of the nuclear family as a viable mode of community only at the expense of Candido's permanent exile; hence the pathos of Candido's exit "up Taft way, where the traffic was and the sunshine." The split or decentered subject (instanced here by Bobby's X-ray vision, the rupture of routine, "Stowaway") collapses back into the mirage of an ego susceptible to "judgment," "balance," "morale." A disappointing dénouement.

Bobby's education into a normal law-abiding citizen is marked by the flesh-wound inflicted on him by Pompoy Morel, his antagonist (the overacting teenager) and the catalyzer of apocalypse: Pompoy Morel's function in the text seems obvious—he embodies the flamboyant exhibitionist (Beatles hair, cowboy boots, Honda, etc.) guilty of "overacting." He thus draws into his figure all the negative qualities and excesses one would associate with the Heredia family and its status summed up by the phrase "fetishism of commodities," with not only labor power (maids, teachers, doctors, etc.) as exchangeable values but also cultural and ideological expressions: music, language, social practices of all kinds. Note that Pompoy Morel is the child of separated parents, scarcely domesticated by his grandmother. What is important, however, is not his allegorical role here as a personification of the false, hypocritical, artificial and unnatural—the surface of a commodified machine vis-à-vis the "Grandmother's timeless rituals" and the depth of her "home"; Pompoy here appears as the trickster Eros, the dionysian seducer of mothers, who then appears as the absolute competitor or danger to Bobby when Bobby sees her mother naked serving Pompoy and Pompoy's gaze ravishing her in Bobby's eyes. it is this look or gaze multiplied, the contrapuntal capture of the mother's body by the bifurcated subject, that engenders the phallic violence performed by the son when he seizes "his father's automatic" and shoots the transgressor of his assumed property. The shooting of Pompoy evokes a profound sense of guilt in Bobby, a sense of his being punished by God for his seeing "through women's clothes," making Pompoy an accomplice, not the outsider-rival.

Contrary to what the orthodox psychologizing reader might suspect, we are not witnessing here the drama of the oedipal crisis being played out nor the simple unfolding of the tensions and transvestite identifications enacted in the pre-oedipal imaginary realm according to Lacan. I think what the text registers beyond the deflection of narcissistic drives shown in Bobby's rejection of parents, house, sophisticated posturings (the combo's stagemanship) and his watching himself—his concern for authenticity and the rejection of the habitual and formal triggers his assumption of the alternative persona Candido—is the protagonist's attempt to construct an oppositional Symbolic Order where commodity fetishism will be replaced by spontaneous and natural transactions, where power would coincide with feelings, and knowledge coalesce with action. This order is fundamentally a utopian subversion of the repressed, bureaucratized and denatured society interpellated by the ideology of the father-governed family, marketplace, authoritarian schools, and a scientific reifying technology (telephones, cars, jargon, etc.) In this approach to a world where, to quote Totong Heredia, "nothing's sure in the world any more," Joaquin aligns himself with the organic romanticism of Coleridge, Wordsworth, William Morris, D.H. Lawrence, and others. But what is singularly ambiguous is the peculiar twist that this debunking polemic displays when it generates its opposite: the quest for the authentic and natural leads to a perception of bodies as contraptions, decrepit machines, unsynchronized parts or fragments, eventually reduced to bones, skulls, skeletons performing a medieval dance of death unknown to themselves. Technology equals death–a typical Luddite reaction.

I should stress here that the decentering of the subject, the dichotomizing of consciousness we see in Bobby Heredia, occurs not because of a gap that opens between the age of seventeen and eighteen but because of the sociocultural dislocations and deterritorializings noted by the text which has undermined parental authority and tradition, disclosing the rifts between the feudal ties of the clan sanctioned by orthodox dogma and the constantly shifting utilitarian ethos of upwardly mobile families adapting the instrumentalist outlook of the profit/commodity-oriented West. Bobby's alienation, in other words, is not a private malady. It is a sociopolitical symptom of multifaceted contradictions whose most immediate manifestation (though ultimately defined by class conflict) is the tension between the sacramental view of religion and the reductive scientism of modernizing society, between private sentiments and public reputation, between the logic of individualist self-affirmation and the communality of desire.

Now contrary to the expectations of reactionary admirers of Joaquin's putative obsession with the Hispanic legacy and folk Catholicism, this narrative will not deliver the mechanical automatic victory of faith over technology without some ambiguous caveats and tacit reservations. I have already underscored above the striving for an unprovocative closure by a reconciliation of the erstwhile deviant youth and the conformist parents, a closure achieved by the unequivocal exclusion of Candido, of alterity itself, from the scene. The text will yield this semblance of restoring the metaphysical norm by a literal coaxing of perception, sight, vision into a confrontation with death, that is, with lifeless or inorganic matter, as a result of which the spiritually invested body limited and bounded by codes of duplicity regains in a most unexpected fashion its site of invisibility. An ironic termination indeed.

The first object of perception that Bobby, now inhabiting Candido's persona or animating the Candido mask, contemplates is his mother: "He had located with a glance the zone where the youth of her face ended and the oldness of her body began but the core of her burned as young as her face though all around it was beginning to be ashes" (p. 25). This is a gnostic vision of the body as a sedimentation of divergent temporal processes and deviations. Evoking sympathy, the mother's image (the body as a heterogeneous surface) yields to the impotent, defeated body of the father who has evacuated its commanding position now to be occupied by successive stand-ins: doctor, teacher, etc. What steadfastly occupies the center in this text, though somewhat marginalized, is the Grandmother, symbol of continuity and the promise of cyclical renewal: She was genuine because she was *rugged* herself and you could beat her up until she was half dead and she would just rise up afterwards and brush away the dirt and be Grandmother again without even overacting all that" (p. 31). This is the last and ever accessible refuge from corporate liberalism. Except for Bobby's *barkada*—"the only clean things left in the world"—everyone's nakedness discloses some ugly, repulsive secret. It is only after Bobby's contact with Mr. Henson, whose linking of Bobby's scandalous "going for lost" with "the etiquette of the race" and "customs of the tribe" betrays Bobby's complicitous role, that Bobby begins to see the human anatomy as a machine or engine. But it is at this very moment too, confronting his family, when he begins to realize the limit of demanding the unconcealed truth—even as his own truth as fluctuating subject produced by certain discourses is concealed from him—that he shudders and recoils from the nightmare of chaos, of the uniform and homogeneous surface where anonymous parts are dispersed at random. What resists casuistic *ressentiment* turns out to be capitalist milieu of exchangeable parts conceived here as machines:

Surprised but delighted to find here, instead of the scandal of human nakedness, which would have to be judged, the precision of machines, which used no morals, he had yet in the next moment blenched. Some of those machines were his family—but who was who? All the machines were faceless and sexless.

And it came to him that the nakedness of the flesh that so sickened him was yet the shape of the person . . . . If you stripped the skin from a person what remained was anonymous machinery. The big wart on the face of this man made him *this* man; scars and wrinkles and mendings and tumours and all that could mar flesh marked out a character, an identity, *this* life, *this* soul.

Oh, they were wrong, he saw now, oh, they were all wrong. The soul was not anywhere inside—not in the mind, not in the heart, not in the spirit, but here upon the seen flesh that they called carnal: this dirt-prone flesh, this bug-bitten flesh, this animal-hairy flesh, this sexual flesh. The ugliest nakedness was still a holy nakedness because flesh was soul and soul was flesh and if it wasn't there all you had were machines you couldn't tell one from the other. (pp. 41-42)

This sudden recognition that surface determines individuality, that flesh or body differentiates, does not yet suffice to restore Bobby to his normal other-directed sense. The purging of the Gnostic heresy needs foreshadowing. What ensues is the apprehension of death (Minnie's hollow skull, Menchu's jeweled skeleton and Bobby's death dance with her) as "the ultimate strip," an insight exfoliating in the search for God, the transcendental nucleus, the ultimate primordial meaning: "He had learned that skin was the deepest thing of all, deeper than earth, deeper than ocean, deeper than outer space, its depths being the joys of human contact, and if God was to be found at all it could only be in those depths" (pp. 59-60).

Ordinarily Bobby's cure would have been completed upon reaching this level of awareness, but then the secular realm of family, marketplace, church and school and business would remain unredeemed, fallen, mocking simulacra of skeletons and machine parts. He is not pursuing an idealized image of himself (Candido already incarnates this possessor or receiver of truth whose affinity with the Grandmother is easily discernible), nor is he attempting to usurp the father's position—the phallic signifier of the Law (the father's gun) has already been used by Bobby to announce his conquest of the patriarchal space left vacant. What is missing?

I suggest it is the body itself, specifically the mother's body, or the materiality of the text as ceaseless repetition producing difference, which could not be evoked unless and until Bobby/Candido becomes the vessel wounded, pierced and nullified by Pompoy Morel who turns out to be one substitutable face of God, avatar of the totemic patriarch. The text foreshadows this shift in this passage: "Feeling was of the flesh, personality was of the flesh, companionship was of the flesh, contact was of the flesh. They had been told in Religion." Paradoxically, Candido now surrenders to an institutional discourse about the saint who needed the leper's sores to find God. The Bobby-aspect predominates. After collapsing surface and depth at the boundary of the skin, the text suddenly springs the presence *behind*, a contradictory move:

God. My God! *That* was what had been lurking in the chair, when Tita Menchu sat there, and in the room, as she danced around. *That* was what had beckoned to be pursued, wanting to be revealed. *That* is what I have to chase, to hunt, to look for, to find. God has blotted out all other faces so I may see *the* face, the ultimate face—the face of God. (p. 51)

The hunt follows winding through the fallen, blighted world of the market —a veritable inferno of skeletons and death's heads—and the Village, up to the piazza where the dance of death is renamed "God's a-go-go" until the climactic episode where the crucial unveiling transforms Bobby/Candido into the ecstatic, penetrated body:

And as he plunged into the thicket his flesh tingled, his hair bristled, he was warm now, he was close now, God had been tracked down at last, God had been cornered, God was at bay, God was waiting for him who had to bend away this last prickly bamboo, who was parting this last curtain of foliage, who stepped out now from the thicket and saw the wall before him—and there indeed was God, against the wall, waiting for him, and he had smiled at God, he had glowed at God, he had flung his arms out to hail God, but God held a thunderbolt in his hand, and then the thunderbolt blazed lightnings and he felt a fire on his shoulder and cried out in joy, for God had hit him with love, God had pierced him with love, God had burned him with love, and he could feel the smile on his mouth as he staggered and swooned with the rapture, seeing, as he touched ground and the dark came sweeping, that God had the face of Pompoy Morel. (pp. 51-52)

Addressed as "Bobby," Candido offers his body as sacrificial target for the violence which is attributed to Pompoy Morel (the literal enemy) who is the avatar of the castrating father. What we have here is *jouissance* textualized, victimization as the birth of the heterogeneous subject that can never be defined by "God" or by the solicitous parents or by the grandmother whose "war of succession" continually seeks to colonize a pluralized subject which persistently negotiates an escape even under the guise of the conventional rhetoric of sixteenth-century antinomian, negative theology.

Can we then conclude that this narrative articulates Joaquin's project of modernizing faith by the ruse of a tolerant liberalism and humanistic realism enunciated in the concluding episode, with grandmother's ritual eclipsed and marital-parental love endorsed as the stable guarantee of mature identity?

It is evident that the subtext immanent in the narrative cancels the allegation made earlier that the extrapolated myth of the organic society and the humanist affirmation of the body-spirit synthesis resolves the dualism we have explored. For the illusion of balance asserted in the end can be felt as an ironic if not misleading effect of the agonistic metamorphosis suffered by Bobby/Candido, a metamorphosis that in fact precludes maturation as an acceptance of the hegemonic Law (the order of commodified relations) and that implies its annulment and displacement by a new Symbolic Order where the subject is the coalesced male-female subsuming the dualism represented by Bobby and Pompoy Morel. This textualized foregrounding of the subject-in-process preempts the technology-faith contradiction by staging the problem on the level of sexuality and the sociopolitical construction of gender. While the narrative apparatus deploys on the literal level the mystical experience of the post-Oedipal ego split into a double (Candido), which in turn enables the reified phenomena of everyday life to reveal the essence of a market status quo and money economy as inert machine-parts and skeletal detritus, the trope of nakedness is paradoxically undercut by the strategic figuration of Pompoy as the mask or disguise of God, which in the semiotic mode of our reading translates into the totemic father inflicting his revenge on the presumptuous heir. Thus the symbolic castration of Candido in the initiation scene at the edge of the urban sprawl, in a vestigial pastoral retreat to which he finally drives his antithetical Other, turns out to be a magical vindication of a differential system involving kinship, class, and nation constantly threatened by the universalizing forces represented, on the one hand, by a patriarchal "God" and, on the other hand, by the instrumentalizing forces emblematized by the Beatles, Western fashion styles and lexicon, by consumerist obsolescence in general.

I am not arguing here that Joaquin deliberately stages the self-deconstruction of his initial modernizing impulse, his project of salvaging Grandmother's rituals and recontaining them within the folds of a tolerant humanism which accommodates to rapid social changes safely rendered here as superficial phenomena concealing an immutable core of reality underneath. What this analysis demonstrates is the way the orgiastic "martyrdom" of Candido—this double himself being a symptom of Bobby's alienation (the negative) and his grasp of a Christian truth (the positive) at the castrating hands of God masquerading as Pompoy Morel (or vice versa)—dismisses the urgency of the moral dilemma (the authentic whole versus the fraudulent ensemble) and substitutes for it a discourse of bodies spawning monadic identities. This serves in a way to conceal and foreground at the same time the creeping Manicheanism embedded in Candido's own moralizings and the inability of his discriminating apparatus to penetrate Pompoy's disguise. At best the narrative is caught in a double bind: to purge the gnostic heresy and its metaphysical conceit, the text offers a notion of all historical phenomena (including gnostic practices of stigmatizing the body) as participating in God's process of revelation and therefore meaningful in varying degrees. Ultimately, the status quo is reaffirmed, the rite of passage revitalized, the grandmother vindicated at the cost of the reader indulging a guilty conscience. Because Bobby's wound is not fully healed, the scar of loss inscribed in the categorized body can bleed anew and escape the totalizing identification of the hegemonic hierarchy.

In the unfolding of the narrative action, one finds the complex, devious trajectory of Desire whose unpredictable movement not even Joaquin's protean narrative apparatus can fully chart, hypostatize, and forever repress.

"The Order of Melkizedek"

He would hold his secret knowledge and secret power, being as sinless as the innocent: and he would be a priest for ever according to the order of Melchisedek.

—James Joyce, *A Portrait of the Artist as A Young Man*

In that Creation they labored, or were afflicted . . . in that same it is meet for them to receive the fruits of Suffering: . . . and in that creation they endured slavery, in the same they should reign.

—Saint Irenaeus, *Adversus haereses*

The primary and most beautiful of Nature's qualities is motion, which agitates her at all times. But this motion is conserved by means of crime alone.

—Marquis de Sade

In his pathbreaking treatise *The Political Unconscious* (1981), Fredric Jameson argues powerfully for a concept of literature and art as "a symbolic meditation on the destiny of community" within a dialectical reading of history as an extended narrative of the collective struggle to humanize nature and naturalize the human— history as revolutionary praxis. Composed on the eve of the popular uprisings christened the "First Quarter Storm" (1970), Joaquin's novelette "The Order of Melkizedek" may be construed as a sustained meditation on the destiny of a peripheral Third World formation undergoing crisis, relentlessly interrogated by its past and its future. It is a meditation on the fate of the individual subject caught by the reifying and commodifying impact of late capitalism convulsed by internal contradictions. It is, ultimately, a meditation on the collective subject-in-process, negative dialectics, and the utopian subversion of Desire.

For the archetypal modernist artists like Yeats, T.S. Eliot, and Joyce, history is an unmitigated nightmare from which the antiheroic twentieth-century protagonist yearns to escape. And for Marx, the burdensome weight of the past (tradition) weighs like a nightmarish curse on the living who perhaps can only take comfort in the thought that when the tragic circumstances and actions of the past are replicated in contemporary times, they invariably assume the exaggerations and theatricality of farce. This transmogrification, however, is not one of the iron laws of the dialectic, despite perversions made of *The Eighteenth Brumaire* and other texts. In fact it signifies the possible creative nature of human intervention into the open-ended and nonteleological process of world history. History looms as a terror to its victims and an opportunity for the revolutionary protagonists, those who grasp freedom as the "recognition, or taking-in-hand" of necessity (Engels).

A site of the most profoundly kaleidoscopic resurgence of eros and the polymorphous drives of the unconscious, interrogating the matrix and limits of the sign-system which constitutes the Philippine formation and positing its own aesthetic resolution of the contradictions overdetermining the text and its codes, this narrative sums up in archetypal fashion the obsessive themes and motifs comprising the Joaquinian problematic: how to allegorize the process of recovering an organic collective life identified integrally with the past (figured as the realm of the Virgin, absent matriarchs, La Vidal, the Salemites, i.e., Guia and her doubling nemesis in Sonya Borja—the archetype of antinomy) where class conflicts dissolve, where existential life-predicaments find temporal and relative solutions, where the paradoxes of modernist culture (individual freedom in history versus bureaucratic alienation in consumer mass society; monadic solitude versus the ego annulled in action, etc.) may be homogenized in a symbolic or hypothetical realm: the pluralized text of "The Order of Melkizedek." Such a past—the primordial hierophany emblematized by the Three Kings suggests the miracle of the Incarnation as the fruit of peasant rebellions — and its interpenetration with the present and future, that is, the entire temporal dynamics of class struggle which tries to recapitulate the historical dialectic of Philippine society, its transformation and evolving crisis, underlies the plot and character-system of this text in a far more richly ambiguous and multilayered structuring than the ethical binary orientation of the apparatuses operating in "Candido's Apocalypse," or *The Woman Who Had Two Navels*. Whether it is not more reductive or satisfactory in elucidating the nuances of the present conjunctural crisis—the crucible for this demand is Joaquin's recent "mystery/thriller" *Cave and Shadows*—is a corollary question we can explore in a moment.

I would venture at the outset to characterize Joaquin's project in this narrative as essentially a historical-materialist demystification of the humanist illusions of the subject (Sid, the Ferrers). It is also a figural mapping of Desire (Guia, Sonya Borja) as the demystifying but also utopian force which defines itself on three levels: as psychological *ressentiment* on the individual or literal level, as rebellious class consciousness on the political level, and as the impulse of a mode of production which symbolizes a fantasied or imagined completion of the individual subject, the filling up of the space of plenitude with a recovery of that archaic but always present object which has been lost (the mother's body, the organic community). All these three levels become articulated with one another in the literal plot of the Estiva kin's scheme to capture Guia (ironically, the wayward or lost guide) primarily because of the wealth she will inherit when she comes of age but basically because the ego of the putative family unity seeks to reconstitute itself as a desperate last move before either an atomistic seriality completely takes over, or a revivalist movement forever thwarts its dream of restoring its original if make-believe coherence. Bissecting the Sid-Ferrer-Guia constellation are two strands: Fr. Melchor's quest to recruit the disgraced Fr. Lao thwarted by a botched hermeneutics (including Mrs. Banaag's *ressentiment*) coupled with Ferrer's sleuthing, and Sonya Borja's undercover or duplicitous effect on Sid. When these three lines collide, the manichean obsession of Fr. Lao—his "dark night of the soul" coexists and feeds on the image of the "scarlet woman, the whore of Babylon" encountered in a university town in Kansas—purges itself in the killing of Guia, surrogate for evil but also the agent of his salvation. Guia's sacrifice, imaged in that silenced oral/vaginal threshold—"the parted lips were breathless"—marks not the victory of the status quo but its momentary self-negation: the death-drive unmasks itself as patriarchal self-righteousness rendered blind and futile by the female body and its symbolic resonance.

It might be easier for clarity's sake to describe the allegorical function of Sid's family as the text's attempt to establish the centralizing but severely eroded authority embodied by the "Picture of the Founder" presiding over Adela's den. When Guia is captured and brought back to Adela's house, "a mere child" in Sid's arms "when they returned from their father's funeral" (this incestuous image compensates at once for the loss of the totem), we read: "Adela waited in her den: all their gatherings seemed to require their father's tuxedo'd presence, hugely there on the wall." The patriarch's marriage to three wealthy women from the North (tobacco money), the South (Visayan sugar) and the Center (Ermita, real estate) not only suggests the potency of the clan founder, the ecumenical explorations of the "sexual geographer" and "sexual economist" but also projects the hypothetical unity of the nation as a synthesis founded on the marital transactions of the landlord-comprador classes, including the *rentier* class of pre-World War II Manila. It might be noted that this merger is thematized by the conversations about the past and blood filiations among the Ferrer's circle over which the Father's "eternal tuxedo" hovered. This exhumed past will generate three spectral auras: Fr. Melchor, Fr. Lao and the two testimonies of Dr. Lagman and Fray Calezon. The Father's presence is purged in that neutral site born not only from real estate speculation but also from transnational/global finance: Makati where Sid and Guia talk about the "Carnal Christ" and the deadly decorum of the Ferrers. Note the transitional if ambiguous quality of this location where Fr. Melchor also appears with his thugs delivering the warning of the Furies: "This new heart of Makati was a transplant of American downtown—from treelined curb to penthouse'd roof—but glittered anomalously between the rank provincial decay of Manila and the lordly tin roofs of the suburbs" (p. 250).

The patriarchal genealogy is affirmed in Santiago Ferrer, papal knight, and his wife Adela, a Daughter of Isabela; and in the "middle-aged collection" which "moved with an ease fibered by money in the bank and food from supermarkets," the bureaucratic-professional intermediate strata from which Sid exiled himself to the United Nations in New York. While ten years separate Sid from his elder sister Adela, these "clean, decent, reasonably honest folk: salt of the earth agleam," whose self-congratulating looks "produced their collective aura," share Sid's noninvolvement. Their chic slogan of "No Comment," if asked about the Vietnam War or any current event, updates Sid's "prophylactic" attitude to the world—even though its odd emblem, the toothbrush he waves at the airport, misread and confiscated, becomes a phallic surrogate at the end. The Kafkaesque hero, "harassed by the native gods of customs" after which the taxi driver is sacrificed, becomes a candidate for succeeding the father when Adela Ferrer urges Sid to assert their filial power: "Papa put us in charge of her. Are we to abdicate, declare her of age, turn over the estate to her as she now demands, though we know perfectly well she'll only turn it over to that crazy sect of hers?" (p. 214). For Sid, this involvement in the killing of the taxi driver serves as the pivotal node where the father's ghost intrudes and filiations (kinship) threaten affiliation (taboo on incest). It anticipates the return of the last of the Three Kings (avatar of the Son in orthodox dogma, of the Holy Spirit in the eschatology of Joachim of Floris). Sonya Borja, the frontier woman crying in the wilderness, reminds Sid of his ambiguous nostalgia and provokes a renunciation and an acceptance of irony as irrational necessity:

"How about that young go-go for old things?"
"The safely dead past. Kicks from ikons. Yeh, man, we dig. Hah. Daring of me, wasn't it? Besides, that wasn't me really, only my father in me. He was a vulgar adventurer, the kind they say battens on experience. If anything scared me off, it was the thought of his coming back. Like, now, in my sister Guia. I think she's the only one of us who's our father's child."
"We are all of us our fathers," sighed Sonya Borja, "though we don't know it." (p. 217)

Of Sonya Borja's role as the agent of confirming Sid's virility and her epiphanic departure at the end with an epistle both apologetic and prophetic, more later. Sid's attempt to exorcise the ghost of the patriarch by exile and noninvolvement fails: "I always try not to be where the action is, ... so now I'm up to my neck in it." His return together with Fr. Lao from the U.S., site of Fr. Lao's "fall" and Sid's separation from his wife, resurrects the past through Guia and the Salemites. Fr. Melchor claims him to be on their side: "You are of those who called me back." Sid's inquiry (inquest, by hindsight) into Guia's stages of development—recapitulating three phases (from stowaway Ginny to Gigi to the nationalist Guiang and finally Sister Guia; 1950s to early seventies)—dramatizes his affinity with the Adamic impulse of the Salemites, an archaeological pursuit which exhumes the traces of origins. Fr. Melchor says:

Ah, Mr. Estiva, if you go back at all it's impossible to set a limit: up to this point and no farther. If you dig up one grave you have also unlocked the ones that lie below. You've heard of the diggings during the Renaissance: how it was feared that with the resurrection of their vessels and ikons the old gods that had gone underground had surfaced again? (p. 255)

Sid verbally rejects Fr. Melchor's warning "not to block her [Guia's] path," but in truth it is Sonya Borja who disrupts the communication between Adela and Sid (the filial tie) during the winter solstice of their sexual transaction; and it is Fr. Lao who deprives Sid and Adela and Santiago of their object: control of Guia's will and property. In effect, Fr. Melchor's prophecy in the text is fulfilled: "I must warn you, Mr. Estiva, that you are invoking forces that are without mercy . . . If you and yours move, so will the furies."

Sid's ambition to affirm the patriarchal duty fails—he has abjured it in his Manhattan exile—only to succeed: the return home deciphers the thickness and incoherence of the contemporary social text, revealing the intertextuality (in historical materialist terms, the totality constituted by manifold inner contradictions) of individual psyche and reified milieu, of memory and Desire. Is Sid's vocation at the end the abolition of history, of linear progression, and the reinstallment of the cyclic repetition of cosmogony and the archetypes? Before endeavoring to answer this question, we might delineate Sid's position as the locus of ironic reversal and the matrix of the historicist vision which, in the last analysis, informs the structuring energies of the text.

While the narrative progression—an alternation of Sid's coming to awareness of his body in society through Adela's cry for assistance in bringing Guia back to the fold, and the struggle of the Salemites to recruit Fr. Lao, the "sinner" from the New World—is crisscrossed and bifurcated by innumerable parallelisms of various kinds, this network of analogues seeks to impose a static or recurrent pattern on the multiplicity of events. On the whole, the narrative mechanism is designed to constitute the relationship between the ego/subject and its social grounding which hinges on two lines of development. The first, obviously, concerns the return of Sid Estiva in response to a call from his stepsister Adela to help "straighten out" the errant Guia whose maturation (and accession to legal property-owning age) leads through initiation into a primitivistic sectarian movement led by an enigmatic figure, Fr. Melchor. Such a return, duplicated by Fr. Lao's flight and its immediate reversal at the very moment of their landing (both Sid Estiva and Fr. Lao came "down from heaven but unwinged by the general guilt)," is premised on a possible recuperation of the past, or a reassumption of direction and guidance of Guia's growth (hitherto determined by circumstances dictated by peripheral economics). And, with it, there unfolds the stabilization of the family's property which is a last-ditch attempt by the comprador class to moderate the excesses of the *rentier* faction, real estate speculation here representing time as a cornucopia of infinite profit.

To oppose Guia's drift into the Salemite community on the eve of its going underground and postpone the falling apart of the clan (the social compromise of the elite), Sid tries to don the mantle of the patriarch in order to effect the recovery of Guia from the forces of the Other (for the elite, the impostor and agent of the underclasses; for Fr. Lao, evil incarnate). Coalescing with this project of rescue or salvaging, which pits the pettybourgeois secularizing milieu of the Ferrers (the husband's role as *Santiago Matamores* replicates the Hispanic crusade against the infidel Moors, a replay of St. James slaying the Moors—the archetype of the manichean logic contradicting the theology of the Incarnation) against the deviant forces gravitating around the overdetermined figure of Fr. Melchor, is the process of inquiry into his identity–an intrinsically dialogic discourse to be terminated by the retelling or narrativization by Fr. Lao (the bias in point of view is clear) of the sect's rites, his escape, the prophet's disappearance, and his conversion through Sid's contingent display of his toothbrush ("the miracle of the coincidence"). These two lines converge as soon as Sid alights on the ground, his emblem of identity the source of the initial hermeneutic error which splits the actant (returning native) into two and allows conventional realistic representation to produce its illusions of verisimilitude.

It is revealing how this gratuitous act of brandishing a prophylactic, an innocent gesture which generates the sudden conversion of Fr. Lao and leads to his role as the nemesis of Guia, the object of the psychomachic combat, crystallizes for us the paradoxical but somehow inescapable thematic resolution to which Joaquin is compelled, given the limits and efficacy of his ideological-aesthetic codes. We shall see the complex ironies of fate locked with free will when we chart how the coincidences of the plot originate from an argument profoundly subversive of its surface meaning.

It might be useful as a hermeneutic device to encapsulate the impetus of the narrative development in the proposition that what the text is wrestling with involves on one level the purgation of a body politic of guilt (moral paralysis) and, on another level, the expulsion of a specific threat posed by history, more frightening when such a buried temporal realm is characterized by the domination of tribal daemons or archaic forces which pervade a pre-Christian community. We can interpret these forces which synecdochically evoke Nature as motion or pure spontaneous will, as impulses textualized here in the intercourse of Sonya and Sid (pp. 257-58) where the fire's incandescence distills carnal passion and heralds the advent of the spirit, and in Sid's escape from his captors (the Salemite corps) who has restored him to his original nakedness:

Joint and muscle, not thought, catapulted him from clearing to shrubbery. His body had become pure speed, unstoppable, crashing into bush and vine, rushing through undergrowth. His limbs acted by themselves, each dash or swerve spontaneous. This being was but movement, instinct, impulse, engine, and could have split a tree. Only when it had torn through a thicket into a second clearing did the brute energy, recovering mind, sputter to a halt, gradually embarrassed, knowing itself naked before people. (p. 203)

This is the reduction of the body into pure motion, albeit defined by a purpose: the Cartesian ego disappears, just as in the sexual embrace and in primitive dance-rituals the property-owning "I" dissolves into what Sonya calls possession by "the dark gods of the blood" (D.H. Lawrence).

An act of purgation transpires with Fr. Lao's exorcism of the past, his killing of the archetypal "whore of Babylon" in the guise of Guia, and the arrest of Fr. Melchor's followers. On one level, Fr. Lao here personifies the self-destructive potential of a hypostatized will that still animates traditional neocolonial thinking. This will is also diagnosed by Guia in the polemical exchange between Guia and her kin oscillating between the trapped sterile existence of the Ferrers and the self-indulgence of Sid:

What's this about me and you holding up in Manhattan? With me as what? The baby you wouldn't have, the wife you couldn't keep, the mistresses who have to rape you? ... I'm the one girl you can be sure will have to love you always, and the perfect partner in solitude because I'm almost not another person, I'm almost only you again. Picture the two of us so nicely becoming old maids together—" (p. 265)

When Fr. Lao discovers God in the person of the "angel" Sid who is being used without his knowing it—proof of the structural determination of the empirical self by the conjuncture of events— this discovery entails a delayed effect mediated through the Salemites and their metonymic extension,

Guia. This is the model of the overdetermined historical process filling in the substance of the actant (Sid as the empty vehicle or signifier) and defining his ultimate status as player in the drama of antagonistic class forces and competing modes of production.

With the vindictive drives of reified tradition (Fr. Lao's fixation may be construed as the instrumentality of a patriarchal regime) released in Guia's slaying, we are left with a situation where the stage is set for a beginning. A New Year's Day comes when finally the chief protagonist, doubling back and rehearsing his initial visit to Salem House (the Adamic hearth of the vestal virgins), transvalues his individual past and parodically enacts a vow of recognition whereby the reified world is cancelled, preserved but sublated into a milieu of transparent meanings:

It didn't seem right to go without making a gesture. He put hand to pocket, fetched out the toothbrush and stood it up in the niche, sticking the handle in a crack of rock.

But something else was needed. He pulled out the plane ticket, crumpled it into a wad, placed it in the niche and lit a match to it. He waited for it to burn before walking away.

At the edge of the ring he paused to look back, looking back across the still evening at the wedge of wall where the wad of plane ticket burned, a flame tall in the void, steady before the standing toothbrush. (pp. 269-70)

But before this, using the keys (the deciphering knowledge) entrusted to him by Fr. Melchor, the melancholic Sid returns to Salem House, a reprise of his first visit "guided" by Guia when he was shocked by "an Igorot-style wooden carving of the Virgin pregnant, asquat on her haunches, halo of stars round her head." This time the light before the pregnant Virgin has been extinguished; Sid surveys the cloister and the backyard with its ring of ruins. The Stonehenge-like adobe blocks have been moved to the Antipolo orchard, a sign that the libidinal investment is flexible and mobile. The indigenous Christ with phallic icon exposed has also been transported so that the empty niche now looms like a gaping womb which, to the messenger-heir-violator of that once sacred space, now becomes a mouth revivifying Guia's voice and, with it, the intertextuality of pagan rite and Christian (Feast of the Circumcision) liturgy:

The niche was the void where night had begun, though it was another night he hears.
— *When do you celebrate it?*
— *New Year's Day, you donkey. Now shut up and let's go.*
— *Why New Year's Day? That's not liturgical. Oh yes it is. Feast of the Circumcision.*
— *And you're cordially invited to our patronal festivities, donkey. Now, let's go in. I'm cold.*

We can take this passage as the epitome of the existential predicament in which the subject is forced to interpret, to produce meanings, but only in the context of the established linguistic and cultural codes so that at any given moment class struggle proceeds through an articulation of several ideological practices sharing the same code (the Puritan versus Royalist conflict during the English Civil War, for example) but inflecting it in antithetical ways. That last scene of the story may also be conceived as the crucial moment of the production of meaning as repetition with significant variation, the germ of novelty, in which the possibility of a new society is intimated no longer by a solitary individual consciousness but by the whole network of relationships equivalent to Sid's evolving identity. Sid's gesture of converting toothbrush and plane ticket into votive paraphernalia confirms the text's autoreferential thrust even as it repudiates humanistic-empiricistic positivism, here signified by the reality-effect of the description.

Indeed, what the narrative sets out to accomplish as one of its "unconscious" tasks is to shatter the myth of the Cartesian cogito, the autonomous monadic ego; to disintegrate the atomized but self-generating sensibility and insert the fragments into the evolving structure of the narrative discourse itself. It is anti-Kafkaesque motive, as alluded to at the beginning when Sid reflects that his crime, for which he had been kidnapped and denuded of his worldly trappings (both an initiation process and device to abolish history and reenact the periodic cosmogony), is precisely his cosmopolitan "non-involvement." Why his exile? The rationale is flimsy: "If he lived abroad it was because being alien committed you to nothing local. You couldn't read a newspaper at home without upping your body pressure; abroad, newspapers read like anthropology" (p. 215). This pretext, however, duplicates the alienation of the Filipino himself as immigrant/exile and also as colonized subject rendered impotent in his homeland. Sid is preconscious of this determination by context; full awareness comes when he takes up the task entrusted by the institutional/familial power structure which affords him a tortuous learning experience. Sanitized, isolated as a fragmented consciousness which apprehends the "world's hurt" as a procession of "papers moving from office to office, a figure in a report, a line on a graph" (so much for Weber's rationality)—the phenomenon of reification now recontained in a retrospective analysis—Sid is programmed through the accident of being the victim of a hermeneutic error, bodily stowed away in a taxi he thought he was directing, then stripped bare. Reduced to the alien in his homeland, Sid is further transformed into the unmasked inhabitant of a fallen Eden whose escape reveals the Adamic motif which links him to the Salemites and the archetypal Melkizedek.

The next time Sid is undressed, the night before consulting Dr. Lagman and Fray Calezon about the truth concerning Fr. Melchor, he experiences his first "wet dream" since puberty and the sublimation of erotic fantasy in the UN agency; and his inability to recover the triggering event of which the wetness is the trace suggests the predicament of a whole society suspended in a postadolescent inertia, unable to comprehend the sources of its unease: "He tried to recall the dream, in which he had watched a confused procession coming up from darkness; but nothing in the dream explained its effect." Dramatizing the precarious and contingent nature of one's role, this gratuitous stripping of Sid by the Salemites introduces him to Sonya Borja, the "Eve" on the edge of the urban jungle and confidante-turned-lover—the shadowy ally of Sid the sleuth who turns out to be an intuitive sympathizer of his enemy.

Sonya's rescue of Sid from baptismal violence and his reintroduction into society through provision of his son's clothes can be tied with her mediating function as the disguised force of the pleasure principle which validates Sid's sexuality and affirms the submerged continuity of what Mrs. Banaag calls "the felt wisdom in the blood . . . in the flesh." Her sexual communion with Sid, which occurs on winter solstice as a rite to "help the sun be born again," burns out Sid's mnemonic stasis and disrupts his contact with the everyday fallen world. Sid discovers Sonya's duplicity afterward; her sudden retreat or ascent to Baguio evokes Lawrence's "dark gods of the blood" which (she writes) presided over their "gluttony." Her letter of farewell —another voice or inscription which tries to fill up the absence of Guia, and also heal the cleavage of suspicion in Sid's mind — testifies to a fissured self, the dissolution of a coherent autonomous ego identifiable as mother, wife, or daughter. Escaping all those gender categories, Sonya reenacts the inaugural gesture of Hegel's "unhappy consciousness," this time hounded by the specter of her own past marked by separation, isolation, guilt:

Afterwards, of course, I was horrified. One doesn't chuck mind that fast. My husband said he could hear my mind at work even when he was making love to me; so he ran away. Now it's I am running away. What I do now seems so silly. We play with the past, making chi-chi fashions out of it, or decor for a party. Maybe I'm being punished for having used it so frivolously, as mere bric-a-brac.
But it was madness to come up here. This is their country, their terrain, the dark gods. I was in Bontoc and Sagada and up to Ifugao country and they were all about me. Remember telling me how, as you ran from these goons, you felt your naked body had become pure movement, without a mind, every limb thinking for-itself? That's how I feel now, as I run and run but always find myself where I would run away from.

Tied with Guia's syndrome when excited—"she went still all over, the parted lips breathless"—in which erotic release spells death (pp. 225, 251, 266), and her musing approval of repudiating all by immersing one's whole being in a large dynamic movement (p. 230), this passage performs at least two functions: first, it affirms what it rejects by the Freudian mode of negation where the repressed adheres to and contours the surface so that Sonya can then condemn the valorization of the primitive as madness; and, second, it spatializes the temporal by locating the archaic in a geographic site in contrast to the mountainous terrain of Ifugao country accessible to anyone (in contrast to the exclusive baroque club of Santiago Ferrer which parodies history) so that we no longer need to retreat into the past—that past is right there in the present, coexisting with it as in a palimpsest where traces of earlier inscriptions show through. In the first, the text seeks to exorcise the terror of history and the burden of a decadent tradition; while in the second, the notion of the present as an overdetermined confluence of past and future liberates the will from a fatalistic determinism whose most compulsive symptom is the successive appearance of the Three Kings, avatars and bearers of the epiphanic message.

On the surface, we perceive in Sonya's letter how space and time have been collapsed into circular motion, with beginning and ending fused together. This is evident in the scene where, immersed in the vertigo of complicitous ramifications, we perceive a mother's pursuit reaching a climax, a wife whose husband has fled, this woman vacating the scene but asserting her presence in script, in the marks on the letter which Sid interprets. His act of deciphering recuperates that differential process which the narrative in turn thematizes as the ordeal of the subject to free itself from its traumatic quest for refuge in the illusion of self-presence. This woman's confession of her anguish to escape from the past when the past turns out to be the future juxtaposed spatially to her present, ushers in the prophet Fr. Melchor who now becomes the figure of a transcendence ironically parasitic on circumstance and the bodies of unwitting participants in a drama that subsumes all. Fr. Melchor's parting statement strikes me as the most succinct formulation of history as incarnational happening in a fallen, guilt-stricken world where a *deus absconditus* keeps surveillance and waits for the ripe moment:

"You think I have changed, Mr. Estiva? Yes, the weariness comes when one fails and has to hide again. But I have come back before, I shall come back again. A faith thrives on the blood of its witnesses. And we have a new one. Saint Guia, virgin and martyr." (p. 268)

Not the denudation of the neocolonial native but the death of the taxi driver is what permits the course of prehistory to begin, for the self-appointed outsider Sid to wake up and grasp the paradox of positionality: "I always try not to be where the action is...so, now, I'm up to my neck in it." If opposites beget each other, if all identities are produced by differential relations—more precisely, if discrete entities do not exist but only the flux of relations, then the loss of identity Sid temporarily suffers becomes the propaedeutic, fertile ground for his understanding his position through the coordinates of place invested with the aura of art, a position sensitive however to unexpected mutations and novelties:

> This was, thought Sid, jolting through downtown, a Manila his backside did not recall. If I closed my eyes, this could be the dirt road to a childhood summer in the provinces. But how shut eyes as agape now as then at the primitive? Rizal's image of the city as a frail girl wearing her grandmother's finery no longer fitted; this was a dirty old broad got up all wrong in the yé-yé girl's clothes. The old city walls that came into view across the soiled air and a bridgeful of chaos astonished with their look of calm and dignity. (p. 219)

There's still the familiar mystique of nostalgia for Intramuros; the presence of the Cathedral affords a convergence of "memory and appearance," a privileged instant to be displaced, occluded and dispersed by the relentless stratifying sedimentation of the text.

Absent welcomers, mistaken identity, loss of control, abduction and stripping, and eventually death and solitude mark the nonchronological unfolding of a narrative whose initial pretext is the familial imperative to secure the cohesion of property by separating the adolescent Guia from the affiliative group from which she derives her sense of vocation ("I've found myself," p. 226). In effect, the elders are wresting for control and judgment of the future. In spite of their massive effort to suppress the past (Guia recollects her past as groundwork for the present, while Sid and the Ferrers strive to neutralize it by exploiting it), the elders disinter it in their puritanical authoritarianism and thus unleash the avenging furies of the Other inscribed here in the collective praxis of Fr. Melchor's sect. The scheme succeeds at the cost of destroying Guia—she herself predicts the result by warning Sid that he's sending her back not to "decorum" but to death (pp. 252-53). In Adela's den where he reconstructs his past, Fr. Lao condemns the sectarian talk of "history and renewal and the native soul" as diabolic and subsequently releases the violence of his despair ("because God had withdrawn" in Kansas, USA) on Guia, the unrepentant and rebellious offspring. Filiation triumphs over affiliation.

On closer inspection, we discover another implicit dimension: Guia, the embodiment of populist tendencies in the youthful generation and of a whole society endeavoring to shake off the tyranny of the patriarchs and the power-knowledge complex of imperialist hegemony, is also the sign of absence/negation which subsumes the narcissistic complacency of Sid and the Ferrers, of a whole commodified milieu. Refusing her role as the prized possession over which Sid and Adela haggle, nourishing the uncircumscribed "anger and passions" released in the naked dancing of the virgins during Halloween, the intact Guia cannot be allowed to circulate freely since her use-value can only be exchanged by the patriarchal surrogates, hence her destruction as the tabooed witch and "scarlet whore" necessary for the ethics of a market-society to continue. Without the "gleam of her mother's jewels," Guia stands for an aborted community in the process of becoming, for charisma about to materialize: "All the limbs and organs in wild prayer." Guia is the metamorphosing signifier—the whole Philippine formation in the fifties and sixties—still heterogeneous, not yet transgressing, still intact, progressing toward a reconstitution of its subjectivity in a collective regeneration of the race which, assuming a revivalist organizational form with authority crystallizing in one person, cannot but incur the repressive wrath of Establishment power. Guia's actantial function subdivides into the nationalist activism of Mrs. Banaag and the more subtly insidious if cathartic seductiveness of Sonya Borja. Both matriarchs escape the verdict of Fr. Lao and the oedipal machine of the state police, thwarting the pathos of a conservative realist closure.

Notwithstanding the crafty intertwining of narrative strands leading to the breakup of the Salemites' orgy, the release of Fr. Lao and the punishment of Guia—resolutions that would satisfy the superegoistic public—there still remains the excess of questions and wishes immanent in the surplus of textualization surrounding the enigmatic prophet. This logocentrism has not run aground against the Real, the unrepresentable limits of history, the absent cause whose configuration and texture can be mapped out only by the *écriture* of Desire. And this is where the phantasmal figure of Fr. Melchor intrudes, his last meeting with Sid being the narrative's own valorization of its self-sufficiency and an exegesis of how the Real is registered in its disseminating effects. Fr. Melchor's promise is fulfilled in the return of Sid's belongings (contradistinguished from the prophet's stigmata which now no longer signifies):

> Sid was staring at the things on the table. Then, ruefully, he picked up the green prophylactic with the frayed bristles.
> "My symbol of non-involvement..." he murmured.
> "We made it mean the means to deepest commitment."
> "But what a coincidence that I—"
> "There are no coincidences, Mr. Estiva. When you called us back years ago you set in motion certain forces that made inevitable, not only that you should come home, but that you should come home bearing a sign aloft to proclaim a connection you were unaware of; and that, like magnet or lodestone, or the smell of blood that attracts the creatures of the deep, you should draw all about you the other participants in this drama that you initiated. It was no coincidence when they—But why do you stare at me so, Mr. Estiva?" (p. 268)

On the surface, Fr. Melchor asserts here the idea of determinism by hindsight and the patent/latent inevitability of what happens, an idea whose philosophic version is none other than Hegel's reading of history as a revelation of necessity in which every historical event becomes a manifestation of the Universal Spirit. Sid's invocation of the past (read: Joaquin's glorification of the Hispanic legacy) has summoned this primitivistic trend which, in its periodic annulment of profane time and virtual eternalization of man's cosmic existence, preempts the need for any redeemer. Of what then is Fr. Melchor a prophet?

In the twelfth century, the Cisterian monk Joachim of Floris in Calabria introduced a radically progressive, trinitarian conception of world history which revised the hegemonic Augustinian doctrine of temporal change expressed in the *City of God* (Book 32, Chapter 30). Amid the intense persecution of the Franciscan Spirituals and the miseries brought about by the papal-imperial wars in Italy, together with peasant jacqueries and the People's Crusade at the end of the eleventh century, Joachim conceived his age as witness to the impending decisive war between the forces of Anti-Christ and the emergent disciples of the true spiritual Church. It was the penultimate phase of the second age, the Age of the Son (New Testament) dominated by clerics of the "carnal church," the "Whore of Babylon"; this age having succeeded the Age of the Father (the period of the Old Testament) presided by the patriarchs or married men. While the first age had been characterized by law (knowledge) and the second under grace and partial wisdom (resembling the Augustinian notion of the millennium begun by Christ and maintained in the sacramental life of the Church), the third would witness the ascendancy of liberty over filial servitude, the spirit over the letter, and the negation of the flesh/spirit dualism which vitiated the Age of the Son. Such a transition would occur through a ferocious struggle between the old and the new, recapitulating the Jewish eschatological combat in the Book of Daniel and the Christian Revelation of St. John of the Apocalypse. In the years 1200 to 1260, the Babylonian captivity of peoples under the first Anti-Christ would prevail until the second incarnation of Christ and the period of sabbatical peace and justice which would inaugurate the supreme rule of the Spirit. What is immediately consequential to our purpose here is the impact of this heretical vision in the thirteenth century, when Gerard of Borgo San Donnino in 1254 adapted Joachim's "eternal gospel" to sanction the practice of the followers of Saint Francis (1182-1226) and their ideal of absolute poverty as against the spectacle of the degenerate, avaricious, worldly Roman church. Gerard of Borgo was promptly condemned and imprisoned for this revisionism, followed by the intense persecution of the Franciscan Spirituals in the later decades of the century, with their subversive and dissenting impetus persisting in the Flagelant movement of 1260 (the ending of the Age of the Son), in the semi-Joachist sect of the False Apostles anathematized in 1274, and in various prophecies merging with the Sybilline writings. (Note that in our time of the "reinvention" of *el dios pobre* by Latin American theologians of liberation, we should remind ourselves of Pope John XXII's condemnation in 1323 of the Franciscan doctrine of Christ's absolute poverty as heretical.) What runs through the whole heterodox current in the fourteenth and fifteenth centuries, in which the Anti-Christ was apprehended in the Great Schism (1378-1417) and its two contending popes, in the Black Death (1348-50) and endemic social and political disturbances culminating in the Anabaptist Rebellion led by Thomas Munzer (1489-1525) in Germany, is the Joachist expectation of the imminent termination of the present age through a catastrophic upheaval and its replacement by a new golden age of peace, harmony and abundance.

It is in this context that the elaborate hermeneutic exercise of interpretation and decoding around which Sid's homecoming as alienated native, Guia's search for herself, and Fr. Melchor's real identity turns, discloses its proper mission as a displacement of that anxiety concerning what's to come, a transposition of drives to compensate for an originary loss first imaged in the psychic splitting of Sid and Fr. Lao, Sid's denudation, and the multiple scissions and deracinations which climax in Guia's death and Fr. Melchor's disappearance, for which the mask or cover of a back-to-primitivism sect serves as a distracting if sublimating alibi. Under the guise of an indigenizing religious movement complete with pagan folk art Mrs. Banaag labels as "a magical nature religion" imbued with a nationalistic vocation—the Salemite brotherhood, with its iconology of the phallic Christ and its apotheosis if instinct, serves as the libidinally charged site where the prophet, a filial heir of the original, first manifests himself. What appears as a simple inquiry into Fr. Melchor's past—Sid learns in his first visit to their shrine that Fr. Melchor (now a layman) was ordained in Fookien province, China, served in Tibet during the Chinese civil war, and then dropped by his order for complicity with a schismatic church—becomes an archaeological hunt as the layman exfoliates into the prophet Melkizedek, a mask or front (the misplaced message carries the address "At the Sign of the Milky Seed. Deck Six!") which is one polar sign opposite the heraldic conversion of the Three Kings. On the one hand, we have the biblical archetype of Melkizedek, priest and king without father or mother, in charge of the body of Adam and head of a sect which worshipped Adam's body (Fray Calezon adds: "Adam is the only other character in the Bible who had neither father nor mother.") When Sid accuses Fr. Melchor of using violence and women to implant a heathen cult, deluding people of a "new image of Christ," Fr. Melchor retorts:

"*Deluding*-tch, tch Mr. Estiva. You know that's not so. The god is worshipped, the true god. Does it matter if we call him Baal or Bathala, Priapus or Christ? What is the point of that passage in the Bible where Abraham and Melkizedek worshipped together. Melkizedek invoked his heathen god El or Zaduk; Abraham prayed to Yahweh. But the Bible makes no distinction between the deities calling Melkizedek, too, a priest of the most high God. And when St. Paul placed Christ himself in the line of

Melkizedek, was this not a recognition that the pagan priesthood was resumed in Christ, that the old cults were being continued in the new faith? Abraham had already made such a recognition: he paid a tithe to the pagan high priest Melkizedek. It didn't matter to Abraham who Melkizedek was or in what name he worshipped God."

"And it doesn't matter who *you* are?"

"Yes, I hear you have been making inquiries. No, Mr. Estiva, I don't think it matters. What mattered to Abraham was that Melkizedek was on his side. the important thing here is that I am on your side."

"My side!"

"You are of those who called me back."

"I don't think I ever went that far back."

"Ah, Mr. Estiva, if you go back at all it's impossible to set a limit: Up to this point and no farther. If you dig up one grave you have also unlocked the ones that lie below. You've heard of the diggings during the Renaissance: how it was feared that with the resurrection of their vessels and ikons the old gods that had gone underground had surfaced again?'

"And you think that's happening here now?'

"Oh, I don't pretend to be one of the old gods. Merely to be in their service—as you are, though you may refuse to admit it. And as your sister will be, when she has gone beyond the Christian image and learns by herself what is the question that must be asked: the name of the god she worships. It will be her illumination. Therefore, I ask you not to block her path." (pp. 255-56)

Conflating the two genealogies, the figure of Melkizedek symbolizes the syncretic process in which the old is subsumed in the new without being modified or distorted, the old referring to the prelapsarian Adam or Melkizedek without male or female progenitor, without the impregnating patriarch or the pregnant matriarch: Infinity itself without beginning or end, the folding of exterior and interior and of soul and flesh into each other – in effect, Joachim's reign of the Holy Spirit realized. On the other hank, Fr. Melchor can be viewed as the last of the pagan Three Kings delivering the good news of the advent of the son of Man, the Christos-redeemer who will inaugurate the millennial age for the oppressed peasants and victimized underclasses. He will establish the messianic kingdom of the promise that will reverse history, dispossess the privileged property-owners, and emancipate the suffering just and virtuous saints from bondage. Here, in this reworking of the apocalyptic and chiliastic tradition from the Book of Daniel to Revelation and its historicist articulation by Joachim of Floris, the narrative secretes its "political unconscious" for which the thematized topics of "restoring paganism" and revitalizing autochthonous faith, while symptomatic of institutional Christianity's crisis in late global capitalism, serve as plausible and manipulable counters.

For what name indeed can we give to the avatar summoned by Dr. Lagman's recollection and to the images of the Exodus and New Jerusalem that his voice renders in communicating less to Sid and Sonya than to a collective audience of listeners whose solidarity emerges from the promise his text simultaneously fulfills and disappoints? One of the few surviving witnesses to a peasant religious uprising in Pangasinan in 1900, Dr. Lagman recounts the founding of a Christian communist settlement of poor peasants "escaping from the capataces of the landlords and the Yanquis of MacArthur," an egalitarian paradise of plenty, where "every day was fiesta," a sacred spot where Christ, the Virgin Mary, the Holy Ghost, the Twelve Apostles and God have taken bodily forms, all only to be destroyed in March 1901 by the American invaders led by General Otis who then hangs Christ and the Holy Ghost in public and jails the rest. As for the god of this Eden, the voice attempts to erase the lacuna:

"At the trials before the military court it was learned that his real name was Baltazar. He did not seem to have any other name. Nobody could say where he came from. He had simply appeared during the Revolution, in the Central Plain, exhorting the peasants to rise, but in the name of his religion. And the peasants began to follow him until he had an army of his own that would harass both Aguinaldo and the Americans. By 1897 he had established his headquarters in this place that was to become the New Jerusalem. At that time, according to testimony, he was already more than forty years old.

"As I said, his end is as mysterious as his beginning. One day he was there, the next day he was not. But many of those who were in his New Jerusalem believed all their lives that he would return one day and call them back to his kingdom." (p. 245)

Two years ago (Dr. Lagman brings us to the present), Baltazar surfaces:

"He said he had come back as he promised, under another name, Melkizedek, to start the rebuilding of his kingdom. Would I join him again? I tell you, if I were not crippled, I would have stood up that instant and followed him. But all I could do was try to remember for him where this or that survivor of the New Jerusalem had last been heard from. He thanked me and left. He has not come back, but I hear about him. I hear he has been in the provinces tracking down the children or grandchildren of those who were his followers and that many of these young ones, for whom, of course, he is a family legend, are joining him. In what? A new uprising? A new Kingdom? That, I cannot tell, but sometimes, as I sit here musing, I wonder if they are to come back, truly, again: the great days, the Revolution—and how I wish I were young again!" (p. 246)

Notice that Dr. Lagman is not referring here to Aguinaldo's straggling forces in retreat but to that whole complex duration of rapid changes, in particular the millenarian rupture, which can only be poorly and inexactly designated by the term "Revolution." The narrative apparatus reacts to this dangerous possibility when Sonya dismisses Dr. Lagman's mnemonic recreation of the past as "exultant nostalgia," a sanitizing epithet to purge

Baltazar/ Melchor of any possible association with paradigms like Thomas Munzer memorialized in Engels' *Peasant War in Germany* (1850).

The signifier "Fr. Melchor" now undergoes further sliding and elision in succeeding texts: first, in Fray Calezon's document about Melchor de la Epifanio, an Indio layman assigned to Fookien and later ordained into priesthood in 1796 despite his ugly birthmark (the substitute navel), after which he disappears in Tibet "after joining an esoteric Buddhist sect there." Except for the updating of "Indo-China in 1800" to the Communist victory in 1949, a stigmatizing association, this tallies with and echoes Fr. Melchor's statement to Sid earlier. Second, in the history of his order, Fray Calezon exhumes a record of an armed resistance to the Hispanic conquistadors in the late 1500s led by a high priest of the old cult bearing the same stigmata—limp, mark on forehead; then, in the 1690s, another uprising of Christians regressing to paganism led by a "Christian by the name of Gaspar who claims he has all along been a high priest of the old cults." The archaeologist of texts offers his authenticating voice: "Gaspar declares that the time has come to restore his kingdom, and we have this revolt, again in the Central Plain—oh, quite an uprising." With the uprising suppressed and Gaspar vanishing, the conclusion Fray Calezon draws is that "there has been a series of impostors copying the message and the appearance of a pagan original, and with a predilection for the names of the Three Kings: Melchor, Gaspar, Baltazar." And the latest impostor is Fr. Melchor, alias Melkizedek, the head of the New Salem community, whose biblical resonance foregrounds the quasi-Pelagian and naturalistic notion of Adam as not only without forebears but also without sin and therefore needing no future redemption. At this point we arrive at that incommensurable aporia, a zone of transgressed limits and boundaries where all the contradictions fuse to block the narrative apparatus from functioning further toward logical synthesis of which the friar's gothicism of "Heathenisms emerging from consecrated ground" can only be a pallid approximation, and his concluding judgment—a quotation from the Bible of Melkizedek's permanent priesthood—a textualizing vindication of the prelapsarian cosmic creation: either Nietzsche's Eternal Recurrence, or Joachim's Third Age of the Holy Spirit.

Such deliberate collation and alignment of texts yields the insight that it is in this undecidable moment that the myth of eternal recurrence (Melkizedek as the self-renewing, ever present Adam *in illo tempore* or dreamtime) irreconcilably collides with the Christian doctrine of the Incarnation as a unique event, not repeatable, since Christ died for our sins "once only, once for all" (The Epistle to the Hebrews 9; 1 Peter 3:18). In the narrative, this event is prefigured by the succession of the Three Kings irrupting at epiphanic moments of native history, the chiliastic thresholds when the masses of exploited and oppressed toiling in a fallen temporality process of collective self-directed renewal. With Guia's body recaptured or reterritoralized by the familial, exegetic machine through Fr Lao's act of salvation, desire is once more pacified; but Fr. Melchor, the announcer of authentic redemption, disappears and Sonya Borja decamps, permitting the flow of deterritorializing desire and inscribing the ubiquity of charismatic power in her flight. We can provisionally schematize the semantic pattern of the narrative thus:

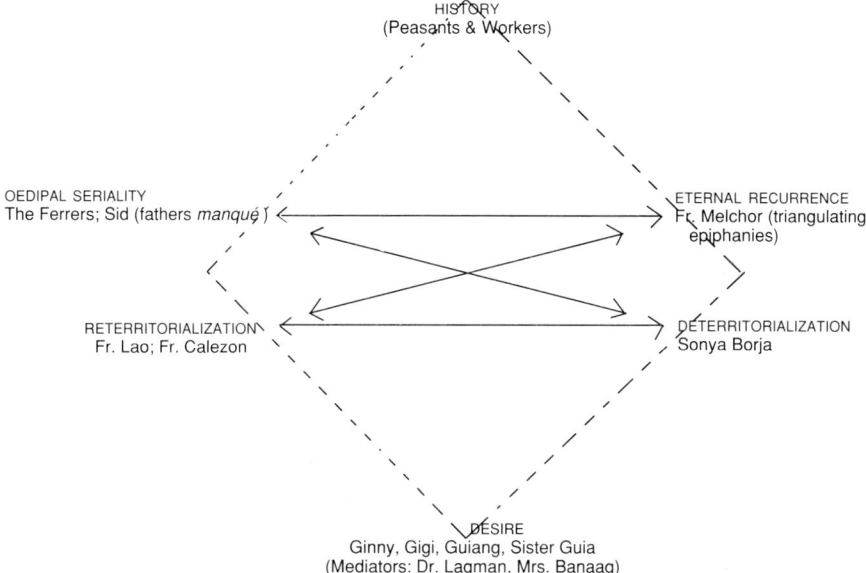

It will be obvious by now that the periodic irruptions of the avant-garde prophet-kings into the "fallen" world of routine and bureaucratic power relations are not occasioned by the nativist transvaluation of Christianity into pagan cults, although that is how the dispersion of the monotheistic/monolithic power center manifests itself; rather it is occasioned by the upsurge of the politicized masses, their reappropriation of their alienated will-to-power via nationalist and radicalized class consciousness. And for want of a better complex term other than the Real, I use "History" to designate here the absent cause for the hierophany of Baltazar, Gaspar and Melchor who are frustrated repeatedly when they endeavor to announce in action the advent not of the Son/Christos messiah but the collective agent allegorized by Joachim of Floris as the Holy Spirit. Such frustration takes the form of "eternal recurrence" not in its Nietzschean import but as a quasi-Freudian moment of deferral or displacement. We can further appreciate the uncanny aura that envelops the manifold coincidences and ironies that overtake Sid–Fr. Melchor imputes to him something excessive: "You are of those who called me back . . ."—when we consider his obsession for the intact virginity of his half sister Guia and his resumption of "legal guardian" status as a sign of the return of the Patriarch, the reinstallation of the oedipal machine whose efficient administrator is Fr. Lao, among others, and whose textualizing product is the dead body of the heiress Guia and the evacuated Shrine. We may then read all the successive hermeneutic attempts at naming, defining, interpreting, deciphering and identifying as instrumentalities of the reality principle, what Deleuze and Guattari call the "paranoiac transcendental law" in contrast to the "immanent schizo-law" (the demands of the unconscious) whose corresponding figuration here is the sexual play of Sid and Sonya and the description of pure motion (Sid's fleeing; participatory politics; orgy) which modulates the institutional monologues into dialogic, heteroglotic carniva—the Rabelaisian vision of a ludic community where the body / soul conflict evaporates into sheer cries of pleasure.

In trying to fix the connotative topography of themes and the density of character relations, I may have opened graves piled on top of one another —Fray Calezon and Fr. Melchor's metaphor for dialectics and intertextuality. But this mode of interpellating textual units and tropes is dictated by Joaquin's project of trying to say everything at once in a single utterance, exemplified by Guia's aphorism, "Whatever is Mod is God," or the cryptic synthesizing image: "Whenever she was very excited she went still all over, the parted lips breathless." Such stylistic indices may be grasped as the markers "on the road to Damascus," particularly when we historicize its beginning from a tribal agricultural stage proceeding toward an industrial capitalist national polity–a progress aborted by U.S. imperialist intervention, so now the Philippine formation unfolds itself as a constellation of unevenly juxtaposed, nonsynchronic regressive progressive tendencies, always on the verge of achieving the integrity of an independent nation (Corpus Christi) but always halted at the Feast of the Circumcision, with the aboriginal furies turning out to be nothing but the apostles of Father's revenge. The text dramatizes this subterranean continuum of the struggle periodically manifested in nativist protests and phenomenal revolts (see the airport hunt, p.199), the ebbs and flows of collective Desire finding multiple incarnations that disrupt the operations of the death-worshipping technocratic machine. The trajectory of the utopian wish-fulfillment and demand for partisanship (commitment to a vocation) undermining the realist status quo in this narrative may now be finally represented in this heuristic diagram:

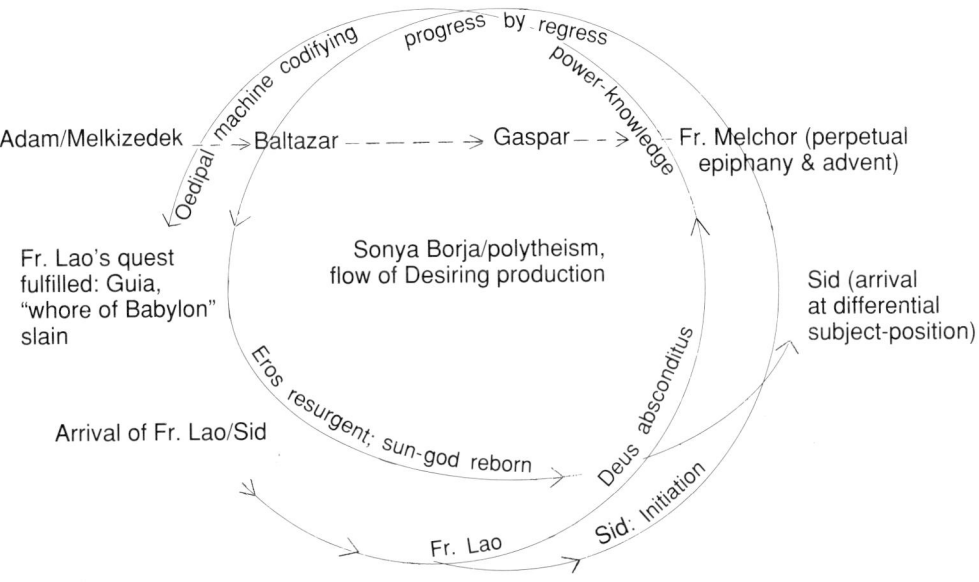

With two bodies (Guia's stilled and Fr. Melchor's performing its disappearing act) erased, and their traces buried in the ruins of Salem House and the womblike niche of the shrine whose corresponding mimesis are disembodied voices addressing from their absence the oedipal body/phallus circumcised, the reflective and embryonic ego now begins its agonistic shadow dance as it denies the multiplicity and heterogeneity of desire and in the same act affirms its irrepressible immediacy. Joaquin's next therapeutic mediation, *Cave and Shadows,* will pursue its project of exorcising Oedipus and salvaging what Deleuze and Guattari call "the body without organs" —a utopian plenum long vanished in a past forever anticipated, a future nostalgically embraced.

4 Simulacra of the Sublime: Deconstructing Joaquin's Poetics

The emotions always have a quite definite class basis; the form they take at any time is historical, restricted and limited in specific ways. The emotions are in no sense universally human and timeless.

—Bertolt Brecht

The phantasy of poetry is a social image.

—Christopher Caudwell

Reach for your pen only when there is no other way of saying something except verse. You must work up things you've prepared only when you feel a clear social command. To understand the social command accurately, a poet must be in the middle of things and events.

—Vladimir Mayakovsky

IN THE NINETEEN POEMS included in the 1952 Graphic House edition of *Prose and Poems*, we find recapitulated and distilled in concentrated semiotic models Joaquin's problematized response to a world bifurcated by irreconcilably antagonistic forces and precipitated into anarchy. This anarchy manifests itself (in the pre-1940 period) as "dissociation of sensibility" in "Six P.M." and "Song Between Wars," the unconscionable sacrifice of youth to war, the devouring Minotaur. Opposed to this sense of entrapment (between the Second World War and an impending nuclear Armageddon between the U.S. and the Soviet Union at the beginning of the Cold War circa 1950)—"the labyrinth behind / and the Beast ahead"—is what we might call an apocalyptic or prophetic vision which, through various mimetic and didactic modes, affirms the rootedness of the spirit in conscious matter, in the body's well-nigh unrepresentable constellation of desire.

We might consider a late poem in the canon, "Stubbs Road Cantos," dated Hong Kong 1949, as an illustration of Joaquin's instrinsically materialist perspective (all page references are to the 1987 edition of Joaquin's

Collected Verse, published by Ateneo de Manila University Press). Unlike "Verde Yo Te Quiero Verde," this poem departs from the classic decorum of tightly patterned stanzas and witty rhyme schemes characteristic of Joaquin's versifying practice in general. Here, bursting the constraints of conventional rhyming schemes, the poet structures his narration of the seminarian's routine around the predictable turn of the seasons and the repetition of key images, in particular "the yard with sunflowers / and the hillsides with tiny bitter blackberries." Time here acquires flesh and meaning through the mediation of organic life and sensuous phenomena so that even its denial by the "Rule of St. Augustine" is equated with winter "stripping / the yard and the hillsides, prohibiting further / leisure on the seashore and the Sunday tigers" (p. 7).

The second verse paragraph consisting of twenty-eight lines, the longest section, departs from the collective awareness noted in the first verse paragraph. Here the persona or speaker describes his feeling of isolation, and here the juxtaposition of the novice projecting himself as a St. John the Baptist at Christmas time, heard only by God and himself, and the approaching victory of Mao's revolutionary Communist forces in mainland China, suggests that the personal dilemma of the speaker—the last verse paragraph forecloses this perception—still cognizes the real world not just of seasonal change but of historical development as its arena:

> Dawn broke; and sunlight fell on the hillsides
> where no berries were; the race-horses
> stamped in their stables in Happy Valley hearing
> the first hawker abroad, the first whistle of the ferry boats
> and the sound of guns on the mainland approaching
> as I stood in a wilderness worshipping secretly:
> as I stood in a desert expectant (it was the Time of Advent):
> as I closed the book and bowed and returned to position,
> who had sung in secret and received no answer. (p. 8)

The last line, an anticlimactic expression of nonfulfillment, of expectation foiled amid the signs of renewal—dawn, sunlight, the Communist victory, reinserts the speaker back into the group's discipline. But it fails to suppress the dissonances of the body, the corporeal boundaries and potential of transcendence:

> The mystical
> mirth of the springtime lover in the canticles
> turned hoarse in our throats, turned into sobs in sore throats,
> that sang the Lenten office to an obligatto
> of coughs and sniffles and noise of noses blown furtively
> as we stooped to the Glorias. (p. 8)

Spring, instead of inducing ecstatic anticipation, produces "damp miseries." However, it also evokes "memories / of the heat and the Passion palms of the homeland: / we ached for the green heat under the palms of the homeland / as we huddled indoors." With the Communist guns safely silenced, the novitiates obey the authority of the Father Master (alluded to in the first verse paragraph) and, confined to a kind of pregnant hoping, become the feminine vessels waiting for Christ's resurrection

> from the red yard and red hillsides, waiting
> in the supper chamber, the windows bolted, the lights on,
> our lamps lighted, wise virgins, the mystical
> brides of the springtime Lover of the canticles. (p. 8)

In contrast to these "wise virgins" adoring the "springtime Lover of the canticles," however, the speaker gives us "Stubbs Road Cantos" which undermines the predictable cycle of the seasons by its hint of linear and irreversible development ("the voice that cried in the wilderness," "and the sound of guns on the mainland approaching"), by its dramatic if unintended confession of a rupture between the mythical archetype and the existential protagonist (last four lines of the second paragraph), and by its positing of marriage, albeit a mystical one, as a break in nature's organic circularity: the wild prophet merged with the virginal brides. Eros here conquers the "Rule of St. Augustine."

Obviously summarizing this interregnum of Joaquin's life as a seminarian in St. Albert's College in Hong Kong (from 1947 to 1950), "Stubbs Road Cantos" and its dialectical overcoming of asceticism and the otherworldly regimen by a foregrounding of the Incarnation as central trope confirms the supremacy of the comic temper, an essentially utopian orientation, in Joaquin's art. The two poems printed before and after this poem testify to this orientation as affording a strategy for reconciling real-life contradictions, or sublimating these contradictions onto a higher plane of understanding.

In "Landscape Without Figures," the poet locates the future underground, in "neolithic caves" instanced by "bomb-shelter, catacomb, foxhole / and fathomings ever more profound"—a future "where even man will not be vile." With the fourth stanza, the focus shifts from the movement underground to the surface: "The Future's rapping at the door." The poet then abandons the impersonal allegory, unable to sustain the rhetorical tirade reminiscent of genteel *New Yorker* moralizing. In "mankind's eventual hegira" to a future cursed with nuclear destruction, "your sad eyes, staring, make this room / the memory's viaticum." Whose "sad eyes"? This strange hiatus is passed over in the last stanza where the metaphor of burrowing underground is sustained:

> A stone heart's in the stricken flesh
> that craves a miner for its health
> but hears no miner's axe—unless
> Christ, with his customary stealth,
> comes cleaving through the heart's material
> the twin caves of his birth and burial. (p. 53)

This conception of "the heart's material" and its dual usefulness informs the thematic center of "O Death Be Proud" (dated 1947), reversing Donne's famous sonnet "Death Be Not Proud."

In this poem Joaquin celebrates the lyric potential of organic matter, its metamorphosis into different forms insinuating the collapse of gnostic hierarchy; Caesar's and Agammemnon's "relics arise to replenish a grocery." The witticisms and burlesques of cliché are meant not just to invoke death as the proverbial great equalizer but, more integrally, to emphasize the transitoriness of social and political structures, as well as the inevitability of reversal and change:

> Because it is man's fortune kitchenward to decline
> I am fed on my dead father's unstable status:
> I break his body and drink his blood, turned bread and wine.

The eucharistic analogy conceals the violent act of revolt, the reduction of titles and power elites to the level of consuming humanity. In this poem, the impact of death and destruction by war—registered in "Song Between Wars" (1946), together with "On Public Speech," perhaps the bleakest of them all—is neutralized, absorbed into the organic cycle of decaying-recomposing matter: "O Death, thou art the edible apparatus / we eat, and that shall eat us by and by."

Joaquin's antimetaphysical sonnet, a counterpastoral antidote to pious sentimentality, subsumes also the distantiating perspective of "The Years" (1945) where the supernatural vanishes amid "the plight, the fright, the flight / of mortals on a small star sailing sugar and shoes" (p. 50). Life's continuity overwhelms the landscape of holocaust where war, "the bull that's human," roams freely. This Rabelaisian humanism—a fanatical intoxication with the pleasures of the senses sharpening the awareness of mortality—is what probably attracted Joaquin to Rizal's already fetishized "Last Farewell." Composed in 1944, in the last year of the Japanese occupation of the Philippines, "Jose Rizal's Valedictory Poem" is already removed from the original text by attribution, already alienated and converted into a space for postmortem articulation. It is charged with a Lucretian fervor, a celebration of the kaleidoscopic mutability of matter which overshadows its overt metaphysical connotations:

> And when my grave is wholly unremembered
> and unlocated (no cross upon it, no stone there plain):
> let the site be wracked by the plow and cracked by the spade
> and let my ashes, before they vanish into nothing,
> as dust be formed a part of your carpet again.
>
> Nothing then will it matter to place me in oblivion!
> Across your air, your space, your valleys shall pass my wraith!
> A pure chord, strong and resonant, shall I be in your ears:
> fragrance, light and color: whisper, lyric and sigh:
> constantly repeating the essence of my faith!

Contrary to the etherealizing and disembodied impulse exalted in the above stanza, the poem reiterates the act of reposing ("To die is to repose" with the play on shift of position), the task of reconstituting a landscape whose attentive listening to the language of the patriot-martyr will occasion its rebirth: "O lovely; how lovely: to fall that you may rise! / to perish that you may live!" Rizal's parting words summon the "Eden lost to your blood" to a presence which, amid the rubble of 1944, asserts the principle of hope and future regeneration in the verbalized gesture of renewal: dead language is reincarnated in the speech of the conqueror in at least three dimensions.

From the 1939 poem "Now Sound the Flutes" to the 1943 poem "The 14 Stations of the Cross," six poetic attempts are made to exorcise the terror and confusion, the demonic perversions, of a system which can only appreciate "golden boys and girls" because, as "Song Between Wars" puts it, "they are molten money and their bones are cash." This Swiftian indictment of a commodity-dominated society demonstrates itself earlier as a demand for distinction, for a reappraisal, in "Now Sound the Flutes": the time has come "to break the spell / and find what's real and what's fable." The speaker begins with a confession of self-doubt which is immediately dissolved by a dream on Pentecostide:

> Fire did waste my flesh to nothing
> till there, purged beyond love or loathing,
> the skeleton, fair like a bride,
> shone forth, redeemed from temporal clothing. (p. 41)

This leads to a confrontation: "And how can you wed me to your pleasure / Earth? for now the secular span / of flesh is not my spirit's measure." And yet, somehow believing that "Time" will not exhaust his inner core, he calls the community at the end for a wedding—a marriage of the durable and pristine skeleton with dreaming, transient flesh.

The dreamer of "Now Sound the Flutes" who still upholds the primacy of sharing his private illumination, begins to elaborate this experience in "The Visitation," written in 1941, in the year when conflagration from bombs swept Pearl Harbor, Manila, and other cities. Here, the fiery havoc becomes a sign, a visual icon, which makes language superfluous: "Grace, unexpected and pure Grace, / flame-swift descending." Redemption heralds itself as "white bird or white flame" in the moment of silence when, in a revealing look of recognition, the lawgiving father is acknowledged "as though Love, birdwise manifesting, / bird-tangible had gone / forth from a father to a son" (p. 46). Since epiphany allows the "bitter tongue" to unloosen "praise and wild song," uniting "flame and dove," "the peace devouring fire of Love / and Love's cool-breasted solace," the aegis of grace offers for the distraught and delirious speaker of "On Public Speech" and "Life and Letters" a privileged haven of contemplation and retreat from the wasteland in which "the senses have become a burden: what's thought but sensual slavery?"

"On Public Speech" rejects any possibility of clarifying the tangle of appearances and truths in the skein of ordinary existence; it upholds a resignation to blindness and despair, given the bankruptcy of the liberal discourse of the marketplace "to serve us in our spiritual hunger / a slightly acid Mother Goose." A gloomy debilitating forecast is uttered in "Life and Letters": "The streams from the heart have nourished / out of this stagnant clay / the old evil of dreams." The speaker meditates on the futility of resistance to the decadence of the modern world: "nothing we do can stay / the forest nor restrain / the utter twilight / creeping upon the brain" (p. 45).

Confronted with the disasters of bourgeois societies in Europe and Japan overtaken by fascist barbarism and compelled to rescue the human spirit from utter surrender to nihilism, Joaquin is driven to two strategic modes of resolution. One is the traditional vindication of God's justice most eloquently expressed in "The 14 Stations of the Cross" where the act of Jesus' sacrifice stands, in part, for humanity's determination to subdue the negative and to demarcate its existence as a function of its opposite:

12. JESUS DIES

> Now, as a radiance
> round this wracked Form appears
> and lightnings aureole Man's
> high Champion—shrouded in fierce
> night, thunderous and wind-split,
> the shocked world shuddering hears
> as its quaking floors retreat:
> Hell opening under God's feet.

It is Christ as "stealthy miner" in Joaquin's last poem "Landscape Without Figures" who cuts in the human heart "the twin caves of his birth and burial," tomb and womb coalescing in the flesh. The drama of Christ's passion culminates in a circular return, a repetition, in which Christ is mourned as "Great Pan" who dies but who comes back "till Easter's holy mirth / a new world brings to birth." A supranatural organicism supervenes here—the second mode of harmonizing if not sublimating contradictions.

In "Life and Letters," we discern a nascent primitivism—"Give up to forest / this acre of decay"—a melancholy, somewhat Tennysonian yearning for a primordial stage now superseded: "O light of a younger day / that fades on the highlands, / never to burn again!" This impulse becomes the full-blown eulogizing of the aboriginal in the antielegiac "Ballade": the Aetas' land "seems more than we can break." Waves of conquerors—Malays, Spaniards, Japanese, Yanks—have disturbed the slumbering hills and valleys with "human woes," usurping instead of inhabiting the place: "We scared them flying and now we quake / because *their* land upholds our house."

It is in "Verde Yo Te Quiero Verde" where we find the impassioned valorization of the body and the revitalization of all the senses in the power of language to invent time-space as a sensory continuum, the immersion of consciousness in the pulsating matrix of creation: "The river-cool sea-serpent skin / of your deep arms enfolds my flesh in silence." But, as in Joaquin's typically dialectical apprehension, this recovery of a virginal territory decoded by Desire, a space sanctified for *jouissance*, can only evolve from experiences designated by red (ripeness and terror of death), white ("wisdom, the scourge of God"), and blue (thought, despair, mold)—the red, white and blue combination not unaccidentally coincides with the colonial power's insignia of hegemony:

> Yet from these senses, though in their
> decadence, still rises fourfold
> a hunger for that other color, virgin, girlish!
>
> That abrupt, sharp waking up, bare
> of blankets, of all dreams—with dawn
> on the grasses: all water, air
> and earth caught for an instant clean and careless! (pp. 38-39)

But this vision is forged in the tension of an ordeal, in a poignant awareness of the fallen, nude, sterile surroundings which constantly threaten it:

> Yea, this my world—spun, sped between
> fire branching under, fire above. You
> are its whisper of Eden, Queen
> crowned over color:
> > Color of Green:
> > > I love you! (p. 39)

This hymn to the maternal and generative spirit (green as the incarnation of Eros) recuperates the rhapsodic celebration of the wisdom of the flesh in Joaquin's first poem "The Innocence of Solomon." There the polarity of wisdom (spirit) and innocence (flesh) structures this ego-decentering affirmation of youth and all that it symbolizes; of its seductive accessibility— instanced here as a pilgrimage back to the source of the primeval river— through sexual bliss, with the wise king "chaliced drowsily" in Sheba's arms, his "own deep sepulcher" (p. 31). This bias for exuberant release, for the annihilation of the deluded consciousness in sexual rapture is echoed in "Saint Thais" whose hetera's love is "like the serpent wise" yet is frail as the frail / blue doves of Aphrodite" (p. 33). After "Verde Yo Te Quiero Verde," dated 1939, Joaquin suffers the seizure of "bad conscience," precipitated perhaps by the apocalyptic wrath of war, and retreats to a manichean vision witnessed in "On Public Speech" and in "Song Between Wars." In this context, the intervention of Rizal restores a balance, awakening the heterogeneous drives of the psyche, the mythopoeic sensibility called to reinvent the unspoiled beauty of a land in the past (as in "Ballade," a foreshadowing of the later *The Ballad of the Five Battles* glorifying the Virgin's intercession) and revitalize the senses removed from nature's rhythm ("The Years," "O Death Be Proud," and "Stubbs Road Cantos"). But after the war, after the project of imposing classic restraint on the energies of the unconscious hinted by "A Morality" (where the poet makes a pact with the Devil to claim the harvest of May-wealth) and by "The 14 Stations of the Cross," Joaquin's voice can only rehearse the tired Eliotesque lines of "Song Between Wars" and the discordant, non-sequitur narrative of "Landscape Without Figures." Unable to recapture the decentering spasm of pleasure registered in "Verde Yo Te Quiero Verde," the poet seeks refuge in the cynical-stoic tone of "Ballade" and "The Years," and the banal witticism of "O Death Be Proud." "Stubbs Road Cantos" may be read as a symbolic castration of Solomon or of the virile bard of "Verde Yo Te Quiero Verde," the poet having lost the power of articulating the substance of time and now is reduced to the silence of "wise virgins, the mystical / brides of the springtime Lover of the canticles."

What has occurred in between? It would be too easy and evasive to state that Joaquin, in confronting with his artisanal standard of moral judgment the crisis of global capitalism, equates the war with the vulgar materialism and worldliness of pre-1941 society. We can measure the distance Joaquin had traveled from 1939 to 1946: the boys and girls who grew up after the war, "whose green hearts are / peacocks perched upon apes / and pigs that feed on pearls" ("Song Between Wars"), have become victims to the sacrilege that Solomon can still observe from a distance: "The apes have ravished the inner temple, / the peacocks rend the sacred veil" ("The Innocence of Solomon"). In "Landscape Without Figures," the poet conjectures that man's underground probing may "find his live limbs eagerly / intruding on Persephone" (p. 52). Contrast the forced rhyming here and the bluntly ornamental use of the mythical figure with the dramatic appearance of Persephone (the Mother/Virgin Gestalt bifurcated) in "The Comment Ungallant" (1939), a parable of discovery. The speaker addresses the beloved woman, piercing her pride in "every raven strand" so that "my love turned into stone in my heart for I saw / not your proud face in that brook's mirror but Medusa's." The "rich and treasured hair," reminiscent of Saint Thais' "lost locks," does not hide a "leaf-voiced shrine" nor moss grown wells, raw fruits, slopes hung with curtains, as in "Verde Yo Te Quiero Verde," but the opposite:

> and my face buried in your hair, I, laughing, studied
> ways down to your breasts with my mouth when suddenly,
> drowned in your hair as in black waters disembodied,
> I felt (but too late then to draw back), horror-flooded,
> at my hot lips the cold lips of Persephone.

Even before the war, Joaquin has manipulated the sonnet form to deliver this vignette with an oxymoronic quality investing all erotic and utopian projects, a quality which he envisages as an irrevocable dualism in "Six P.M." and as an apocalyptic wager in "Pascua Flamenca."

A seminal but insidious paradox defying the formalist procedure of interpretation lies at the heart of these two poems which are strikingly exceptional in betraying the tangle of antinomies from which the speaking subject, divided by the unconscious, strives to free itself. At issue is the power of language to represent experience and to reconstitute a dispersed subject, a consciousness volatilized by the force of difference both internal and external; and whether the daemonic will can overcome the disrupting semiosis of the chain of signifiers by extrarhetorical persuasive devices or by the fiat of myth and phallocratic decree.

Obviously organized around the disparity between two antithetical selves or personae, the daytime and nightime roles, "Six P.M." posits a site for the production of ideology and the doubled subject. It soliloquizes the dilemma thus: the play of language ("ruefully architecting syllables") can erect only an "ivory tower" circumscribed by rational daylight awareness. This grammarian-speaker can only register bare sensory data heedless of what the "Angelus" suggests, that is, the punctual mark of sacred duration which commemorates the incarnation, the possibility of apparently trivial phenomena becoming radiant with archetypal meaning and thus intimating plenitude. The octave of this Petrarchan sonnet is fissured here, at the seventh line when the equivocal question is posed: "But I—where am I bound?" In both senses of "destination" and "confinement," "bound" establishes the necessity and permanence of alienation. Without the "four walls," the imagination—figured here as the Other ("and you project strange shores upon my yearning")—cannot unleash its licentious oneiric energies. This "yearning" thrives on limits which afford the luxury of extrapolations and the recovery of the legendary (Atlantis, Cathay). But the easy rhyming of "Cathay" and "Sinai" signals the endeavor to erase difference by establishing identity, the goal of the Same avidly sought but in the same breath deferred, permanently postponed. The "I" has gradually lapsed into passivity. And its surrender to the revelation of sexuality casts doubt on the identification of the speaker as "Trouvere at night" and "conquistador"; the labels are meant ironically, for the claims of performing epic conquests or heroic gestures are belied by the confession:

> Apocalypse awaits me: urgent my sorrow
> towards the undiscovered world that I
> from warm responding flesh for a while shall borrow:
> conquistador tonight, clock-puncher tomorrow. (p. 34)

Because the antithetical balance initiated in the first line of this poem, paralleling the dualism of trouvere/grammarian, dictates the arrangement of the last line, the text vindicates the power of rhetoric to maintain the split psyche under the rubric of what is usually categorized as modernist sensibility. But it cannot hide the spurious nature of the dualism. The speaker is neither conquistador nor trouvere. And the apocalypse he arrives at, parodying the angelus, stages the mute revenge of the "warm responding flesh" as nameless and depersonalized, leaving us with the conclusion that here the poet is bound to reach the impasse of recognizing the futility of escape through language. He may also realize at last his boundedness as a self-enclosed monad in a world defined by the ethos of clock-punching, the world of alienated labor and its mirror opposite, the phantasmatic and hallucinatory realm of the primal lost love object. Apocalypse becomes the discovery of the world lodged in the "warm responding flesh." But that experience is limited by the demarcation of time imposed by the calculating rationality of the business schedule and by the categories of market-exchange: "borrow" thus encapsulates "sorrow" and dominates the feminine end-rhyme: "tomorrow." Ultimately the daemonic persona, which proclaims its capacity to repossess unfallen immediacy (possession of the unknown, the new or undiscovered), becomes hostage to the victimized rider of the bus whose conduct and destination escapes the poet's will; the exigencies of the text triumphs precisely at this juncture.

Ten years separate "Six P.M." from "O Death Be Proud," but one can detect the classic decorum prevailing in the antithetical phrasing and parallel syntax, the play of puns and synecdochic continuities which give a semblance of the poet in control of the semantic energies unleashed in the process. But in the latter sonnet, the thematic coherence and the satiric wit are marred by the intrusion of the "I" with a forthright conversion of death as a revolutionary moment, the overthrow of the patriarchal reign legitimized by the eucharistic allusion:

> Because it is man's fortune kitchenward to decline
> I am fed on my dead father's unstable status:
> I break his body and drink his blood, turned bread and wine.

Consequently the epitaph (the last four lines) denies the primacy of myth and seeks to naturalize historical change. For here the predicament now involves the familial constellation of relations, no longer the solipsistic and imaginary conflicts laid out in "Six P.M."

It is only in "Six P.M." that we find Joaquin fully engaged with the modernist topos of heroic will versus bureaucratized mentality familiar in T.S. Eliot, Ezra Pound, Hart Crane, etc. We can gauge its peculiar position in the canon by comparison with "Pascua Flamenca," written two years after, in which the dissociation of sensibility personified by Balthassar reflects the disintegration of the milieu, a shattering of the concord between God and man memorialized in biblical legend. Here the dramatization of the "I's" dilemma is fixed by a prior model, Balthassar's position, until the "I" assumes the burden of the past and defines the hidden covenant in discontinuity.

In the first part of the poem entitled "Procession of the Holy Kings," the tactic of laconic reporting and disapproving tone aims to isolate Balthassar as "that cruel man," equipped only with "sardonic sapience." Balthassar is portrayed as a freak, the odd guy of the three magi (compare this poem as understudy for the story "The Order of Melkizedek") who discerned not the star of Melchor and Gaspar but

> a gibbet—and from the gibbet heard a cry....
> Wherefore he rose, called for his men, and far
> and wide did travel, searching for the Lord. (p. 42)

It is in fact this vision of the gallows which makes necessary the Lord's advent, generating the purgation of sins and overcoming injustice, cruelty, and oppression. Balthassar's faith is confirmed by his perseverance, his offering moved to an underground site prefiguring Christ's death, his rebirth:

> And far and wide he beheld, always and everywhere,
> the mighty gibbet burning in the air:
> god cried to god, the Father foreswore the Word....
> In a cavern, deep under the ground, the third
> wise man knelt down and offered God—despair.

The second part, "Procession of the Holy Women," shifts the stage from Christmas to Easter where the speaker confesses to Balthassar, "bitter to the bone":

> I have gone down to the cave, I have seen the tomb's
> emptiness the emptiness that dooms
> the spiritual Arabia of my own.

Renouncing a merely private fantasy realm, the speaker here laments the absence of a numinous and transcendent power, an absence which for the three Marias becomes anticipation of a young bride for her coming bridegroom. He is unmoved by the women's humility and faith, unable even to offer despair to God because, contrary to what he professes, he is no longer like Balthassar but an inhabitant of an entirely new epoch devoid of any hope for a collective renewal, a "gypsy" consciousness isolated from others and whose allusion to Balthassar only reveals the gap which separates the time when gods still contended for believers and an epoch of total unbelief:

> But I am Balthassar, cracked with years and learning,
> lost in a world where all the gods have died:
> always and everywhere, I must see a gibbet burning. (p. 43)

For Joaquin, the paradigm of Christ's incarnation and sacrifice cannot but sublimate this "gibbet burning" with a trope, a signature of things to come, in the same spirit that in "Landscape Without Figures," the empty space insinuates subterranean transformations, mutations in "this twin caves of [Christ's] birth and burial." One cannot ignore the desperate imperative of "I must see a gibbet burning" as a clue to the need for a chiliastic resolution, the figure of a pentecostal gallow inaugurating a second advent. Even in a time which rejects continuity and origins, the subject-position here manifests its function as the site of ideology (nostalgia, hope, desire) which mediates between the speaker and the Real (history). The subject-position is constructed by an institutional Christian mythology which, on the face of its contemporary rehabilitation as "theology of liberation," may provide the key to resolving the aporia of texts that deconstruct the subject, repudiating coherence and referentiality as survivals of a bygone era.

In Joaquin's poetry so far (excluding the new poems in *Collected Verse*, 1987), one can grasp the obsessive engagement with the vicissitudes of materiality and nature permeated with a dynamic spiritual élan as in "Verde Yo Te Quiero Verde" or bereft of it as in "Landscape Without Figures." While the early poems—"The Innocence of Solomon," "Six P.M.," "Saint Thais," "Verde," and "The Comment Ungallant"—invariably valorize the primacy of sensuous experience as containing its own purposiveness, the secularizing drive is not a naive commitment. It is qualified by the allegorizing drive of "A Morality," "Now Sound the Flutes," "On Public Speech," and "The Visitation." The utopian impetus of "Verde" withstands the irony of the double in "The Comment Ungallant" and "Pascua Flamenca" but erupts as a primitivistic protest in "Life and Letters," "Jose Rizal's Valedictory Poem, " "Ballade," "The Years," and "O Death Be Proud." In spite of the nihilism of "Song Between Wars," Joaquin upholds the viable present and its promise in "Stubbs Road Cantos," a meditation on the inevitable approach of spring. In spite of the ascetic retreat in "Landscape Without Figures," with the distancing technique of allegory cancelling the representational hubris of language, the poet positions two poems of victory over death at the center of his corpus: "The 14 Stations of the Cross" and "Jose Rizal's Valedictory Poem." In their resistance to the reifying tendency of imperialist culture, in their affirmation of utopian materialism— "we ached for the green heat under the palms of the homeland"—and in their critical reflection of the individual psyche determined and shaped by the historical process, Joaquin's poems are worth repossessing in our emancipatory reconstruction of our national culture. What I am proposing is that the poetic texts conceived as aesthetic-ideological discourses be viewed as material practices, subtly equivocal interpellations that mobilize or paralyze readers, thus eliminating the usual epistemological privileging of the aesthetic over the ideological. From a semiotic perspective, Joaquin's baroque style here and in his fiction may be deciphered as signs of the crisis of metropolitan (Spanish seventeenth-century decadence) power surviving in the feudal bureaucracy of the American colonial period up to the Liberation era of the fifties. But I propose here a more dialectical and historical reading so that we can articulate more purposefully that crux of class struggle as it takes place between our critical discourses and the texts themselves, thereby actualizing their subversive and emancipatory potential.

5 Joaquin's Theater of Transgression and Sacrifice

Being human means joyfully throwing your whole life "on the scales of destiny" when need be but all the while rejoicing in every sunny day and every beautiful cloud.

—Rosa Luxemburg

A colossal upheaval of the entire social and economic structure was required before women could begin to retrieve the significance and independence they had lost.

—Alexandra Kollontai

Do we fully understand that we aim at nothing less than an entire subversion of the present order of society, a dissolution of the whole existing social compact?

—Elizabeth Oakes Smith

CELEBRATING THE PERIPHERAL SETTLEMENT outpost, Intramuros, the old Manila, as the emblem of an unforgettable aporia—"For three centuries this medieval town was a Babylon in its commerce and a New Jerusalem in its faith"—and thus the symbolic goal if not political objective of a vision of radical transformation, *A Portrait of the Artist as Filipino* (1952) is Joaquin's fullest dramatic rendering of the memorializing telos of his artistic vocation. Evoking the Virgilian rehabilitation of nostalgia, the tone of the play's choral voice Bitoy Camacho resounds with a pathos less prophetic than resigned: "While I live, you live," Bitoy addresses the twin "vestal virgins" of the city reduced to ruins, "—and this dear city of our affections shall rise again—if only in my song!"[30] Unlike Virgil, however, Bitoy (Joaquin's ventriloquist) sings not of *Pax Romana* under Augustus' reign but of a memory intensely self-aware of its precarious, aleatory duration and anguished by the alterity of its interpellating rhetoric.[31]

Like the portrait Don Lorenzo has painted to synthesize the segments of his career and of the Philippine struggle, the framing device Joaquin uses here—Bitoy's elegiac invocation on "The Noble and Ever Loyal City" and of the Marasigan house as the fountainhead of virtue, of "custom and ceremony" which begets innocence and beauty (to quote the Yeatsian epigraph)—betrays the triumph of that paradoxical inwardness of mind and action that the colonial prewar "jungle of slums" was then already fostering and that the heyday of postwar U.S. corporate dominance would heighten into ferocious individualistic competition. We witness here the incontrovertible symptom of the split in modern life between private conscience and civic duty, a cleavage whose antithesis is the *Gemeinschaft* Bitoy tries to recover in memory "where it lives; still young, still great, still the Noble and Ever Loyal City. And whenever I remember it, the skies above are dark; a typhoon wind is blowing; it is October; it is the feast of the Naval." Here, the syntax of his meditation reveals that the polis and its mock-image as symbol serve as the fertile matrix of realism: the vertical and horizontal lines of language, the paradigmatic and syntagmatic horizons of thought, aptly converge because the individual and the collective still coalesce in the ritual of faith. Art thus recuperates the etymologic import of religion as linking or binding of disparate elements. But Bitoy himself not as choral commentator but as specific character is profoundly decentered. Orphaned at fifteen, Bitoy parallels Tony Javier as the psychic register of the commodity-dominated milieu; but unlike the transient lodger with the ambition of rising from vaudeville piano player to "big, rich crooked lawyer," Bitoy in part represents the thoroughly disillusioned urban worker whose impulse to demystify appearances may ironically be his most cogent credential for the artistic vocation.

From History to Myth

At the beginning of the second scene of *Portrait*, Bitoy prepares us for the encroachment of Pepang and Manolo and the sisters' desperation:

I had said goodbye to that house, goodbye to that world—the world of Don Lorenzo, the world of my father. I was bitter against it; it had deceived me. I told myself that Don Lorenzo and my father had taught me nothing but lies. My childhood was a lie, the nineteen-twenties were a lie; beauty and faith and courtesy and honor and innocence were all just lies.

The truth was fear—always fear—fear of the boss, of the landlord, of the police, of being late, of being sick, of losing one's job. The truth was no shoes, no money, no smoking, no loitering, no vacancy, no trespassing, and beware of the dog.

When the nineteen-forties came along, I had become a finished product of my age. I accepted it completely, and I believed in it. It was a hard world but it was the truth—and I wanted nothing but the truth. (pp. 24-25)

Here society manifests itself as a network of regulations, taboos and prohibitions; a vast labyrinth of codes and discourses, a hierarchy of authorities that reduces the individual into a passive, obedient subject of a world where objects (commodity-fetishism) now dictate and where institutions once invented by humans acquire an uncontrollable life of their own. Bitoy of course is not a protagonist but a marginal observer, the somewhat detached reporter whose distance from the play's moral conflicts is precisely what privileges him to empathize and also elegize the glories of a unified sensibility now only recuperable through the allegorizing, pedagogical apparatus Joaquin deploys here.

Immediately one can pose questions about the "unified sensibility" which, personified by the two sisters and Don Lorenzo's aging circle of friends, seems residual in retrospect compared to the hegemonic petty bourgeois, opportunistic ethos of Don Perico, Pepang, Manolo and Tony Javier; for obviously that model of organic society epitomized by "The original Manila" has become eroded with the insertion of the country into the contigencies of world trade after the opening of the Suez Canal in 1869, and its domination by U.S. monopoly capitalism after 1898. The once cohesive Marasigan family itself has disintegrated with the absorption of Pepang and Manolo into a market economy that has in turn driven Candida and Paula to take in lodgers and try to sell their labor-power. With his "charming democratic friendliness with which the very rich and powerful delight to astonish their inferiors," Don Perico embodies the successful compromise of the "residual" organic with the dominant culture of exchangeable and quantifiable values. Except for the traditional festivity surrounding the October feast of La Naval de Manila, the practices of a kinship-based community have disappeared from Joaquin's stage; only its aura lingers on.

This aura of vanished tradition, what Walter Benjamin refers to as the questioning look of the original, is what Paula and Candida have in mind when they imagine how "the shadow of this house" arouses fear and shame and guilt in Manolo, Pepang and their ilk:

Aristeo: You mean, they are afraid of this house?
Candida: And they want it destroyed!
Alvaro: But why?
Paula: Bacause it is their conscience!
Manolo and Pepang: PAULA! (The drums are now rumbling right under the balconies.)

Paula (advancing slowly): Yes, Manolo! Yes, Pepang! This house is your conscience and that is why you hate it, that is why you fear it, that is why you have been craving so long and so desperately to destroy it! No, you cannot afford it! You cannot afford to have a conscience! Because you know you will have no—

Manolo (stepping back): SHUT UP! SHUT UP!
Paula (standing still): You know you will have no peace as long as this house stands here to rebuke you!
Manolo (raising his fists): SHUT UP—or, by God, I'm going to—(The balconies light up dazzlingly as the procession passes below.) (p. 63)

Judging from the violent gesture of suppression it triggers, this valorization of the Marasigan house as the repository of a lost familial coherence, as the conscience still partly alive in Manolo and Pepang, demonstrates most explicitly the contradiction in Joaquin's subliminal myth: the inner voice of moral judgment is externalized in a "house" which is less a physical construct than a whole ethos, a constellation of beliefs and practices concretized by the solidarity of Don Lorenzo's friends and the two sisters (inside) versus Manolo's market-calculating machine (outside). Conscience appears *contra mundum* but can only exist within that world it condemns. A further irony—perhaps the overriding trope in all of Joaquin's writings—is the circumstantial juxtaposition of the Father's heralded but not actualized emergence into the scene with the Holy Virgin's passage, her advent itself enlisted in the fight against secular individualism, as I will explain later.

In the resolution of the sisters' predicament, as Paula and Candida in orgiastic pleasure behold their father's coming, Joaquin shrewdly reaffirms patriarchal power sanctioned by the Virgin as the foundation of a morally superior dispensation. With feminine Otherness—the heterogeneous creative potential of matter—circumscribed, and possibly displaced in the artist Bitoy as vessel/receptacle for the libido disseminated here, the order of a hierarchical, tribalized city is reinstated as the telos of art and the destiny of Filipinos. Could we assent to this progmammatic drive subtly invested in our sympathy with the beleaguered sisters and our admiration for the heroic father-artist?

There is no doubt that Joaquin's implicit project here is to exorcise the demon of the cash-nexus, vulgar materialism, or, in more exact terminology, the ideology and practices of comprador capitalism in a U.S. colony, under the guise of indicting the selfish utilitarianism of Manolo and Pepang and lauding the defenseless charms of Candida and Paula. Put more simply, the dramatic action aims to generate inwardness and psychological depth in a world that ceaselessly flattens everything and reduces all qualitative differences into abstract, exchangeable equivalence—the dynamic of reification converts humans into objects and in turn fetishizes thought, institutions, feelings. But in the execution of this project, a series of ironies and paradoxes are generated that introduces an element of indeterminacy undermining the play's thematic consistency.

Earlier I have called attention to the framing device of Bitoy's narration whereby his postwar perspective (the weeds and rubble of war-devastated Manila) distances in time the moral and ethical dilemmas of Paula, Candida and Tony, and at the same time infuses them with prophetic, eschatological density. By demarcating the outside as senseless "destruction" and the inside as order ("everything in its proper place"), and by apostrophizing the continuity of that order at the end, Bitoy creates "a portrait" that doubles the original mimetically in capturing the experience of the middle stratum in postwar Manila and also distorts it by stylistic equivocations. This portrait is both true and false at the same time.

We know that the pivotal moment in the play arrives when Paula, after her seduction, reappears in the third scene looking "very young, happy and tranquil." Her description suggests the triumph of the woman over all worldly temptations, the purgation of the curse: "She has fought, she has conquered; now she comes back radiant—merciless as a child; ruthless as innocence; terrible as an army with banners." She announces that she has destroyed the portrait, a report that produces the anguish and remorse—the conscience—of Tony and precipitates the sisters' discovery of free choice and the assumption of their existential worth, uniqueness and responsibility:

Paula: And now they will say we have lost our senses. Remember: we have destroyed a piece of property worth ten thousand dollars. That is something they will never understand. They will say we are mad, they will say we are dangerous! And Candida—they may be right after all—eventually . . .
Candida: I am willing to take the risk.
Paula: We are free again! We are together again—you and I and father. Yes—and father too! Don't you see, Candida? This is the sign he has been waiting for—ever since he gave us that picture, ever since he offered us our release—the sign that we had found our faith again, that we had found our courage again! Oh, he was waiting for us to take this step, to make this gesture—this final, absolute, magnificent, unmistakable gesture!
Candida: And now we have done it!
Paula: And we will stand with him?
Candida: *Contra mundum!*
Paula: Oh Candida, let us drink to it! (She pours out drinks.)
Candida: Yes—we have been born again—not of his flesh but of his spirit!
Paula: Then let us drink to our birthday! Happy Birthday, Candida!
Candida: Happy Birthday, Paula! (pp. 56-57)

If not as midwife then as the fertilizing agent, the Father's artwork which has been reified by the standards of colonial market society into U.S. dollars "delivers" the two sisters as two restored spirits able to make moral distinctions and decide their fates because they have regained their courage and faith by destroying that artwork. Can we then do the same to Joaquin's portrait so that we can liberate our spirit from bondage to an illusory corporatist model of community premised on a renunciation of pleasure and the abandonment of critical thought?

Just as Paula and Candida release themselves from secular bondage through a gesture of destruction, the inventing of a sign (the act itself) interpretable in various ways, we can perhaps free ourselves from the mesmerizing idea that in the face of an acquisitive, commodity-centered society, the only viable response is a retreat to, if not reinstatement of, a harmonious idealized past where labor is not alienated, where free will is predicated on objectively defined moral obligations, where beauty and happiness blossom in hallowed ritual and tradition.

In contrast to the mainly conservative outlook informing the play, Paula's sudden, inexplicable act of destroying the sacralized art object, the Father's irreplaceable artifice—the daughter's revolt against patriarchal despotism—is itself a radical rupture which, though made plausible by her earlier disruption of habit in submitting to the rejuvenating magic of Tony (as trickster/shaman), cannot be fully rationalized in the context of the sisters' previous behavior. Anything is possible with women, as the prejudice goes; but this seemingly gratuitous act, on second thought, springs from that submerged resentment and anger against the Father expressed in the sisters' accusation that their father has ruined their lives, a protest acted out in destroying the painting which they conceived earlier as their punishment. By negating that punishment and forfeiting the Father's hypothetical forgiveness, the sisters commit an unprecedented act of violating custom and ceremony. Ironically, this act of liberation fuses them with the Father vis-à-vis a hostile, profit-oriented society where a commemorated event like the feast of La Naval has become empty, mechanical ritual.

The Wedding of Eros and Death

When Paula and Candida destroy the "Retrato del Artista Como Filipino," what is it they are rejecting? As Bitoy and the sisters describe it, the painting depicts a non-Filipino scene where a young man carries an old man on his back fleeing from a burning city; both young and old faces belong to the Father, intimating that the youthful past is the redeemer of the moribund present. This painting drastically modifies the Virgilian original of Aeneas, the prototype of the ideal Roman ruler, rescuing his father Anchises on his back from burning Troy, with his son by his side and his wife trailing behind. Unlike the Homeric heroes Achilles or Odysseus whose individual wills animate their collective missions, Virgil, the poet of the metropolitan center of Empire, completely suppresses Aeneas' personality and sacrifices inwardness to a strict devotion to duty. The purpose of the Trojan prince's journey is to found a city where the household gods can be reinstalled to affirm the continuity of generations and the immortality of the family. He suffers and fights not for himself but for the future: the Roman State, *Pax Romana* under the Emperor Augustus—a future imaged on his shield and also prefigured by his descent to the underworld and his colloquy with his father. This imperial burden of the hero, however, cannot be simply replicated for the obvious reason that the fathers in Philippine history (including Lorenzo Marasigan) have been defeated, have not founded cities or empires, have been killed, co-opted or exiled. Candida's impression of a two-headed monster depicted in the painting expresses her distance and her exclusion: the painting images the circuit of the Imaginary (Lacan), the past incestuously bound to the present, the hypostasis of primordial inspiration.[32] In effect, the painting encapsulates the anti-Virgilian message of the present mature artist parasitic on the young, a dependency complex symptomatically misread by its viewers.

Unlike the refugees in the "Retrato," the painter and his daughters are caught in the burning city and met (according to Bitoy the chronicler) "a horrible death—by sword and fire," their house and city perishing with them. Originally, the painting was a gift and also a farewell message before the painter tries to commit suicide. It induces the sisters' need for atonement and forgiveness. The Father has a right to be cruel, Candida says, because "his conscience is clear." This conscience exercises hegemonic sway in scene 1, vividly felt in the shame the sisters experience when they thought themselves singled out during the blackout, a separation from the city which spells death for them.

In the second scene, this conscience enables Tony to perform a dance of enchantment before Paula, luring her into pursuing the dream of innocence and youth and happiness. This disintegration of Paula's link with Candida and her father comes after Candida's frustration in getting a job, aggravated by her sense of being completely useless, after which follows her ambiguous sacrifice of Paula. Before this, Don Perico's "worldliness" softens the ground for accommodation: "No man has a right to stand apart from the world as though he were a god" (p. 35). His apology for his life captures the determinism connoted by the portrait, the fatality of fragmented and atomized lives in the modern world:

Oh Candida, life is not so simple as it is in Art! We do not choose consciously, we do not choose deliberately—as we like to think we do. Our lives are shaped, our decisions are made by forces outside ourselves—by the world in which we live, by the people we love, by the events and fashions of our times—and by many, many other things we are hardly conscious of. Believe me: I never actually said to myself, "I do not wish to be a poet anymore because I will only starve. I shall become a politician because I want to get rich." Too often, one is only an innocent bystander at one's own fate . . . (p. 36)

Don Perico implores Candida's forgiveness and, as the Father's surrogate, enunciates the totemic law of the Symbolic Order: "Paula—Candida—stand with your father. . . . *contra mundum!*" Rejecting Pepang's dismissal of Don Perico as an opportunist double-crosser, Candida vows to fulfill the promise they make; but with Paula's tone of "parodying Don Perico," one can glimpse the internal fissure in the complicity of the subalterns.

In the third scene, the moral and cultural predicaments of Don Lorenzo and the two sisters suffer unexpected twists: Candida's confession that she surrendered to worldly temptation, to evil, because ultimately she wanted to free herself from the cash-nexus acquires its antinomic rationale in the principle she utters to justify their abandoning the house: "Because to save one's life is to lose it!" Consequently, Paula's loss of her virginity yields not only Candida's act of passive choice (releasing her sister from the circuit of the Imaginary) but also Tony's splitting and the emergence of a double: the guilty aspect which seeks forgiveness from Paula, and the ethical persona whose parting words—"I want to go to the devil! I'll enjoy it, I'll have the time of my life, I'll simply love—Oh, damn you, damn you!"—bring about the sisters' reconciliation. They begin to grapple with the existential wager of risking the future. When Paula taunts Tony, "You will never forgive me, Tony, for what I have done to you," she assumes the role of initiator: she declares that Tony "will never be the same again" because, first, he has acquired the stigma of a past; and, second, his carnal contact with the "enchanted" virgin imposes on him the ordeal of compensating for the loss of the innocence (the loss of the portrait) manifest in his complete identification with the status quo and its norms before he assumes the role of the suitor who pronounces the right words.

What results, then, is not Paula's violation or her secularization but Tony's redemptive castration ("He has found his tears") coincident with, and superimposed on, Paula's destruction of the Father's masterwork, the decisive stroke of cancelling the patriarchal gift/curse (the incestuous Narcissism of the "two-headed monster") and inaugurating a new dispensation, as the sisters announce that the "evil spell has been broken! The enchantment has dissolved!" What kind of dispensation succeeds, is suggested by Paula's half-playful reply to Bitoy: "Our kingdom is a barren land, and the king, our father, an old man." A promise of regeneration still needs to be fulfilled.

Contrary to the orthodox opinion that this play elegizes "lost virtues" and "inherited values ... dignified by daily custom and ceremony" and presents the timeless values signified by "Intramuros" as an emblem of human creativity, what the play's dénouement foregrounds after exhibiting the sisters' capacity for instituting a differential system of actions is the recovery of communal solidarity occasioned and sanctioned by the Virgin Mother. It is the celebration of La Naval de la Virgen which confirms the feminine matrix of the metropolis in which nature and pleasure coalesce, where sociality is born. Hence Manolo's impotence in expelling the bearers of conscience: Paula and Candida. But it is precisely into this nourishing and unnameable maternal space (the Platonic chora anterior to Logos or God), prefigured by the metaphor of loss and castration (the painting's disappearance) that the dying but resurrected Father is welcomed—the Father as literally and symbolically engendered by the women and the Virgin. The construction of the symbolic—language, art, society—depends then on the sacrifice of the woman's body coeval with the time of fulfillment and totality (the city), a sacrifice which establishes the Father's Law insofar as this is acknowledged by the tribe. I should like to emphasize that the Father is censored, prevented deliberately to appear in person on the stage. He is the absent presence; this primal loss or lack is the archetypal figure of Desire. He is destroyed by war associated with cursive or linear time (time as project, teleology, the prospective unfolding of history). There is no beatific vision of the Father crystallizing here as the procession of the Virgin reaches a climax because Joaquin refuses that father who is himself annihilated by the virile forces of war which destroy the privileged matriarchal space, the city. Note that Bitoy Camacho addresses Paula and Candida as the muses of memory and imagination who constitute him as subject (artist, Filipino), the Orphic child forever bound to the earth and whose hysteric song traverses the space of cyclical, monumental time.

I would therefore conclude that *Portrait* exemplifies a characteristic Joaquinian strategy of radical exorcism: patriarchal Christianity imposed by violence is neutralized by and recontained in the body of the Virgin Mother (space triumphant) coeval with the city, and the figure of the maternal city then becomes the site of the play of difference, of ludic games and destabilizing, antiobsessional *jouissance*..[33]

Metamorphosis of the Other

Which leads us to *The Beatas* (written November-December 1975), Joaquin's genealogy less of the modern women's liberation movement than of the ineluctable conjuncture of race and sexuality in the Filipino struggle against patriarchal Western colonialism.

Ostensibly this is Joaquin's assimilative gesture of modernization, positing the seventeenth century *beaterio* as a totally new creation: the "mystical community of lay folk" whose oxymoronic novelty inheres in its producing "intrepid God-seekers who battled viceroy and archbishop, insisted on the autonomy of conscience, gaily affronted the prejudices of their times, and were the first to exercise the right of suffrage in the Philippines." In his discourse on "Beatas: The Intrepid God-seekers of 17th-century Manila," Joaquin stresses the modernist thrust of the secularizing and racially integrative impact of the beaterio movement which later on registered its charismatic influence in the *cofradia* of Apolinario de la Cruz (1740), the Guardia de Honor sects (1890), the secret Masonic lodges and eventually the Katipunan where the initiates envisioned themselves members of a "secular Communion of Saints." But it is not the oppositional or revolutionary dimension Joaquin foregrounds in the essay; it is the implacable mysticism, albeit a worldly and humanistic kind, that Joaquin endorses, finally attributing the discipline and prophetic gifts of the initial inspirer, the native Hermana Sebastiana, to the miraculous power of the Holy Ghost. Of this underground movement which rejected the commercial pride and martial extravagance of seventeenth-century society, Joaquin elaborates further: "These mystics, too, expressed the vitality of their day in the very passion of their protest to it, as well as the paradox that ages of great physical vehemence seems to produce, automatically, the most ethereal mysticism," as witness St. Teresa, St. John of the Cross, and the poet John Donne."[35]

Conceived as metaphor=history, the play *The Beatas* offers a revealing counterpoint to the indiscriminate triumphalist mysticism of the essay which one can glimpse as a residual trend here in the quasi-ordination of Hermana Francisca to Sebastiana (end of stanza 1) and the death-rebirth choreography of Francisca Fuentes who experiences transfiguration into Francisca del Espiritu Santo through the mediation of Fr. Domingo (end of stanza 3). As historical evidence and theatrical spectacle, the costumes and coded patterns of movement may be considered the metaphoric correlatives to the substantive *agon*: the gynocentric revolt against patriarchal authority, the native protest against colonial tyranny. What undergirds these two revolts and undercuts the putative mysticism of the protagonists Sebastiana and Francisca is the much more scandalous cry of the flesh and matter—the pagan Great Mother's revenge on gnostic Hellenism (the Holy Ghost invoked by Fr. Domingo), the earth inflected by human desire into city and world, which the Beatas' slogan "Urbi et Orbi!" articulates as a profoundly subversive manifesto. This cry may be the prophetic announcement of the coming of the female Christos to renew a world blighted by a force like Blake's Urizen, the male egotistic reason legitimizing institutions of power. In this context, the Holy Ghost assumes a female identity.

In an accompanying note to the play, the author suggests that the first "stanza" of this poem hymning these blessed heroines can be presented by itself as a complete one-act play. This may be considered a pacifying tactic. The theme of God as pneumatic Lover rivalling the carnal Eros over Doña Mariana de Salcedo and eventually winning possession, surfaces here; but although this "flesh-and-blood" lover whom the Mystery Man (ambiguous if not androgynous) challenges is assigned a male gender, the Mystery Man is transformed into the "quarry," overwhelmed by the tangible presence of not a single person but, in effect, of the assembled women whose covenant expels the Mystery Man physically. This covenant is the "mystery" of native, creole, aristocratic women meeting together to form a counterchurch. In one sense, the dramatic ruse of the Mystery Man as the demonstration of male authority utilizing a folk festival (the Carnival, a saturnalia of "farewell to flesh") before Lent may be construed further as the figure of, first, the classic Eros as opposed to Christian *agape* confining women to the status of objects of self-centered sexual gratification; and, second, as the police instrumentality of church and state identifying the women as extensions of their husbands (freed only in their widowhood). The Mystery Man as the categorizer of social role functions then as the disruptor of female bonding, denouncing most severely his antithesis, the Hermana Sebastiana de Santa Maria whose magian or prophetic virtue earns her the ostracizing label "witch." That the covenant partakes of a witches' coven, may be discerned in the incantatory sororal divination rite around Sebastiana whom Antonia, the recluse-solitary who has returned to the world, calls the "Gypsy from India."

The play begins with a confusion of identities, the concealment of apparent knowledge, in the spirit of abolishing taboos and laws and hierarchies; this carnival break in time, a prelude to a more radical transposition of rank and places, allows the definition of "good works" as worldly acts of charity. This affirms the linkage of faith and works (praxis, labor).[36] A glimpse of Antonia's initial choice of withdrawal into a nunnery as a result of her vision of the "transience of all joy and beauty" is provided us, the other Antonia transcended by the carnival alter ego who at the end releases her servant Hermana Lorenza from servitude. It is Antonia who heeds Sebastiana's urging to cut off the masquerade, emerge from the underground, and "thus make today the last day of our own fearful Carnival" by setting up the archaic rite of "fortune-telling," an unmasking of the Mystery Man as a brother blinded by passion and pride, by illusion. What is striking about the magical fortune-telling is the evocation of the female presence, the unnameable presence that cancels the dichotomy of light and dark (the source of scapegoat casuistry): "May the light conceal her! May the dark not reveal her!... Darkness, keep her! Light, be her jailer!"

One detects an excess of connotations and innuendoes in Sebastiana's allusion to the Mystery Man's object of pursuit: "My dear, dear brother—we are all of us loved, and all unworthy of being loved. Even you and she. So, shadow us, if you must . . . but not in a rage of pride. Believe me: when you have tracked her down and exposed us, your quest will just have started. The road you have taken does not lead where you think it leads; nor will it end where you think it must end." If this does not hint at the allegorizing irony of the whole action characterized by reversals and transvaluations, at least it demarcates the limit of androcentric thought and intention.

Fr. Domingo exposes the women's subterfuge, the first mark of reversal, in which parties, balls, the carnival are employed to thwart the prohibition of women meeting together—this transgression generates a retributive force that converts the hunter-Mystery Man into a pursued target—and violate what Fr. Domingo calls the "basic law of society," woman's subordination to either father, husband, brother or son. His judgment reflects how the patriarchal order can claim to be natural by its own fiat: "In effect, dear ladies, you would make your own laws! Such female independence is unnatural; it is sheer sexual rebellion and can only bring confusion to society." To Fr. Domingo's advice to the Indias (Juana and Sebastiana) excluded from the nunnery to fashion their own private hermitages, Francisca, Antonia and Luisa all reply by asserting their need for "a mystical community," for after all "religion is but a heightened, an intensified awareness that we belong to the human community." This beaterio they seek to organize with the permission of the ecclesiastical authority will be open to all women "whatever the color of their skin," their vocation springing from what Juana calls "the right of the amateur to be spontaneous."

Before this first stanza ends, we recognize the authentic vocation of these women as priestesses of a fiery spirit initially alluded to in their reference to the Lord of the Carnival, the dionysian Lord of mocking, transgressive laughter which wrecks all barriers, taboos, injunctions. The aristocratic Doña Luisa de Losada expresses the antihierarchical thrust of feminist love as the women initiate the servant Lorenza into the collective: "Among us, may love notice no mistress or servant, no rich or poor, no color or class—." After electing Hermana Francisca as their leader, and after the invocation of the "great Spirit" and all the holy women of now and yesterday which instances the group's self-induced thaumaturgic power, Francisca is reborn as "Hermana Francisca del Espiritu Santo" whose beginning is embedded already in the past of Hermana Sebastiana. The calling of the beatas as "spies" and "secret agents" of the underground amid the carnival of mundane existence receives a genealogy and program from Sebastiana's life as model and Antonia's pedagogical catechism derived from it:

Sebastiana (waving towards view outside balcony): Look, Hermana—gaze upon this bright city in fiesta, a city ever in carnival, being rich and prodigal. It is a great city—and a mean one; a beautiful city—and a vile one; a noble city—and a cruel one. But whatever it may be, this city is our world—and in that world must begin all our labors. Unless we love this city more even than we love our souls, we work and pray in vain.

Antonia: Listen, when Hermana Sebastiana first came to this city she was so moved by it that she prayed God to discharge on herself the punishments for all the sins committed in this city, in this land.

Sebastiana: And therefore did I feel responsible whenever disaster visited this city, or any part of this land, because it meant that I had not proved worthy enough to be a vicarious victim.

Antonia: And that is what all of us must strive to be: worthy victims but in secret. For we are, as it were, secret agents sent forth to spy out this city and deliver it to heaven. It's why we were called forth from hermitage and solitude: to form a vanguard of love to invade the city called secular.

Sebastiana: Let no one scoff that we are so few. Remember: ten just men could have saved Sodom.

Antonia: So must we move through this city—in secret, as it were, or underground—and try to be the ten just persons for whose sake this city and this land will be spared the fires of heavenly anger.

Sebastiana: What we must cherish, in short, is the idea of human community—the belief that we human beings are so *linked* to one another that we can, through the good we do, nourish each other here in the world and even beyond the grave. Solidarity! People and their wonderful solidarity! What some of us lack, others can make up for; and the entire body draws health from the virtue of each member. It is what religion calls the Communion of Saints.

Francisca: And it is thus that I and my labors must be oriented? To the city and to the world?

Sebastiana: To the city and to the world!

Antonia: And not only you but all of us. Let all our efforts be addressed—

The Beatas Behind: To the city and to the world! (pp. 179-80)

In spite of the tone of conspiratorial vanguardism shrouding the concept of "worthy victims" of sacrifice, ultimately it is the belief in human community that removes this project from the individualist, monadic space of baroque mysticism and inscribes it within the tradition of utopian-millennial, populist thinking in Western history. No transcendental intervention here but the immanent working of the human creative spirit in matter, the transforming sensuous practice of organized toilers.

Beat, Beaten Up, Beatitude

I submit that Joaquin's notion of secularization accords with what Harvey Cox, in *The Secular City*, regards as the conception of the profound historicity of life, the deliverance of society and culture from "tutelage to religious control and closed metaphysical world views" to evolving openness and freedom. [37] Insofar as human praxis for Joaquin inhabits the spheres of temporality and ecological change, which Fr. Domingo at the end apprehends as the balance "between action and contemplation, between the wind of loving and the fire of love," then such praxis is revolutionary and Joaquin is its prophet.

In stanza 2, we find the beatas assuming the role of the Old Testament "emissary prophets," conforming to the Pauline renunciation of the legalistic commandments of Judaism in favor of "liberty in Christ" when they admit the Japanese Hermana Jacinta into their fold: "Asia is a great world. . . ." Here sounds the catholicity and expansionism of this messianic faith now challenged by the father's wrath (Captain Prieto trying to recover his daughter Rosa), the political authority of the Governor and death. Rosa easily disposes of the father; the Governor's accusation that the beatas "deny [themselves] to the male sex" is implicitly admitted by Francisca, and when she is disheartened by the hostility of the city and the world, Fr. Domingo's statement that women should not try anything novel or audacious which betokens independence, provokes her defiant testament: "Women have been, and will go on being, involved in dangerous ventures—." The will of the community is consulted in a secret ballot; what is at stake is the "freedom within the law of this house." Consensual politics validates the autonomy of the community and sanctions the principle of self-determination enunciated by Francisca: "Our license grants us certain rights and immunities; but once we begin to surrender those rights, once we begin to submit in fear or from caution to interference from outside, then this house may lose the freedom it should enjoy and we may find ourselves becoming but the tools of the powerful" (p. 199). To underline the vigor and futurist orientation of gynocratic unity, their singing of the Magnificat is made to blend with the construction noise so that in effect the Virgin Mother is the genius who presides as simultaneously the productive mediator of a new society and matrix of a new subjectivity.

When Francisca confronts the Governor to refute the charge of illegal construction—"Are we on trial here because we hired some carpenters, or because we will not hire some husbands?"—after the Governor's acknowledging the beata personality as "new construction," we see the plot staging the theme of constituting a new subject-position for woman as social construct whose genesis and metamorphosis occur in time. The Father's Law, the symbolic regime upheld by the Governor, is interrogated and exposed as partial and prejudgmental. While Francisca suffers an internal cleavage in the face of Jacinta's illness (the body's fragility), Fr. Domingo's catalyzing challenge heals the split; Francisca's psychomachia—the irony present whenever the meaning of one's action depends on an external interpreter (the patriarchal regime) is overcome by the beatas' reaffirmation of their self-legitimizing enterprise which, opposed to any self-indulgent mysticism, is ultimately committed "to the city and to the world."

Situated in an allegorizing context, the opening of stanza 3 with the allusion to the ghost of the Japanese beata points to a relentless historicizing drive that counters any possibility of irony as a mode of reducing life to the single moment or instant present where the divided subject (divided in body and spirit) persists in its irresolvable dilemma. Death, the limit of the organic, is annulled by memory—a memory sustained by the sacrifice of female bodies—so that it is not the ghost of the dead that completes the community (fifteen places after the "mysteries of the rosary") but the permanent possibility of what Sartre calls a "third," those who have participated in the ongoing task of liberating women and those who will awaken later, death and deferral guaranteeing the narrative momentum and the authentic historical continuity of the beatas' adventure.

In the third stanza, with the erotic lover (Mystery Man), father (Prieto) and Governor repulsed, the anticipated psychic demon of mystical quietism rears its head in the person of Barbara. Joined by Pilar and Belen, Barbara eternalizes that immanent tendency in Francisca and others to opt for solitude, the quiet acceptance of guilt by Eve's daughter. Here then we witness the beatas' profoundly renovative transvaluation, their communal uprising against the male Incarnation myth in this sisterhood's abolition of "all distinctions between sacred and profane," the bottom line dichotomizing which sustains power societies. Hermana Francisca eloquently proclaims the vocation of the beata, "the secular as saint":

> In the Third Order, the vocation is to service *in* the world, or the secular life. While remaining with the world and of the world, anybody and everybody—the married and the unmarried, the servile and the noble, the educated and the unlettered—can aspire to spiritual perfection by simply pursuing as devoutly as possible the particular way of life each has been called to. But since the Third Order remains in the world, it must expect—as Hermana Barbara, alas, did not expect— trouble, trouble, and more trouble, with the resultant war and tear on the nerves. But I thought this house had made its nature so clear that anybody joining it would expect, not an escape from the world but rather a deeper involvement in the world; not peace and quiet, but rather unceasing struggle—or, as Hermana Barbara would put it: a perpetual state of war. Which is why an almost military discipline has been required of us. (p. 204)

Because the interior demon of fear and guilt has been exorcised with the overthrow of the sexist postulate of Eve's origin, the leader of this community can logically envisage the fulfillment of their "emissary" role in leaving the beaterio and plunging into the "hustle and bustle of life." Of their Babylonian captivity—since the Dominican authorities have decided to dissolve their house—Francisca uncovers its hidden truth which attests to the fundamental discontinuity between the sign and its plural significations: "And remember: even a journey into exile is but another going forth to the city and to the world!"

In the confrontation between Francisca and the Archbishop, what the theologian Mary Daly calls the singular aim of feminism as "the creation of new space . . . at the boundary of patriarchal space," is thematized as a rejection of the Archbishop's "laws of God and man" which define the female gender as "hysterical": "And because this is your basic nature, you need, you *crave,* something stable to steady you—and that has ever been the cooler mind of man's government."[38] Francisca verbalizes the symbolic import of the *beaterio* as an antiworld where the future is lived now and the cosmos renamed:

This is a house that would disprove all the hoary theories about women. For here is a house where women refuse to live in cages because they would prove to the world that they can be as responsible as any man, and as capable of a free life. Here they have set up their own government, they are making their own laws. Here, they remain in the world and yet are under no father, no husband, no brother, no son. Here they elect their own officers, make their own decisions, support themselves through their own labor, and create their own way of life. (p. 211)

"And most of all because we would lead our own lives," Francisca continues, men resent the beatas. The Archbishop's concessive paternalism is revealed as a thin mask on his sexist animus, his chauvinism now dominant in the continuing sex war. In conducting this war, the beata (like Rosa) takes on a soldier's bearing and discipline that make her equal to men in the regimented mentality of the father Captain Prieto.

To grant intelligibility to the beatas' involvement in politics, Fr. Domingo invokes the respected name of St. Catherine of Siena before the skeptical Captain Prieto without realizing the shrewd co-opting tactics deployed by the Establishment in sanitizing the iconoclastic potential of such "insurgents."

Before the beatas' journey into exile, Joaquin insinuates his own Christology in Fr. Domingo's exposition that Christ is present in the "act of communication, of communion, of contact," analogizing it to the erotic fusion of lovers in the same breath that he insists on the renunciation of the system of rewards in "the dark night of the soul," when God is occluded or does not seem to exist. Fr. Domingo's Pascalian wager easily lends itself to pregnant misreadings:

What we call Christ is the union, the communion, of each with all, and all with each, in that crowd. Or let me put it another way. In a kiss between lovers, can we tell who gives the kiss and who receives it? All we can say is that both are the message and also its messengers. And when our communication with the world attains this quality of love's kiss, then that charity has been achieved which does not compute itself in terms of favors done or merits gained. And in that spacious charity are we released from the self and liberated from loneliness.

Why should Fr. Domingo impute selfishness to Hermana Francisca, and then persuade her that her "smug triumphalism" is an obsession with "confounding the male sex in general with [her] female abilities"? Here the text betrays a strategy of recontainment and immunization: the feminist revolt is defused and its subversive impulse channeled into an abstract mysticism whose model is one of the intransigent misogynists of the Judaeo-Christian tradition: St. Paul.

Should we not suspect the presence of a secret agent in the person of Fr. Domingo even though he has been tutored by Beata Sebastiana's example to disavow rewards? His working out of a personal predicament—to escape from "cosmic loneliness" by "the ability to regard this world as though it were an end in itself and not only means"—testifies to this worldly asceticism where excessive guilt or anxiety is displaced by a fanatical devotion to a "calling" in the face of a hidden God's inscrutable will: "The final meaning of virtue as a life to be led as though, or even if, there were no salvation, no heaven or hell, no life everlasting." What is the goal then? Release from the self through communion and communication. But why should the Hermana Francisca submit to the pressures felt by Fr. Domingo who, unlike the Hermana, lacks the emotional and spiritual support of a militant, besieged community?

Fr. Domingo's rechristening of Francisca contrasts sharply with her first baptism by Hermana Sebastiana and the other beatas in stanza 1. This death and rebirth process, an exorcising of the woman Francisca Fuentes and her return as "Francisca del Espiritu Santo" mediated through the male priest Fr. Domingo, suggests the reimposition of patriarchal control under the guise of Francisca assuming the evangelical mission of planetary unity with "the continent that is mankind." While the global or international arena acquires centrality as the breeding ground of the modern *beatas* operating "outside the official Jerusalems and in the gentile world," whose "spiritual life is their workaday life," the colonial and theocratic milieu of Manila and the Philippines as the site of terror linked with utter parochialism or narrow-minded bigotry is marginalized if not ignored. Clearly, loneliness is not the beatas' problem, as Fr. Domingo claims; their problem is the male authority of the Archbishop, Governor, fathers and priests whose antisecular mystifications seek to circumscribe the horizon of women and reduce them to an inferior, subaltern caste.

What I would argue here at this juncture of the play concerns Joaquin's existential "bad faith" in finally aborting the process of women's becoming, which is implicit in the beatas' project of "facing nothingness and discovering the power of being" (to quote Mary Daly) by inventing the fiction that the beatas' idea of "the world" does not encompass Asia, the Americas and Europe. Has he forgotten the Japanese beata Jacinta whose death engenders the ghost that completes the community? By evoking the specter of Paul the Apostle, whose admonition that it is better to marry than to burn rings vividly in our ears still, Joaquin displaces the struggle against patriarchal domination into an interior, psychic war of the members generating all the expected antinomies and dualisms (solitude and society, action and contemplation, etc.) that mirror all the material and ideological contradictions in actual society. The beatas, submerged in "this larger community that is the Tribe of Tarsus, the children of the Pauline Era," lose their raison d'être, their revolutionary vocation, and subsist as one more military detachment of the faithful under the bureaucratic supervision of androcentric institutions and the hegemonic Law of the Father.

Is it possible to extract from the parting words of Francisca to her sisters as they go into exile the embryo of a prefigurative, egalitarian politics; intimations of overcoming Joaquin's false transcendence and premature universalism (Hegel's "bad infinite") and valorizing the heterogeneous and unpredictable, the vertiginous and inexhaustible creativity of feminine difference? Francisca foresees and foretells joyous reunion as well as death:

> If you mean to go where I go, then you must be prepared to take a risk, you must be willing to take chances. Even if I could, I would give you no pledges, no assurances, no certainties of any kind. All I can surely promise you is . . . unsureness; unsafety; insecurity; suspense and hope—the terrible suspense called hope, which can be more harrowing than despair. If you are prepared to endure the ordeal. (p. 223)

Before she exits, Francisca calls on Sebastiana and Antonia, a gesture of remembering-looking forward which warns us that the repressed takes vengeance when we least expect it, when we are most unprepared.

Rhetoric of Castration

In her pathbreaking treatise *Sexism and God-Talk: Toward a Feminist Theology*, Rosemary Ruether traces the rise of "Spirit Christologies" in the movement initiated by Joachim of Floris (cited in the chapter on "The Order of Melkizedek") who conceived of the Spirit as "the principle of revolt against a past perfect Christology" which will usher in a new stage of redemption not through the "Son" but through the "Spirit." Joaquin's Holy Ghost with its polyvalent gender finds its genealogy in this vision. Some Joachites anticipated the new disclosure of the Spirit as female; countless post-Reformation movements—French utopian socialists, St. Simonians, New England transcendentalists—and post-Enlightenment radicalism in general derive their messianic impetus from Joachite prophecy. Ruether describes nineteenth-century reformist feminists speculating that "the emancipation of woman represents the fulfillment of the prophecy of Joel in which the pouring forth of the prophetic spirit upon women will usher in the final era of world salvation. . . . Radical feminism, which announces the 'return of the Goddess' with woman as her representative, continues a line of modern revolts against the Christian world in the name of a new disclosure of unfulfilled human possibilities."[39] Thus Hermana Sebastiana can be seen to presage Maria Lorena Barros and the women's detachments of the New People's Army and other insurgents today.

If Joaquin is not a conscious Joachite propagandist, the best we can say of the antiphallocentric tendency in *The Beatas* and its approximation to the concept of a subject-in-process/subject-on-trial which one finds in dialectical materialism, is its thematic affinity with one motif of *l'écriture féminine*, woman's singular libidinal economy as conceived by Helene Cixous in "The Laugh of the Medusa": "Though masculine sexuality gravitates around the penis, engendering that centralized body (in political anatomy) under the dictatorship of its parts, woman does not bring about the same regionalization which serves the couple head / genitals and which is inscribed only within boundaries. Her libido is cosmic, just as her unconscious is worldwide."[40] Instead of "libido," Joaquin employs the trope of "the Holy Ghost" and the imagery of the "wedding of wind and fire."

In his dramatic rendering of "The Summer Solstice" entitled *Tatarin*, openly annotated as "A Witches' Sabbath in Three Acts," Joaquin modifies the story's ending which describes Doña Lupe's response to her husband's reptilian submission. The original attempt to capture her victory deploys a prudent rhetorical tactic of metonymically blending the woman's streaming loose hair against "the white night where the huge moon glowed like a sun," thus displacing John the Baptist, paganized here as a fertility (dionysian) deity. In the play, Doña Lupe "suddenly bursts into a mighty scream, weird and prolonged, exultant and orgasmic, terrible and triumphant. . . ." If the worshipped fetish here, the woman's foot, serves as the inflamed phallus, then what we have is not female ascendancy but narcissism—the woman as an extension of the man's virile honor—or, else, a conflation of the man as child to the wife as mother, the child chastised for presumed independence and individuality. With the symbolically castrated husband escaping from the orgiastic procession of maenads and bacchantes, what we behold at the end is the chastened male child seeking the comfort of the maternal flesh.

Why should Joaquin return to his two stories, this one and "Three Generations" transposed into dramatic form in *Fathers and Sons*, after over twenty years since their first publication if they did not harbor rich possibilities for resolving the problem of the self's temporality, of historical discontinuity and death and wished-for renewal? But do we see only a mechanical replication or a marked change, given the qualitative philosophical adjustments and technical experimentation displayed in *Cave and Shadows*?

In *Tatarin*, the time period has been moved from the 1850s to the mid-1920s so that the characters of Micaela and Maggie, expatriates from the U.S., can be introduced to personify the skeptical, enlightened temper and express those sardonic thoughts on machismo attributed to Doña Lupe, the discreet and charming wife of the story: "And *who* built up this male poise of yours? Women! This bluff male health of yours is founded on the impregnable virtue of generations of good women." Micaela is made to emphasize the logical consequence of the combat of the sexes: "Ah, and if it is women who built it up, it is also women who can destroy it—this male poise, this male confidence" (p. 78). We have in Micaela a speaking version of Alfreda Coogan who, like Micaela, abandoned her husband Jack Henson in *Cave and Shadows*; Micaela shocks Paeng when she vows to get married again. She exits after voicing disgust at Paeng's urging Entoy to beat up his wife Amada and admonishing him: "Ah, but Rafael, you forget one thing. Every woman is a tatarin. So . . . let every man beware!" (p. 81)

Aside from the invention of the housemaids as choric narrators to provide the social context and the use of the adolescent Juanito's playful seduction of Rosa as a counterpoint to the rather ineffectual Guido who becomes the Byronic foil to the Lord of Summer he rhapsodizes about, Joaquin faithfully reproduces the content of the story here. He attempts to epitomize the pervasive influence of the tatarin mystery in Amada's voluptuous dance around the *balite* tree and her husband's entranced wonder.

Whereas in the story Don Paeng presents an opaque surface untroubled by any doubting memory or prospect, the husband in the drama acquires depth as he unfolds in confession to his wife a youthful experience as awed, innocent spectator to the tatarin procession, particularly his combined emotions of fear and rage as he watched the little black image of the Baptist borne by the howling women:

Well, I saw it coming—a crude, primitive, grotesque image, its big-eyed head too big for its puny naked torso—bobbing and swaying above the hysterical female horde, and looking at once so comical and so pathetic that, watching on the sidewalk, I felt *outraged*! The image seemed to be crying for help, to be struggling to escape—a St. John indeed in the hands of Herod's women; a doomed captive these women were subjecting first to their derision; a gross and brutal caricature of his sex. As I said: my very soul was shaken. I flushed hotly. I felt as if all those women had personally *insulted me*! And how could I let pass such an insult to *me* . . . that was, somehow, at the same time, an insult to the entire male sex? I burned with rage— oh, how I burned! And yet I dared not make a move. No, no, believe me, it was not fear that stopped me—although, yes, I felt that if I should lift a finger in protest, those women would have torn me to pieces . . . would have torn my manhood to pieces. (p. 97)

Don Paeng anticipates thus his near lynching as he pursues his wife in the crowd of frenzied celebrants, seized here with the unmanning insight of the tatarin as an explosion of the androcentric social code, a subversion of the phallogocentric symbolic order (emblematized by the diminutive Baptist icon) by the dissident energies of the female psyche.

Even as the sarcastic retrospect of his young manhood summons the crowd of women to the conjugal threshold, Don Paeng appears "castrated" in his impotence at forbidding his wife to join the procession. At the beginning of act 3, we learn that Don Paeng's "position" has been "imperiled," as his wife puts it, by Guido and Micaela at his father's party. And so it is not only nineteenth-century romantic aggrandizement of the "eternal Feminine" (Goethe, Byron) and the precapitalist, artisanal sensibility represented by Guido but also the individualism of Anglo-Saxon culture in the person of Micaela that have converged to circumscribe Don Paeng's authority. They have also opened the space where the primitive cathexis of the tatarin cult and the unorchestrated voices of women can discharge their numinous force. The significant content of the form here is therefore what underlies the antagonism of the sexes, what lends it the supraindividual resonance that complicates the mere sensational baroque texture/spectacle for which Joaquin has been praised: patriarchal hegemony inhabits the site of a mode of production where property is determined by patrilineal inheritance, where the phallus establishes a self-reproducing autarky.

Given the plurality of bourgeois feminisms hawked in the market today, it is imperative to underscore the principle of overdetermined contextualization I apply here, a principle distilled for example in Monique Wittig's reminder: "Our first task is thoroughly to dissociate 'women' (the class within which we fight) and 'woman,' the myth. For 'woman' does not exist for us; it is only an imaginary formation, while 'women' is the product of a social relationship."[41] Doña Lupe here may be grasped as the nodal intersection of social relationships exfoliating from the conjuncture of feudal, comprador-colonial, capitalist, and prefeudal ideological practices. Resisting sublimation in paternal discourse, Doña Lupe's either/or language becomes gestural, rhythmic, and finally hysteric: the shriek of *jouissance.*

Only the fluid, polymorphous, nomenclature-defying festivity of women can deflate Don Paeng's chauvinist ego and dismantle its pretended sovereignty by exposing its dependence on the body whose metamorphosis (life-death-rebirth) is subsumed within the collectivist feminine milieu of the tatarin. No longer is the mythical father, conjured by Freud in *Totem and Taboo,* responsible for the threat of castration that founds society, language, morals; it is now, in Joaquin's reckoning, the Demeter-Persephone alliance (the concurrent young, mature and old women in the tatarin) that allows John the Baptist to christen and name the world, and so proceed to announce the advent of the Messiah.

By analogy with the tatarin's naturalizing of the prophetic, antiorganic St. John the Baptist, Doña Lupe's estrangement (Don Paeng blurts out, "But now you are as distant and strange to me as . . . as . . . some female Turk in Africa!") from the conjugal bond, mediated through the body and female solidarity, annihilates male supremacy and unleashes the heterogenous drives from an unnameable and unrepresentable matrix. The beatas have thus joined the witches' sabbath as the fertility earth goddess overthrows the sociosymbolic contract.

Exorcising Phallocentrism

Instead of mobilizing here the Freudian problematic of the unconscious and the Oedipus complex, I would like to bring Max Weber's reflections on the sublimation of natural sexual relation into the erotic to bear on the dynamics of the passions in *Tatarin* and the dialectical trajectory of desire in *Fathers and Sons*:

> From the point of view of any religious ethic of brotherhood, the erotic relation must remain attached, in a certain sophisticated measure, to brutality. The more sublimated it is, the more brutal. Unavoidably, it is considered to be a relation of conflict. This conflict is not only, or even predominantly, jealousy and the will to possession, excluding third ones. It is far more the most intimate coercion of the soul of the less brutal partner. This coercion exists because it is never noticed by the partners themselves. Pretending to be the most humane devotion, it is a sophisticated enjoyment of oneself in the other. No consummated erotic communion will know itself to be founded in any way other than through a mysterious *destination* for one another: *fate*, in this highest sense of the word. Thereby, it will know itself to be "legitimized" (in an entirely amoral sense).

It seems that in *Fathers and Sons*, the parasitic and defensive rule of the fathers exercised through violence ironically stems from the failure to subdue the women, hence its sublimation and brutal vindictiveness. The patrician-looking Sofia queries the masculinist repression of the animal: "I often wonder why men, for whom sex is so easy, are so much more intolerant about it than women, who are supposed to be so strict on the matter. There seems to be a . . . a *nakedness* in our minds . . . an amused irony . . . even a deliberate coarseness . . . that they can never allow themselves, not even in their own minds, or with other men" (p. 131).

Ostensibly dealing with generational conflict and the proverbial revolt of the sons against the fathers, this play, unlike the story, contrives the patriarch Monzon's death and, in reel 3, thematizes Joaquin's obsessive preoccupation with an individual's quest for a vocation in a world where family, community and religion are fast disintegrating. Here, of course, the patricentered family is vindicated in that, first, Zacarias Monzon transforms Bessie into a "woman" and shapes her into a more conscientious, loving prostitute (Magdalene's charity surpassed!); second, Chitong discovers that he is the authentic progeny of his father:

Look, Father, I had felt myself a zero, a cipher, a nothing. And so I thought that my own vocation was just another trying to run away. Until you told me. And now I know I am *something* after all. I am that youthful desire of yours, Father, that you have fleshed alive. It sprang from you, it began with you: *this* which I now will myself to be.

Celo: What was . . . sensuality in the fathers can, in the sons, become a way to God?

Chitong: So it seems, Father, so it seems! God mixes his own asphalt from such materials.

Sofia (*sotto voce*): Like the whip, the table and the bed. (p. 153)

Given his aesthetic path to priesthood, Chitong empathizes with the grandfather and thus delivers Bessie to him, a violation of his father's command but also a fulfillment of his secret desire. His wife Sofia scrupulously demystifies the innerworldly asceticism of the corporate executive, this time in her "ruthless" voice: "Oh yes, Marcelo Monzon: clean as a puritan are you—but *not* because you love purity! Only because you hate your own flesh!" The third form of vindication of this father-centered family is Celo's reconciliation with his lusty father by finally allowing Bessie to minister to the old Monzon in his dying moments.

In the framework of an implicit incarnational aesthetics, Joaquin strives to valorize human experience, its egotism and worldliness, as charged with so many divergent possibilities for participating in cosmic grace. He seeks to validate every choice and action as so many legitimate roads to salvation. Less promiscuous than indiscriminate, this inexhaustible reservoir of charity seems a mimicry of entrepreneurial liberalism in the heyday of laissez-faire petty commodity capitalism. It is able to tolerate Bessie's trade as a humanitarian enterprise. It finally entertains the possibility that fornication may lead to otherworldly transcendence. But it stops short at allowing the "long table" of the Carretela King to remain as an enduring token of the personalistic, Renaissance-like *virtù* and autochthonous exuberance of the self-made man.

As we watch the concluding scene where Chitong the novice recites the psalm for the dead before the family congregates in the grandfather's room, followed by the laborers chopping the long table, we begin to suspect that underlying the metaphysics of vocation and guilt and remorse, the allegorical stratum of meaning in the text involves the contradiction-filled social formation of the Philippines in the seventies (1974 is the time assigned to the events). When Celo expends vindictive wrath on the "long table," he expresses the buried but smoldering resentment of the postwar "organization man" or corporate functionary toward the gregarious, shrewd, caciquelike entrepreneurs of the twenties and thirties, as well as his envy or admiration of their enormous appetite for accumulation and extravagance. His ambivalent attitude manifests itself in a guilty concern for the old man's health and his will to deprive him of his woman. Unable to fully dominate his wife Sofia, Celo struggles to compensate for his failings (he confesses to being a "spoiled priest" to his son) by an innerworldly asceticism coupled with a compulsive anxiety to justify one's calling in terms of material wealth. At the end of reel 3, Celo's asceticism demands usurping the father's position and exchanging places: "No... Not his table... Mine! Mine! I am he! I am he!" (p. 143). Such a claim of equivalence is clearly symptomatic. The son Chitong exemplifies the ethical subjectivism of the third generation upper-class children, open to novelty and "the vocation of love" but susceptible to pragmatism and compromise which allow status quo injustice, class violence and exploitation to prevail.

This minor reservation about Chitong's function in the play should not however obscure Joaquin's antimanichean but unorthodox materialism:

> **Sofia**: Ah, yes... Every day, every single day, needs extreme unction. Every night needs a viaticum.
> **Chitong**: And if the soul is provided with sustenance for its last journey, why not the body as well? This poor body that has served us so faithfully: when the time comes to dismiss and discard it... when it has to go out into the cold and the dark... alone and afraid... how can we deny it its own pitiful viaticum: a last communion of the flesh? (p. 149)

Through Chitong, Joaquin repudiates a superstitious, dogmatic clinging to the past and extols the innovative resourcefulness of humans: "Character is not something we inherit. It is something we create." If these utterances confirm the progressive Enlightenment thrust of Joaquin's inheritance—after all, the 1896 Revolution is a late child of Rousseau, Voltaire, Montesquieu—they acquire their persuasiveness because of their opposition to an essentialist psychology which obscures the complex motivation of the characters and oversimply explains the ethics and politics of action in terms of psychic blindness or evasion:

> **Celo** (*in tones of real curiosity*): And suppose I give up now... stop fighting... submit—would I be at peace?
> **Sofia**: I doubt it. You'd probably be as *miserable* in your surrender to your body as you have been in your struggle against it. Besides, it is too late. Men like your father find their brief escapes in the whip, the table and the bed. That rapt young man out there in the kitchen—your son!—is now groping for a more complete release. For him also there shall be peace. But for you—... It was *not* Chitong you struck.
> **Celo** (*staring*): Not Chitong?
> **Sofia**: It was yourself you hit with the whip, Marcelo. Yes, yourself, that self of yours, inherited, long resisted... that self of yours ever in fury against "animal" girls ... that self of yours which perpetuates your father—it was *that* you lifted your hand against. But it was your son who received the blow.
> **Celo** (*hardening*): That's enough, Sofia.
> **Sofia**: And the blow is a confession of your whole life. You were not angry with Chitong for bringing that girl here. You were angry with yourself, Marcelo, for desiring her—
> **Celo** (*shouting*): Stop it, Sofia! (pp. 145-46)

This psychoanalytic exegesis by Sofia presupposes a fixated libidinal economy sealed from the temptation of free will, accident and historical becoming. But it is precisely the text's subordination/marginalization of Sofia (her wisdom is upstaged by Bessie's candor) that reveals the intractable absence, the conspicuous lacuna defining the limits of Joaquin's regressive world view.

From the claustrophobic ambience of *Portrait* and its paradoxical undermining of Virgilian *pietas*—tradition and social contract as a father-son paradigm of continuity—in order to extol the much more totalizing power of the Virgin, to the cautiously hedged iconoclasm of *The Beatas*, Joaquin has been wrestling with the antinomies and heteroglotic tensions of the specific Philippine problematic where Enlightenment ideals of personal freedom and the pursuit of secular ideals are imperceptibly meshed with authoritarian practices and institutions. What strikes us so memorably in *Portrait* is the focus on a painting (fortuitously and crucially invisible) where the image of the burning city seems to have made more compulsive the willed assertion of paternity (note how the mother is missing) in the "two-headed monster." That image is juxtaposed with an action which bifurcates the Paula-Candida monolith—thanks to the opportunity afforded by the trickster-shaman Tony Javier—and engenders "conscience" (the father is resurrected when Paula-Candida fuse, the wounded Fisher-King is healed when the iconic alienation is cancelled) through the sisters' personal choices. In this predilection for adumbrating opposites and exploring ambiguities, Joaquin aligns himself with the seventeenth-century European art style called the "baroque" quintessentially illustrated by the mystical inwardness and transcendence of Bernini's St. Theresa, the chiaroscuro and fleshly warmth of Caravaggio's paintings, Monteverdi, operatic recitative, bizarre conceits, the figured bass in Bach. What seems more elucidating for our purpose here is the historic contextualization of baroque understood "as a last energetic assertion of the Renaissance faith in the fundamental interconnectedness of phenomena— one that is conveyed above all in a fleshly solidity of realization, accessible (and unavoidable!) to a wider audience than were the *arcanae* of Florentine neo-Platonists."[42] Refusing such gnostic resolutions observable in the modernist baroque of T.S. Eliot, Graham Greene, and others, Joaquin strives to recover that wholeness of sensibility, that fusion of public and private, of self and community, which is inflected in *The Beatas* as the equivalence of secular and saint, in *The Portrait* as reconciliation of past and present, and in *Fathers and Sons* as restored harmony of patriarchs and offspring. The obvious exception is *Tatarin* with matricentric semiosis informing stylized distortions, pleonasms, the calculated mannerism of idioms, gestures, and hieratic movements.

In spite of the adherence to the conventions of expressive realism, in particular the privileging of normative moral discourse, illusory verisimilitude, and unequivocal closure, Joaquin succeeds in registering the nuances, dynamic oscillations and overdetermined contradictions of the historical conjunctures he has selected as *mise en scene,* diagnostic test cases.[43] But in the same process, his attempt to comprehend contradictions of class, gender, race, etc. as somehow all condensed into the flesh-spirit antithesis and resolve them through "custom and ceremony"—the Virgin's felicitous intercession!—falls into the hackneyed essentializing metaphysics he often condemns. Joaquin is thus a victim of his "freedom," his baroque intensity subsiding into gothic melodrama complete with the iconography of decay and horror.

Once again we arrive at the theoretical recognition that despite the heroic efforts of Joaquin, the intuitive and conscious artist, to distance himself from the ethical and political dilemmas of his contemporaries, the ideology and textual practice of superimposing idealist resolutions to such dilemmas is vitiated by its own hubris and loses what Brecht calls its *Verfremdungseffekt* or alienation-effect. Probably the most perspicuous theatrical deconstruction Joaquin executes here is the unmasking of paternity, of what Mary O'Brien calls the masculinist "historical project" based on the universal oppression of women.[44] While women "stand in a relation to *time* mediated by experience," men can only transcend his alienation from time and history through knowledge, the idea of paternity serving as a link between conception and sexual intercourse. While Joaquin does not treat directly of the reproduction process (procreation), a recurrent topos in his writing is man's postejaculatory fate and the trauma of overcoming temporal, genetic and natural discontinuities. O'Brien argues further: "Reproductive process is not only material and dialectical, it is historical. The historical discovery of physiological paternity was a determinate transformation in reproductive process, initiating a male praxis that necessarily and radically transformed the social conditions in which this discovery could be expressed. The *idea* of paternity necessarily demands collective *action* to objectify it in the world."[45] The crisis of that unprecedented but now doomed idea and the unchartable vicissitudes of collective action, this time by multigendered participants, has preoccupied Joaquin right from the beginning of his writing career.

6 The Woman Who Had Two Navels: Fable of Patriarchy "Salvaged"

Man as an objective sentient being is a suffering being, and since he feels his suffering, a passionate being. Passion is man's faculties striving to attain their object.

—Karl Marx

The liberation of women necessitates the liberation of all human beings.

—Sheila Rowbotham

Man's desire finds its meaning in the desire of the other . . . because the first object of desire is to be recognized by the other. . . . I think where I am not.

—Jacques Lacan

OF THE HYPOTHETICALLY INFINITE NUMBER of entrances to the labyrinth, the textual fabric, literally the warp and woof meshed in the signifying process which is the text of this novel, the temptingly easiest seems the threshold of theodicy: the problematic of good and evil, the combat between the angelic and diabolic, the antithesis between "Christian freedom" and pagan fatalism, as the received consensus puts it. One permutation of this morality theme would be a hedonistic transposition of the good/evil polarity into a postmedieval utilitarian calculus of pain versus pleasure. What this move reveals is the shift away from that once hegemonic outlook associated with the Augustinian emphasis on original sin and its essentially institutional apologetics to a post-Renaissance individualism and the monadic psyches of our twentieth-century late capitalist incorporative cosmos. This passage of course sums up on a global level the transition from societies centered on the plenitude of myth and ritual to those decentered ones oriented around the void of an all-pervading fetishism of commodities and the reification of everyday life.

In formulating thus the central thematic concern of Joaquin in this novel, we might have reached a limit-point in which our dialectical method can only oscillate between the poles of order and chaos, abstractions equivalent to virtually saying nothing. We would still have to ask: order or chaos for whom? Unless we have completely dissolved the question of the subject as fixed by hierarchical forces or permanently dispersed in social process, constructed in the fabrication and decoding of signs, the integrating mechanisms of thought and practice, we cannot really leap into the realm of the transcendental and forego history, the ultimate ground of any discourse (interpretation, novelistic composition, etc.) that we can possibly engage in.

With the mention of "history" and the corollary terms "culture" and "ideology" as the imaginary resolution of lived contradictions, we evoke here the other polar limit of a particular framework of thinking, namely Nature, which characterizes structuralist anthropology and other disciplines that have since posited the dualism of Nature / Culture as their organizing principle of discourse.

Like the orthodox modernist text we are all familiar with (say Thomas Mann's *Magic Mountain* or Joyce's *Ulysses*), *The Woman Who Had Two Navels* cannot but help thematize its own form and formalize its own content, a semiotic interaction typical of the novel's myth-making strategy of resolving in the imaginary or allegorical sphere the various contradictions generated by social practice. We shall formulate more synthetically this particular mode of confronting the Philippine crisis toward the end of this chapter.

Parallel Lives Converging

Our interpretive strategy here will combine an examination of the narrative apparatus which generates the plot, that is, the sequence of incidents qualitatively ordered as such (differentiated from the story, diegesis), and the character-system invented to play out fully the tensions in the apparatus and bring them to some kind of harmonious closure. It might be appropriate first to begin with the last two chapters, just as the text begins with the last three days in the lives of Dr. Monson, the exiled veteran of the "failed" first Philippine Republic, and Concha Vidal, one embodiment of that historic rupture but also, in another sense, its virtual truth and fulfillment.

Grasping the novel in its totality, one realizes that the preponderant element in the text consists of the summary of "parallel lives," recalls and returns tactically deployed to yield a mirage of temporal continuity; the rest involves dialogue, the process of rhetorical/casuistic search for and retrieval of meanings invested in incidents, ideas, beliefs, etc. subsumed in a past sedimenting or disseminated in the present, in effect a past created and nourished by an ongoing future: Joaquin's project of settling accounts with U.S. imperialist hegemony.

Our initiation into this national allegory of the Filipino condition may be facilitated by first analyzing the function of the crucial fourth chapter, "The Chinese Moon," a pivotal stage of the novel's symbolic action in which the traditional Chinese festival of New Year, an occasion to pay off old debts and wipe the slate clean for a new start—an inaugural rite of decision-making analogous to "The Mass of St. Sylvester"—serves as the temporal frame in which Connie Escobar's predicament, her agonized wrestling over the choice of whether to return to her husband and all he represents or flee with Paco Texeira, the "guileless cosmopolitan" child of a Filipino-Portuguese marriage, submits to a prismatic, carnivalesque unravelling and finally culminates in a kaleidoscopic "assumption" of Connie's spirit—what Deleuze and Guattari would call a deterritorialization of the unconscious and the dance of desiring-production.[46]

What's really happening in this series of tableaux or dialogistic scenes enacted in the transitional stage of Hong Kong, in this schizoid feast of orderly change, where the presiding image is specifically the "Chinese moon" conflating Kwan Yin and the Virgin Mary, the mother cult of fertility and generation with the goddess of destruction and pregnant chaos, may be described as the attempt to reconcile the earth-mother's "flows" (instanced by Concha Vidal) and the Father's Law (Dr. Monson), keystone of the socio-symbolic construct. Connie's dualistic physiognomy (the two navels: belief, reality) is sublimated into the so-called Christian freedom of choosing life, the maternal principle, against the despotic patriarchy of reason, this ethical dilemma being repositioned in turn as a choice between the paranoiac delusion of Macho Escobar and the anti-Oedipal schizoid revolt of Paco Texeira, the orphaned nomad.

The preceding chapter focusing on "La Vidal" ends with Connie submitting her naked body to Pepe Monson's scrutiny after agreeing to Father Tony's urging that she should "choose" and "feel responsible" (p. 137) and thus acquire knowledge of her self through worldly commitments, acknowledging debts and responsibilities. She has promised Father Tony to confess to him at St. Andrew's monastery atop Holy Cross Hill. As she drives to this "tryst," Connie is subjected to the text's mnemonic production, a recapitulation of her life at different stages counterpointed with the possible futures open to her. However, the aleatory and fortuitous are circumscribed by death, by the body's dissolution in the elements. This chapter in effect dramatizes the call to freedom, the exercise of the will to act, suffer and be free; the courage to reject withdrawal into dreams and ascetic renunciation; the courage to risk opening up new spaces for libidinal investment in the social world.

In the first recall, Joaquin introduces Biliken, the presiding carnival deity representing the folk affirmation of the communal body (Bakhtin) and negation of the deceitful order of patriarchal law, to which Connie would later sacrifice her innocence (Minnie), unable to understand her surroundings: recognize her fictions as marked by the lack in the family and limits of her class: "But lies were safety; were ice cream and movies; were the wall and the gates and the armed guard, and the big house ringed about with orchard. Outside was terror—the crosses on the doors, the three hags wandering in the night" (p. 145). Connie decides to refuse accepting her lies: the first possibility is escape by train (into mainland Communist China?) where she happens to join Macho who tells Connie she cannot cut herself off from her husband and mother, reinforcing her belief that her life was predetermined by her parents and her society, that there is no breaking the cycle of initial hurt and *ressentiment* (self-inflicted revenge).

Macho then confesses his desire to help Connie recover her pride, heal the injury of Concha Vidal's refusal, by accepting marriage with Connie not as a substitute but as fetish, a classic case of pursuing the phantasmal object which originally linked the child to the mother's body. Macho accuses Connie: "Oh, it wasn't enough for you to know it was she I took when I took you in bed. You wanted me to know you knew." This desire for the Other's desire—the Hegelian definition of human finitude—is both satisfied and foiled in this imagined encounter: satisfied when Connie embraced Macho as "her childhood," foiled when in doing so she discovers the passion between her husband and her mother.

While Macho uses Connie to "strike back" at Concha, the child trying to ingest the mother through another female body, Connie tries to "possess" her father through Macho who, in a sense, is only her mother's fantasy. Although Macho dares to break the chain (the oedipal coding) between him and Connie's mother, and Connie appears ready to relinquish the "truth" she has found, the text frustrates this "spiritual" way out by their "simultaneous destruction," death by earth, the first of the four elements "squaring the circle" of Connie's pilgrimage.

Violating the familial taboo which sustains the symbolic order by yielding to the mother, Macho, victim of that patriarchal will controlling the corrupt Visayan sugar plantations, is the mutilated sacrifice of the commodity-exchange system. His beatific exultation when he was young with Concha Vidal standing on the Intramuros walls—"exploding in his mind (as though flametrees had ignited a bunch of fireworks) in a great burning shower of joy" (p. 72)—could not make up for his surrender to her. She becomes an emblem of a need for gratification that is forever deferred (like Dr. Monson's on the political level). She prefigures a demand for that object of need which is the whole world of elite colonial society fallen into decay, a moribund world of lustful cruelty and exploitation and deceit incarnated by Manolo Vidal and his generation of collaborators in the pre- and post-Commonwealth eras.

After burial in earth comes annihilation by water, the maternal element. We see Connie at the beginning and end of the war encapsulated in a world premised on the advent of the savior:

Terror now walked the streets not only at night but also in the daytime but in his secret nook in the orchard, under the acacias, Biliken still presided over a carnival, grinning as merrily as ever, and waiting everyday to be told the news. Connie was happy to have a friend again, someone to be together with, someone to whom to repeat the reports (revised every month) that within a nine-day period beginning on such and such a date the Americans would be coming triumphantly back, in clouds of airplanes and mile-long convoys. But the sun faded poor Biliken . . . but still the Americans did not come. (pp. 155-56)

While the Commonwealth crowd of her mother played mah-jong through the ravages of war, Connie nurtured her adolescence in communion with Biliken, totem of an archaic unity and the body's inscription by lunar, cosmic forces. The second mode of rejection forces Connie back to her mother in a ship pervaded by the "smell of the womb, tasting of tears." Connie rejects her mother's plea for pity, for relief of her conscience, by identifying herself as the embodiment of her mother's vanity, malice, cruelty, lust: "I'm the fruit of all the evil you carry in you." Concha Vidal accepts the lies and pretensions, and accuses her daughter of using her as a buffer and defense from the real world: "You don't dare go free, Connie; you don't want to be saved." Concha's charge that Connie hates her because she (the mother) has stopped lying and has thereby liquidated "the sham world" of Esteban Borromeo (Dr. Monson's past) and her childhood, which evokes Connie's appeal for her mother to cease pretending and return to "the natural world." Concha thus refuses to be Connie's mother, seeing her as "all the evil that is in me." With the shipwreck, she exhorts Connie to "save herself," cut loose from the past and release her victims. The simultaneous death of this maternalized self of Connie suggests a plunge into the amniotic fluid of the placenta, a rapturous illumination in the depths of the womb where Connie experiences *jouissance*.

Deciphering the Palimpsest of Traces

Now, in the third hypothetical attempt to decide her future, Connie compromiser and pragmatic politician whose success from the early decades to the thirties is depicted here as an ignominious betrayal of the revolutionary ideals personified by Borromeo and Dr. Monson. It is the year after the war, and Connie discovers Biliken's belly dented by two small black holes from gunfire—the two navels she would adopt for herself. She finds in Biliken the deity of the body and instinctual energy but loses him as symbol of her childhood: "As her childhood playground had turned jungle, so Biliken had turned sinister." Biliken is now a revolting figure; Connie, sensing the irrevocable fading of her childhood illusions, intuits "the darkness advancing" from the ruins of the past. And here the discovery of her mother's letters to her husband intervenes, arousing her anxiety to irrevocable fading of her childhood illusions, intuits "the darkness advancing" from the ruins of the past. And here the discovery of her mother's letters to her husband intervenes, arousing her anxiety to return to an earlier primal stage. After reversing gears, retreating from the "pain, the sorrow, the awareness, the bewilderment," she returns to the painless fold of Biliken, this time imaged here as escape in an airplane: "herself . . . running across the bare ground towards the air creature, clutching at her furs as she swayed to its barbarous breath and holding on to her hat as she ran up the steps into its warm belly." She meets her father in this imaginary space, the pneumatic "aboriginal atmosphere" of the sky. Her prayer — "Our father who art in heaven"—materializes Manolo Vidal, an ironic climax of the daughter's desire at the juncture where Biliken is enshrined in a Chinatown temple.

Connie's father admits that power, not dignity, has primacy for him "now too old to care about anything except this: to stay where I am." Connie then manages to diagnose her alienation and its source in the lacuna between the revolutionary past, its residual aura, and the vulgar present. Her predicament is cast in her ignorance of her physical father and her quest for the patriarch-bearer of the symbolic Law (which she finds later incarnated in the figure of Dr. Monson): "Because I must know what I am," she said, "and how can I know that if I don't know what I came from?"

Souvenirs and relics—sword, pistol, old uniform, flag—coalesce into the portrait of a hero only to be eclipsed by the newspaper image of sleazy abortionist. So then Connie forms a conception that her parents are quintessentially evil; she condemns appearances, the pulp and paste of Biliken. Her father cautions her: "You want heroes—and when you don't get heroes you make up devils. But we're not heroes and we're not devils. We're just people. And you'll have to learn to accept us as we are" (p. 175). No longer inhabiting a milieu which crystallizes the collective energies and wills into heroic subjects on the scale of Greek or Roman epic, given the time when maniacal forces in a reified world now subvert man's rational capacity, Manolo Vidal resigns himself to the contingencies of events. But when the plane crashes and Connie clings to her father, he urges her not to accept him and not to make peace with her elders. The unconscious speaks: "If you must go down, go down raging. Do not lose that ability, like I did. Take things hard, make a fuss, and refuse to accept what we are—no, not even now. Rage, rage against us—even now!" From a plea for tolerance and understanding, the father clamors for upholding the negative, the principle of difference, which then finds its realization in Connie's eventual commitment to a new life with Paco.

With the father distancing the daughter and thwarting the incestuous temptation in a rapturous "death by air," the text finally stages a cathartic transfiguration in the aftermath of Connie's questioning by Joaquin's version of the "grand inquisitor." This "older priest" performs an exorcism,

Even in Filipino hands . . . the music of the modern West did suffer a sea-change a sea-change that might make the American aficionados wince but gave to their too fearfully Jules-Vernish rhythms a homely bamboo murmurousness instantly recognizable to the Hindu, the Chinese and the Malay; the Filipinos being in this department (as well as in a number of others) the agents between the East and West, building the Harlem gods a bamboo habitation this side of the Pacific. (p. 24)

It is Paco's adventure in Manila that concretizes the profoundly diverse effects of bourgeois reification (whose symptom, of course, is Connie's bifurcated sensibility) in semifeudal and semicolonial Philippines. Unlike Macho's or Connie's quest, Paco's aims not to identify the father as lawgiver, the founder of what Lacan designates as the Symbolic Order, but to diagnose the conditions which have prevented the restoration of patriarchal authority (that of Aguinaldo, Borromeo, Doctor Monson) and maintained what he sensed as "unreality."[48]

Saved from the familial curse of castration-anxiety, Paco, however, is led by his father into the more dangerous realm of the Imaginary, this time manifesting itself under the sign of the earth's body. Here the index of the unconscious is a mountain (cross-referenced to the Holy Cross hill of chapter 4, site of Connie's "assumption" and also Doctor Monson's Tirad Pass, both mandala mounts of transcendence) his father alludes to, the physical fact enabling Paco's sensibility to open up and register the peculiar conjuncture of city, nature, and the feminine. It is significantly via the Father's speech that Paco's naturalization process operates, a speech contained in the maternal ambience of a *femme couchant*, the quintessential trope of Desire in the text:

The astonishment had renewed itself all the time he was in Manila, every time he looked up and suddenly saw the sleeping woman outlined against the sky—and it changed the indifference with which he had come to his father's country into a stirring of clan-emotion—a glow, almost, of homecoming.

By the time he met the señora de Vidal he had become deeply interested in Manila and was ready to be interested in any woman who most piquantly suggested that combination of primitive mysticism and slick modernity which he felt to be the special temper of the city and its people: pert girls dancing with abandon all night long in the cabarets and fleeing in black veils to hear the first Mass at dawn; boys in the latest loudest Hollywood styles, with American slang in their mouths and the crucifix on their breasts; streets ornate with movie palaces and jammed with traffic through which leaf-crowned and barefooted penitents carried a Black Christ in procession—and always, up there above the crowds and hot dust and skeleton ruins and gay cabarets: the mountains, and the woman sleeping in a silence mighty with myth and mystery—for she was the ancient goddess of the land (said the people) sleeping out the thousand years of bondage; but when at last she awoke, it would be a Golden Age again for the land: no more suffering; no more toil; no rich and no poor. So that when Paco first met the señora de Vidal (he had been playing in Manila over a month by that time, and had been learning the city block by block and street by street) he had felt the same shock of recognition as when, glancing up from the ship's railing, he had suddenly seen the range of mountains that looked like a woman sleeping. (pp. 27-28)

Here we discern the dialectical, transforming energy of Joaquin's signifying practice. Interweaving myth, geography, instinct, Western technology, religion and prophecy, the narrative suggests the confinement of the maternal body, its marginalization and concealment, a body which is that of the nation-people repressed by imperialist domination. It is the life of desire in bondage, immobilized, vigilant only in Connie's fantasies but incandescent in Concha Vidal's expansive presence.

From here on, the text becomes a probing anatomy of reification. Vividly apprehended as an all-pervasive existential anguish saturating the atmosphere, the social malaise becomes articulated in the middle class' blindness to the stark reality of class divisions, the discrepancy between "garish imitation mansions" and foul "patched-up tenements": "Some venom was at work here, seeping through all the layers, cankering in all directions. The señora's world of mansions might sit uneasily on its avenues; the hovels of the poor squatted no less nervously on their gutters" (p. 31). The sophisticated metaphysics of essentialism afflicting the middle strata cannot of course be generalized so as to implicate the masses of workers, peasants, etc. It is clear that what Joaquin targets here is the ideology of U.S. imperialist domination in the Philippines, the hegemonic style of mass consumption not only of commodities but also of commodified images and spectacles, in contrast to which the passion between Paco and La Vidal seems to transpire in a desert island:

For in the world of their minds, they moved with cool expertness, rich and poor, among marble halls and ivory baths and luxurious wardrobes; through streets that were all Park Avenues, where the men were all Pierpont Morgans, and all the women unaging, unfading movie queens. One might have to eat cold rice and squat on a pail in the outhouse and sleep on a bug-ridden floor: one sighed and pressed a scented handkerchief to one's nose and invoked the vicarious magic of one's wrist-watch (just what all the Wall Street tycoons are wearing now) or of one's evening dress (just what all the New York hostesses are wearing now) against the cold rice, the rank pail, the buggy floor.... One smiled and floated away, insulated from all the drab horror of inadequate reality by the ultra-perfect, colossal, stupendous, technicolored magnificence of the Great American Dream. (p. 32)

The "Great American Dream" is refracted in the text through oedipal fixations, fetishes, neurotic and paranoid symptoms, harassing and tempting Paco to wrestle with them in the form of Connie Escobar. Analogous to the dual-faced cult goddess Demeter-Persephone (and variants), Concha / Connie becomes a manifestation of that phantasmal object of desire which combines for Paco the absent father/mother in their ambivalent guises:

"He felt ill himself from the spiteful desire to get the daughter in his clutches—but in his dreams, restless with flying landscapes, the woman he hunted had two faces; and though he sweated to catch her he dreaded every moment lest she stop and turn her other face around." Contaminated by the extravagant diffusion of energies and unfocused drives, the anarchy of the sublime, Paco locks his attention on Connie whose body induces a temporary catharsis: "The shock of her mouth stunned his mind with such impact, abrupt tears scalded his eyes." And this compels him to play out his curse by imagining himself the doll-victim to the totem-god of carnal bliss and hallucination: "When she told him she had two navels he believed her at once, and felt—not repulsion—but the heat-lightnings of a desire, feverish and electric, that charged his hands with eyes and his eyes with mouths. While she talked—her bowed head turned away; the cigarette glowing between her fingers—he imagined her in the posture of the idol and he stripped her and saw himself as the doll on her lap." By a transversal overturning of hierarchy, Paco grasps the truth: his body is sacrificed to the daemon of fantasy. Sadomasochism then mobilizes the desiring-machine and unleashes an upsurge of pleasure.

In this framework, the combat between Connie and Paco at the heart of this chapter becomes the symbolic translation of the deadly task of grasping the truth of one's discourse, a feat requiring a forcible stripping of the body's authoritarian trappings, the despotism of social tropisms and habits—the proliferating eyes that frighten Paco as he is about to rip off Connie's dress. In the pursuit of the Real—Joaquin's invention of the two-navelled body is modeled on the parabolic duplicity of stigmata, akin to Freud's conception of the paradox of negation— the pursuer (like Paco) only learns the parameters of his consciousness, the limits of his knowledge. He learns how in the end the discovery of one's own position within the sociohistorical totality can be gained at the expense of the annihilation of logocentric reason which conceptualizes, discriminates, and sets up the artificial boundaries between the illusory and the concrete, signifier and signified, sign and referent, etc. In the end, Paco's wrestling with the wish-fulfilling protagonist in order to satisfy the void within (the questions posed by his life history, Manila, etc.) ushers a mock-ecstasy. It begets a loss of consciousness that suggests a truth born in the text: the utopian body of Desire cannot be possessed by individual effort alone without an interrogation and decoding of all the forces that traverse Connie's existence in chapter 4 and that, in the musician Paco, remain mute but visible in the thousand besieging eyes—the inertia of alien matter:

He was alone, he had escaped . . . But looking up and seeing the mountains, his heart stopped, his eyes started out of his head, his throat screamed soundlessly. He had not escaped, he had not fled at all—for there she still was, stretched out under the sky; the sly look in her eyes and the bloody smile on her lips, and her breasts and shoulders naked. He wheeled around to flee, but his legs had liquefied and, as he flailed the air with his arms, the ground suddenly seesawed and slammed against his face; the moonlight blacked out: stars blazed; sand swelled in his mouth and waters roared in his ears—but the next moment there were no more stars, no more sand, no more waters, only a total stillness, a total void. (pp. 40-41)

In contrast to Doctor Monson whose visit has cracked the mirror and pushed him to a room filled with dust and crabs, where all the cult's candles have been extinguished and what was left was "vacant darkness," Paco returns to Mary's fold, safeguarded from the clutches of the female devils. His claim that the two women have got "a stranglehold" on him testifies to the vulnerability of the shamanistic alchemist of incompatible elements.

Without his wife Mary, Paco might have been irretrievably seduced and, in a metaphorical sense, devoured. Pepe Monson thinks of "dear good Mary," her distancing gaze appraising Concha Vidal as "a real beauty—like one of those jewelled madonnas in Spanish churches." Monson regards the Texeiras as brother and sister, "like the stock twins of Italian romances." Mary is the unseduced daughter imbued with a discipline of enforcing her will: she "hugged a thrift of sentiment as grim as his own." Like Paco, she "had stepped over the prostrate bodies of their respective families to marry," abandoning a boozy father whom she had quietly supported since she was fifteen. She refuses the trap of "a happy marriage," traveling to Spain without any leavetaking: "She would not let love impair her independence." Fearful of the loss of her freedom in marriage, she preserves another subterranean self which "was still out in the wind, among the mountains, walking through an eternal summer"—she is Connie's twin sister radiating "pride" and "expression of lonely defiance." The self-possessed Rita Lopez, an exiled inflection of La Vidal, pronounces the last word on Mary: she has become an "unreachable stranger," her silence a repudiation of the narcissistic voice of the male ego.

We find in Paco's thoughts a reflection of Mary dissolved in "us," the conjugal leviathan: "The desire he felt, so irresistible because it was for a new and unknown woman, also seemed less shameful, because she looked familiar." Seeing Connie's face "so serious and so earnest, so innocent and ruthless, he recovered the peace his own home had lost," panicked by the encroachment of the unknown from the tropical enigma. Paco has arrived full circle, possessing a Mary transformed: his mother left in "peaceful, clear and pious Macao" toward which the lovers are headed at the narrative's close.

Conceived at the beginning as the mediator of East and West, discoverer of postwar Philippine reality, and foiled cartographer of Connie's schizoid flow, Paco ends up enchanted by the awakened woman, "innocent and ruthless," not quite the legendary Sleeping Woman of folk superstition. For him, Connie is new, unknown, with a dangerous utopian mana somewhat neutralized by the emancipatory figure of Mary. After the introductory chapter, Paco fades away and we are left alone to grapple with the fiery metamorphic dance of eros in the sacrificial rites of Macho Escobar and La Vidal.

Counterpointing Exterior/Interior

For the stable circle of exiles in Hong Kong—the Monsons and Texeiras—their own wish-fulfilling world of mirrors cracked with the intrusion of the Philippine enigma in the person of mother-daughter fleeing the sadomasochistic violence of Macho Escobar and tracking the fugitive thaumaturge of magical rejuvenation, Paco Texeira.

Macho Escobar's career epitomizes the degeneration of the feudal oligarchy, its bankruptcy, and its ultimate submission to an orgy of violence. The text's strategy foregrounds the regressive impulse of the feudal superstructure: Macho's juvenile pranks, when verbalized and addressed to La Vidal, "suddenly fuse into a pattern, exploding in his mind (as though flametrees had ignited a bunch of fireworks) in a great burning shower of joy" (p. 72), evocative of Connie's fiery transfiguration. This "mystic battle" generates an orgiastic erasure of the woman's presence: "His face lifted to the sun and the wind, the blood ablaze on his cheeks and the tears in his eyes. He was young, it was summer, and the flametrees were in bloom" (p. 73). This singular epiphanic moment becomes fixed, intensely cathected, a Wordsworthian "spot of time": "They had never parted, had never gone down from the walls." Eliminating barriers, the libidinal investment of the son in the mother-figure would neutralize "the gathering darkness of the Forties" and sustain him through the war:

Yet the bliss of that morning on the walls haunted him; in the midst of merriment a sudden ache in the bones, a blaze of flametrees in the mind, would make him stop and look around and wonder: why was I so happy then and what was it I wanted?

The flametrees burned in his mind, and remained unconsumed. (p. 73)

After the war, when Macho beholds her, "shocked awake from a long long dream ... he had suddenly and sharply and exultantly known, with the old ache in the marrow and a blaze of flametrees in the mind, that he had never stopped wanting, he had never stopped desiring this woman." Macho could never forget their first traumatic meeting: "the passion she revealed was so astonishing he might have come to her a complete virgin" (p. 74), the mother's embrace abolishing the virgin-fetish and reinstalling (in Deleuze-Guattari's terminology) the "body without organs" into the full body of the earth.

What could this recuperation of a primordial moment of vitality in which the blasé landlord recaptures his virility mean? On the one hand, we are told that Macho, after three years of hellish guerilla warfare against the Japanese, had been "immunized" against "the social terrors that had so infected their old love affair"; on the other, this desire betrays itself as the index of an absence, a lack inscribed in the core of a decadent social class whose exploitation of peasants, workers and women could only be matched by its paranoiac mania, its self-destructive overcoding of "honor" and blood.

What characterizes further Macho's pathos and his victimization by the parasitism of the sugar barons precariously maintained by the high sugar prices in the world market and U.S. patronage, is a fatal and anguished complicity with the opportunism of the bureaucrat-capitalist fraction of the elite (from Quezon to the present) which surfaces here in Concha's offer of her daughter to appease Macho's lust. It was apparently the mother's conscience-dictated plan, "an impulse of the heart," to "save" Macho who, she believed, was "corrupted far more by her renunciation than by her lust." Ashamed and horrified, Macho nonetheless accepts the "monstrous" proposal, fully knowing that "he would do anything she asked and anything that would keep him in her hands." We encounter again the sadomasochistic leitmotif—"loving her so deeply beneath his loathing"—which marks Joaquin's response to the technocratic, programmed individualism of modernity whereby the role of victimizer is expiated in the movement of internalizing the victim, hence the formula of replication and traumatic retakes, *déjà vu*, compulsive repetition, and the uncanny in Joaquin's writing.

Without Concha Vidal's physical surrender and her matriarchal ascendancy over the now orphaned Macho (his mother is a "disappeared" entity), his life, based on the evocation of epiphanic moments composed of fragmentary bits of experience, loses coherence. Connie's discovery of the letters, the schizz-flow of desire, exposes what she conceives as a conspiracy between her mother and Macho to destroy her and points out how the "ancient history" of the affair continues to determine the present as a betrayal, just as Paco's recollection of his father and mother, and Doctor Monson's reminiscences of Manila and Tirad Pass, all testify to the deferred but insidious reverberations of the repressed unconscious.

In summary then, Macho performs three functions in the complex textualization of the Philippine crisis as Joaquin articulates it through paradigms of duality and pluralizing operations: first, as the stereotyped portrait of the feudal oligarchy which never resisted Spanish and American invaders, paralyzed by the inertia of patriarchal/familial despotism; second, as Concha's lover (the mirror-image of absent son and husband) whose carnivalesque desiring-machine in the thirties yields a vision of a perpetual summer in the city exiled from his father's demesne and constitutes the realm of the Imaginary wish-fulfillment; and third, as Connie's husband—

the crystallization of her revolt against androcentric despotism and self-exclusion from a degraded world—whose own preservation of the letters (the past) duplicates Connie's and Doctor Monson's clinging to the myth of plenitude and self-presence, and also provides the "conscience" that would demystify feudal and colonial pieties.

Thus when Macho shoots Concha Vidal, an act of penetration to cover up the loss of Connie's body, and closes the infinite semiosis of the text, we can only wonder whether this *ressentiment*-filled homicide adumbrates the breakdown of the historic compromise between the feudal oligarchy and the bureaucrat-comprador bourgeoisie, the caretakers of the present dispensation; or repudiates the sensual, guilt-ridden pragmatism represented by Concha Vidal whose role as the sadistic phallic mother is disrupted by the incursions of an eroticizing death drive. It is time now to direct our inquiry into the problematic of La Vidal on which hinges the elaborate, unfixable figuration of Joaquin's deterritorializing (utopian) project.

Catharsis and Transcendence

Just before the close of chapter 2 devoted to Macho, the narrative conducts us into Concha Vidal's consciousness as it explores the paradoxical turnabouts in her life, specifically when her good intention of saving "the two people she loved most" produces the opposite result: "Anguish was manufactured by her benevolence; her private hell was indeed paved with the best intentions" (p. 82). In chapter 3, Concha, talking to the Monson brothers, is reminded of the "happy" past and reflects on how her actions have produced evil consequences so that, for her, "Every night is the Chinese moon . . . time to pay old debts." Her defense of vanity evolves into pan-aestheticism and the valorizing of pure appearance consonant with the old priest's argument: "Beauty is a virtue too—or, anyway, a responsibility; for a woman not to be beautiful would be to commit the 'unforgiveable sin' against the Holy Ghost." *Ressentiment* pervades her character: "Oh Father, can we really end up hating the people for whom we have made sacrifices?"

The kernel of this chapter, the genealogy of Concha Vidal from her childhood immersion in the community to the sacrifice of "God" through abortion to Manolo Vidal, offers a capsule history of the Philippine formation, its contradictions and provisional resolutions, from the defeat of Aguinaldo to the onset of the depression in the thirties, the birth of Connie. It signifies the libidinal investment of the social field, situating the personal in the matrix of class-national struggle embracing the feudal milieu of patriarchal authoritarianism and the degraded society of market-capitalism. In Concha's development bissected by her two marriages, the narrative not only delineates the psychological flux but also traces the material underpinnings of her character in the various social practices associated with gender, race, and class.

We can grasp Joaquin's strategy of reconciling the existential and moral contradictions that decenter Concha Vidal by comparing the two courtships which decode her body. Her response to Esteban Borromeo's passion indicates the woman's participation in an organic milieu of formalized behavior regulated by kinship and ritual filiation: "An empire had perished in the culture of those disciplines; history informed her impulses; and she had turned obedience, a passive virtue, into a performance" (p. 114). As for her husband and his group that once proudly claimed themselves "history in motion," the rapid mutation of colonial politics reduced them to pathetic relics "discarded by history" and consigned to the "anachronistic parlors of the Thirties."

Harnessing the device of the Wordsworthian/Proustian "spot of time" and its ironic declension in Kierkegaardian repetition, the narrative seeks to ascribe to Concha's consciousness at the moment of her choice of Esteban Borromeo a surplus of knowledge, an excess of perception, aimed at cancelling the desiring-production immanent in the mode of territorial representation:

> But that evening on the azotea, among the potted plants and bird cages, he had yet to fear the future, or bewail the present, or venerate the past. . . . She glanced about anxiously, to see what today looked like; turned suddenly away from her lover to the balustrade, to memorize what she saw—a city knee-deep in dusk and crowned with white fire; the roofs and towers still precise, the streets vanishing, as though ink were welling up from the earth. Through the ruins of this city she would one day crawl like an animal, clothes ripped to rags by barbed wire, the bombs bursting all around. Tonight, unafraid, she reached out for the future—reached out and took her lover and confidently embraced him, being assured by all the grandmothers in her blood that, a thousand adventures from now, she would find, as they had found, those old roofs and towers still there, the same bells still ringing at twilight, the same lizards descending to touch their heads to earth. (pp. 115-16)

Here the sheer affirmation of procreative instinct and the rhythmic continuity of life in nature serves to heal any historic rupture and modulates Borromeo's death into a mere punctual moment of transition from the Empire Days to the eve of the Second World War. What is invoked is an Eternal Feminine, a nurturing genius of the city, so that the images and tropes of continuity connected with ritual and architecture become the tokens of permanence, guarantees of meaning and value. Organic filiation subordinates to itself alliance and the phallocentric contract, unleashing the chthonic power of desire.

Prompted by her wish not to dishonor her father's old age, Conching Borromeo contracts with Manolo Vidal for an abortion and is consumed with anguish. In a passage (pp. 121-220) describing her existential agony, we perceive the figure of Concha invested with the patriarchal authority to "unconsciously" maneuver her fate (the moving carriage with a headless driver). Punctuated by the incessant cockcrowing, her terror at being borne headlong into her mother's lap and swallowed by the earth's body—a terror replayed in Connie's ordeal—occasions a *jouissance* of self-negation: when the carriage speeds out to the open country, "A sudden bliss filled her, a warm bliss folding like a fountain, washing away all fear." Her guilt purged, she is ready to enter a convent where Manolo Vidal begins to court her. Although nauseated by his presence, this revulsion precisely initiates the mirror-stage of her life: "his eyes revealed that she was beautiful." Faced with the choice of confinement in a beaterio and accepting the chance for a break in the continuum, Conching Borromeo chooses the latter. She becomes in this gesture the symbol of biocosmic persistence and adaptation, of the flexibility and protean strength of the native psyche to endure the loss (more exactly, the sublimation) of the carnivalesque illusions coeval with the failed 1896 Revolution and purge the stigma of complicity with the conquerors.

It is this same virtue of resilience, of resolutely confronting the perpetual Monday morning tasks—the unceasing process of decoding and deterritorializing, Deleuze-Guattari's term for the capitalist cycle of production-reproduction- circulation—that informs Connie's ultimate, long-meditated decision to elope with Paco.[49] In the following passage, Joaquin indicates the dialectical matrix of his conception of Concha Vidal and Connie Escobar (representing the poles of gynocratic sovereignty and schizz-flow respectively) implicit in a signifying practice that claims to transcribe not only the cunning, subversive stratagem of desiring-production but also its subsumption within a libidinally charged socius, the body without organs. The text unmasks the metaphysics of Desire by unfolding the materiality of the imagination expressed in the notion of responsibility and the pain caused by exercising one's will. This process begets the "terrible knowledge" that the "I" is not a fixed or static signifier but a risky process of exploration and questioning. Motifs of birth and rebirth, life as constant creation and supersession, the sublation of one stage and its conversion into another, blend in the schizz-flow exemplified in this key passage summing up Connie's plight:

Yes, she thought, everything has to be arranged over there; but did not fear the decisions that would still have to be made, in a world where it would always be Monday morning.... She looked at his brown hands lying on the table and thought of the smashed car drifting among the rocks. So much had been destroyed, so much would still have to be destroyed, to produce the woman that she now saw walking in her bright imagined Macao: cobbled streets winding up to a cathedral, white houses on a rocky coast, trees flowering in blue air—it would be springtime in Macao in the morning. She longed for the morning, but not urgently, not anxiously, resting now after her long, long day, delaying awhile the step that would take her into that other woman, the unknown woman whose face she now saw glittering in the sunshine, informed by a terrible knowledge. She did not doubt that the consequences of her act would be terrible; tomorrow would bring pain, she would find the world in ruins. But to all this she had committed herself by refusing the cliff's edge; and she accepted, without a tremor for the world, whatever she had made happen by refusing to die. She felt callous now, and fat with peace; but tomorrow I will be changed, she thought drowsily, finishing her eggs and pouring herself more coffee. The brown hands [of Paco Texeira] her eyes kept watching retreated from the table and reappeared offering cigarettes and fire. (p. 208)

Connie's projection of the Other, no longer an emergent double but a new creation (the novum), is the clearest proof of a climactic deterritorializing stroke sprung from the same *kairos* of nihilism bewailed by orthodox critics. What is anticipated by Connie's reflection is not just the need to posit a radical rupture but to invent a space for annulling the vertical axiomatics of patriarchal authority (including the regime of the phallic mother) and constructing the horizontal or transversal flows of libidinal energy from the unconscious liberated at last from the terror of the Oedipus complex and family triangulation.

Despite the shifting points of view, the totalizing perspective of chapter 4, and the putative "irresolution" somehow regarded as consonant with a "moral memory" where time and eternity intersect, the narrative leads to a convergence of three lines: the sedentary line of Macho and its seal of castration stamped in his youth, the migrant line of Doctor Monson (the Father's Law suspended), and the nomadic aleatory line of Paco Texeira whose genealogy suggests the discounting of filiation by alliance as the foundation of a future symbolic contract. Concha Vidal, who represents the earth-body as the surface of codes and inscriptions, becomes subordinate to Connie's destabilizing thrust finally aligned with Paco's anarchic flight. Contrary to received opinion, Connie Vidal's hysteria and transference— her worship of the grotesque Biliken should be read as the resurrection of the Rabelaisian festival deity; her two navels as point of departure for serial disenchantments, if not renovating alterity—prefigure the overthrow of the regime of representation (logocentric realism, sexism, etc.) and its replacement by the beginnings of desiring-production. This desiring-machine enables Connie, after her conversion and transfiguration on the hill, to embrace Doctor Monson, telescoping in this conjunction (as in "The Chinese Moon") the serialized and dispersed fragments of experience in a synchronic cluster. But this desiring-machine is located at the heart of a social structure already problematized by the disruptive time-space matrix of capitalist profit-making whose operations directly contradict the homogenizing impulse of an organic socius defined by Father Tony in the concluding chapter: "We're all so involved in one another we can hardly draw a breath without making somebody suffer somewhere. In the end we all have to be rather callous and ruthless to be able to act at all. It's the everyday courage we need to live." While this may prefigure a utopian moment of classless solidarity, the moment of Connie forgiving her parents and finding what she has lost, it also foreshadows quite menacingly the emergence of a hierarchizing sovereignty to enforce the subordination of subjects: the oedipal phallus. Over and against the scheme of this utopian resolution which, in a sense, sublimates class divisions into the conventional thematics of diabolic/angelic conflict and dissolves the woman's revolt into a quest for asserting free will and Christian responsibility against heathen fatalism, one might stress here the victory of affiliation over genealogy, the invented abnormal mutation (two navels) over filial repetition. What torments Connie is neither the trauma of discovery (as subject-position, she is constituted by her father's abortion practice and mother's liaisons) nor the guilt stemming from pride but the rifts and schizz-breaks traversing the body politic, the ruptures between 1896 up to the early days of the second Philippine Republic. What afflicts Connie is not the evasion of reality through fantasy, not the lack of love or security, but the threatening Law of the Father (also known as conscience, honor; the mother as Medusa). With her body textualized as the site for inscriptions by sacramentalized elements (earth, air, water, fire coded by Christian hermeneutics), Connie's courage to sin, to shatter the illusory equilibrium of Hong Kong and provoke "hysterical" asymmetries and imbalances among the exiles, may be interpreted as the workings of desire, the unconscious, which prompts her attempted suicide as the nodal breach and the dream-sequence as enactment of the flow. We can now sketch the warring ideologemes the text tries to reconcile in this provisional diagram:

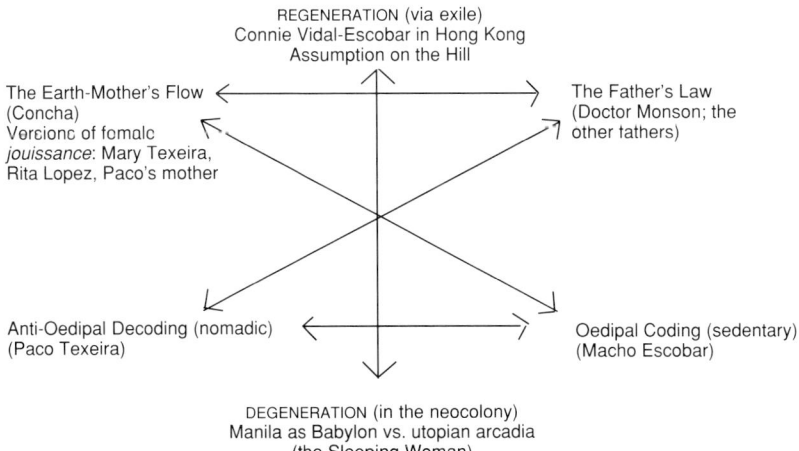

As for the theme of national identity and self-estrangement which, to be sure, tends often to be obscured by the mystery of sin and evil as desiderata for salvation, and displaced by the moral issue of free will vis-à-vis the irredeemable corruption of the world, the text registers an answer neither in Doctor Monson's embrace of Connie nor in the termination of the reign of the phallic law and the terror of oedipal castration (Macho; Concha), but, I would suggest, in the "muffled thunder of guns" from the Chinese civil war then raging, the "distinct boom of cannon" heard clearly by Father Tony Monson in his room at St. Andrew's Convent on Holy Cross Hill (p. 80), the reverberations of an impending revolutionary apocalypse, the fulfillment of a promised renewal heralded later by Connie's "assumption" on that same hill, a lustral rebirth accompanied by the purgatorial, earth-redeeming explosions greeting the un-Christian Chinese New Year.

7 Cave and Shadows: Toward the Production of Utopian Discourse

The old is dying and the new cannot be born; in this interregnum there arises a great diversity of morbid symptoms.

—Antonio Gramsci

Whenever man has thought it necessary to create a memory for himself, his effort has been attended with torture, blood, sacrifice.

—Friedrich Nietzsche

What is originally holy is what we have taken over from the animal kingdom—the bestial.

—Friedrich Engels

The body of the people and of mankind, fertilized by the dead, is eternally renewed and moves forever forward along the historic path of progress.

—Mikhail Bakhtin

SEXUAL POLITICS DRAMATIZED as the struggle for truth, truth as power of discourse and institutional apparatuses; truth as a recovered / uncovered knowledge of events leading toward death with which the chief protagonist Jack Henson seeks to grapple; death as the absent immaculate, pristine body, or the lost mother/wife (the Goddess in her multiple incarnations) and the power of textuality to fill up the absence with some mythical utopian plenitude: these are some of Joaquin's thematic strands woven around the plot-armature of "a thriller in the private-eye mode." But this linear sequence where exchange of bodies and the circulation of language and discourses prevail—the narrative vehicle of capitalist time-space (discontinuous, irreversible, etc.)—is thwarted and undermined by the alternate chapters chronicling the earth's full body and its inscriptions (the fertility cults witnessed in the cave) which evoke an archaic time-space matrix of recurrence, reversibility, etc.—the chronotope of desire, gift, debt. Within this contrapuntal structure, we encounter the ratiocinative mind of empirical-scientific history disintegrated by the flows and impulses of solidarity in the masses and by collective revenge set against the fall into reification and the private solitude of postcolonial, actually neocolonial society today. Behind the archive of inscriptions lurks the allegory of substantive meanings and potent life grasped at the moment of sacrifice.

Intertextual Play

Perception accessible to transcribing in language but uncertain of its origin or destination, with the ego *cogitans* in the process of being posited: this is the Cartesian moment of phantasmatic appearances in the novel. Juxtaposed to this obsessive, even fetishistic visualizing is the body with a name but immediately rendered anonymous, dissolving and haemorrhaging, boundaryless, spun in a ceaseless metonymic displacement and metaphoric doubling: this is the Lacanian moment of the Imaginary and the Symbolic. The initial sentence of the novel epitomizes the narrative's duplicitous intent of healing the bifurcated subjectivity caught in a postfeudal but precapitalist transition by the very process which engenders this fatal split: "The vision—a crab on a string being walked by a naked girl—occurred in deep hotel-corridor twilight and moreover when he, Jack Henson, was feeling himself in a swoon" (p. 1).

We face here the phenomenon of the body as spectacle offstaged only by the emblematic crab and attached to the locus of urban anonymity, the airconditioned hotel, the site of gratuitous conjunctures (Cain the city inhabitant versus Abel the pilgrim) and mysterious initiations. This milieu finds its binary opposite in the unpredictable climate and physical surroundings (Manila versus the island off Davao City) whose detailed description inflected by allusions to the racial experience of "the myth of August as a violent month" provides the alibi of verisimilitude (note Aquino's assassination in August 1983). But it is precisely this assumed convention of expressive realism and the problematic of bourgeois subjectivity that Joaquin's narrative is, as I will demonstrate in this essay, committed to explode even as it paradoxically appeals to it for validation.

Sweat, fatigue, hunger, tactile encroachments, nausea, fever—the body's exorbitant presence, its intractable viscosity and recalcitrant tropisms need to be contained: this is the strategic task of textualization. "Broiled in March, boiled in August. What sins did our forefathers commit, mock-wailed Jack Henson, that we got hell on earth?" (p. 3). Ironically, it is the apparition (claimed later as put on) that stabilizes the apperceiving consciousness whose center of gravity has been shifted to the ecological context (metropolis, seasonal weather)—this shifting of terrain foreshadows the earthquakes and floods later—and subsequently decoded by mythology and Christian prophecy.

Our central intelligence here (Jack Henson) relentlessly decentered by the quest and questioning of the ground of existence resembles Sid Estiva, the returning native of "The Order of Melkizedek": he is exiled from his birthplace by a honeymoon, "treading the ground of his city for the first time in almost twenty-years (he was forty-two)." Back to his old haunt of the fifties after a long exile in a southern island, this entrepreneur engaged in petty production of rubber and cultured pearls finds himself unmoored by the "apparition" whose ambiguous origin is a symptom of what Gramsci calls the morbid "interregnum" symbolized by the double Nenita Coogan/Yvette (the virgin/the whore):

And at the juncture of this T, in the dim light, he saw a big black crab crawling fast across the floor, straining at a leash that was revealed to be held by the girl following behind. She wore pink a-go-go boots, a large pink hat, and nothing else. She and her crab moved from left to right, and disappeared into the arm of the hallway that led to the elevators. (p. 4)

Not innocent but lacking "urban sang-froid," Jack Henson responds to his ex-wife Alfreda's (who eloped with an American Jesuit priest twenty years ago) request to clear up the puzzle of her daughter's death in a cave in the suburbs of Manila. Jack's marital history, already prefiguring the ethicopolitical dispossession of his class and its pursuit of the phantom daughter who has already escaped the stepfather's seduction, is conveyed in the exchange between Jack, the mayor Alfonso "Pocholo" Gatmaitan, the chief of police and the medical officer on the "subject" of the discovery of Nenita (Helen) Coogan's body. So here, at the outset, we confront bourgeois power/ knowledge and its aporia: even as it endows the legal gendered entity Nenita Coogan with appropriate kinship and citizenship qualifiers, the absentiation or emptying of that subject by erasure of the body is accomplished on two levels, first, the mystery of the extinction of her life; and second, the mystery of how she (or her agents) eluded the male guardians/ authorities and deposited her body on the altar of the cave. What the narrative's polyphonic sequence unfolds is the persistent if futile attempt by the feudal patriarchs (personified by Pocholo, the younger and older Manzanos) to recapture and restore the corporeal plenum of the body *mise en abyme*—note that Nenita Coogan mediates on one level the delinquent Filipino wife and an errant American Jesuit priest; and on another, the archaic priestesses and the secular wives and daughters of the major characters—as proof of its undisputed sovereign power over their territory (in both literal and figurative terms).

I will propose here to construe the quest to clarify and resolve the two mysteries which inform the proairetic and hermeneutic codes of the narrative as an attempt by the oligarchic elite and its neocolonial heirs and allies to preserve the dependent or peripheral Philippine formation as a precarious coalition of various reactionary class forces with their varying ideological tendencies temporarily frozen in the present power-bloc. We observe in the novel the Socratic drive to explain and account for the movement and final disposal of Nenita Coogan's body (symbolizing the power of *jouissance,* emancipation from scarcity) from the moment she intrudes into the sphere of patriarchal domination and market exchange. And, intertwined with this maneuver, the text conducts an inquest into the symptomatic failure of the established power-structure to anticipate and abort the Coogan mystery, which now becomes the name for all those repressed forces and deterritorializing energies—the cult of the Goddess, ambivalent Eros, polymorphous desire—that circumscribe the freedom of status quo power and opens up a space for dialogic, multivocal indeterminacies and utopian extrapolations.

From Diachronic Perspective to Synchronic Grid

As a complex of textualizing displacements produced by his probing into the "cause" of the apparition (the anomalous and exorbitant revelation) and the enigma of his disrupted liaison with Alfreda, Jack Henson may be read tentatively as the inchoate bourgeois ego—one version of the Filipino identity aborted/castrated by Spanish and U.S. interventions, unrepresentable as a monadic psyche but recognizable as a subject-in-process. Hence his periodic interpellation by hallucinated phenomena and diacritical citations from legends, annals, folk-memory, etc. He embodies the national future as repressed desire, a deracinated sensibility open to the prospect of the body's resurrection, the unity of *nous* (reason) and psyche (spirit).

While Jack Henson affords a pretext for the mapping of the inviolate female body (the earth; wife, daughter, mother)—the "effigy of a virgin martyr," as the doctor puts it—as a sacred site by the public authorities, it is he who generates the space for an interrogation of the phallocentric order (after all, he has forfeited the father-husband position) and the dismantling of what holds the conjuncture of forces and bodies together, namely, a colonial mimicry of bourgeois discourse whose anatomy (substance and form combined) is diagnosed by Joaquin's practice of writing. For what we have, in Jack Henson's specific dilemma as the disintegrated subject trying to constitute itself in an empirical world of fixed objects is the collective predicament of the Filipino petty bourgeois individual—elements of the middle strata—who cannot represent himself/herself as a speaking or acting subject in a coherent, integral, self-generating mode of signification because the family-kinship network of the feudal past has well-nigh disintegrated but the cash-nexus and the commodifying mechanisms of a fully capitalist industrial society have not fully emerged to homogenize the wreckage spewed by the breakdown of the old order.

In Joaquin's text, that old dispensation (represented by the Manzano dynasty) has collapsed and what has supervened is the rule of the bosses based on expediency, state violence and demagogic populism. These, in large terms, comprise the indices for the novel as "objective correlative" to September 1972. But the middle strata refuse to face this reality. Jack Henson, the nascent bourgeois ego, strives to systematize and organize time (*chronos*) into historical narrative (*kairos*, with *peripeteia* and *anagronisis*), but in so doing he is caught in an impasse, an inescapable double bind since his attempt to forge meaning through the old modes of representation falls into the abyss of difference, anamorphoses and alterity. That is to say, the *cogito*—the autonomous, rational, self-identical ego—can only resort to a relational definition of meaning as figured in the gap between subject and object, signifier and signified; a meaning forever suspended by the constitutive play of presence-absence in language and temporarily hypostatized by power and the will to dominate.

When the status quo of the traditional oligarchy, eroded by ruptures from the oneiric and libidinal flows in folk-memory and mass revolts, finally crumbles, we see also the cogito slide into delirium, into paranoid and schizoid acts while the apparent naturalness of social forms, habits of common sense, thought-patterns and gestures of everyday life evaporate in a thorough carnivalesque unmasking process. In his densely argued study *The Tremulous Private Body*, Francis Barker refers to the "metaphysics of death" underlying the "absentiating mode" of bourgeois discourse which, to effect meaning through representation, "must depend on the absence, the non-being or death, of the very object it seeks to designate."[50] This succinctly elucidates the function of Nenita Coogan's disappeared body and the constellation of undecidables gravitating around it. Given the absence of Alfreda, the nonbeing of the naked woman with the crab, and the nonpresence of Coogan's corpse (ironically replicated in Yvette's sexual rite and profane death), the site for the spontaneous genesis of the rational ego seems assured. But what the text dramatizes is precisely its premeditated abortion or, at best, its premature birth. This, I submit, is the novel's "political unconscious," the untranscendable horizon of its manifold possibilities of signification.

With the revenge of the archaic and the organic community over the patriarchal system (André's drowning), the neocolonial inheritance congealed in the Manzano house and its Alexandrian masculinist supremacy over the female deities of the sacred rivers collapses. So two antagonists remain: Jack Henson, the subject-position of the defamiliarized and uprooted conscience (his ethical affiliation has replaced blood-filiation in his relations with others), and the populist cult of the Ginoong Ina. We can glimpse in this schematic tabulation the possible reading of martial law, constitutional authoritarianism, and dictatorship as signs of a desperate, last-ditch attempt to shore up the ruins of *La Alejandria* but this time on the foundations of a bureaucratic dependency no longer tied to the old sugar barons and landed semifeudal oligarchy. With Alex dead and the clan fragmented and immobilized, Pocholo's swerve from dependency to the underground may serve as the only viable way out for this group.

Jack Henson is the melancholy, fey, somewhat disembodied chronicler of the demise of the *ilustrado* gentry in the wake of the unprecedented revolutionary insurgence of the Filipino masses in the seventies and eighties.

Dialogical Seduction

Activating the generic code of a private detective thriller with its scientistic detached protagonist assigned to redeem a fallen world—W.H. Auden's guilty vicarage—and restore an original but uncomprehended innocence, the text generates this simulacrum of the Cartesian ego, the inductive-deductive organ of a consciousness guaranteed by stable institutional markers: property, marriage, school, etc. But note that for our central protagonist, the initial markers are unstable and pejorative: a solitary cuckold, saddled with a godfather's property in a remote island near Davao City. His claim of self-knowledge is an alibi of which the narrative is Ariadne's thread through the labyrinth: "But now I don't care if it sounds corny to say that losing Alfreda made me find myself on the land."

The confession is revealing: dispossession of/by the woman precedes the former "owner's" spatial orientation and self-discovery. It must be pointed out that Jack Henson is not only repaying Alfreda what he owes her—a symbolic debt, to be sure; he acknowledges the divorce or separation as what in effect constitutes him. Alfreda may be conceived here as desiring-production which cuts and codes the nomadic flow directed toward death: Nenita Coogan's "full body without organs," death-wish incarnate.[51] Jack Henson displays a readiness for the ordeal; the *tabula rasa* of his consciousness becomes the surface on which inscriptions by the socius (*écriture* as difference) are unveiled, as if Jack were a foetus just delivered prematurely so that his quest for Coogan's body becomes his postnatal trauma: as he says, he had "to face all of you," no longer the classic stock figure of "the husband a priest had put horns on." He thus offers himself as a forking signifier gifted with a castration wound, his delusion of wholeness conferred by the play of differential relations (between Pocholo and himself, between Chedeng and the Manzanos and himself, etc.).

So tied with the pursuit of knowledge concerning victim and killer, his experience amounting to a diffuse accumulation of self-cancelling testimonies, is the knower's engagement with his past (childhood memories, the whole postwar milieu described partly in Joaquin's first novel and in "Candido's Apocalypse" and "The Order of Melkizedek"). Despite his disclaimer, this interrogation of his past involves him in a complex ethico-political criticism of friends and kins that exceed a merely satiric framework where the play of desire manifests itself first as wish-fulfillment in the genital (oedipal) stage as he retraces Coogan's path. His drive to "know" this fruit of his wife's divergence, a coupling with a part-object, shifts to the realm of romance (intimated by the historical interludes) where vertiginous fantasies reenact an oral stage occupied by primordial anxieties, where the ominous castrating father-villain (the Manzano elders) is overcome by a shaman-trickster figure (Pocholo, then Isagani Segovia) whose wily ploys are energized by a symbiotic if duplicitous relationship with the mother (Ginoong Ina and her avatars: the Hermana, Jeronima, the warrior-priestess, etc.).

With the epistemological program of the prophet-annalist (parts 2, 4, 6, 8) unfixed and Pocholo's veridical explanations deconstructed by the Ginoong Ina and her explanation in turn rendered suspect by Isagani Segovia, the text displaces the melodramatic structure of representation. The recalls and "flashbacks," in this context, should be considered quanta of intensities interrupting the linear, transparent logos of the collective unconscious, the Filipino racial memory. Now the traditional preoccupation of the romance genre with destiny and providence begins to merge with the formal mutations of psychological realism to produce this graphocentric construction of a simulacrum: Nenita Coogan or the various manifestations of the Goddess, difference itself personified. The simulacrum is the antithesis of the copy or the representation of an original. In their lack of finality, the riddle of Coogan and Ginoong Ina foils any attempt to reduce them to mere icons or reproductions of the original model, the Platonic idea, which the novel's title alludes to. Hence, the text's project is a transgression of telos, *arché*, totality, in foregrounding desire as "the presence of a future in the present," in its counterpointing of perception and memory with hope.[52]

With Alex Manzano's nihilism engendering guilt and self-violence, the voice of patriarchal authority can no longer provide an access to an intelligible, hierarchically arranged cosmos. It is through his refusal to open Alex's letter of confession—death, "the body without organs" invades the living as a ghostly self-presence—that allows Jack Henson's mind to make connections "until the moment came when he looked and saw they composed a chain." Henson's interrogation of Pocholo and his subsequent identification of Pocholo as the perpetrator-manipulator behind the scenes (the *deus ex machina*; causality that converts contingent human existence into necessity, the natural) prompts an inquiry into motives, revealing the mixing of personal grievances with political or ideological convictions. Base and superstructure are tightly imbricated here. But Henson's deductions cannot all be apodictically confirmed, hence his helpless weeping—

"Could time and madness be wept away?"—until the accused, the Other (Pocholo) returns to apparently confirm what would otherwise remain shadowy hypotheses, a heap of floating and undeciphered signifiers (Coogan is the prime "floating signifier").

As the long dialogic confession of the unmasked "author" of the text Henson has been reading and interpreting, Pocholo's reconstruction of the past may be construed as a demonstration of a centralizing will to contrive meaning by cutting the flux of drives investing fragments and part-objects; an assertion of a systematizing and conserving intelligence. But paradoxically enough, Pocholo's recapitulation of what happened spawns the uncanny ruses of textual doubling—his desire for recognition fulfilled, the pleasure of ludic reversals springs from the empty, blank abyss:

I had no particular plan for myself then, certainly no plan to remain in the Church while secretly aiding its enemies. But suddenly, with just that one spiteful act done on the spur of the moment, I was Mr. Hyde, a double agent, moving underground. And how thrilled I was! Never before had I experienced a pleasure so exciting, so intense, as at that moment when, at the Cardinal's villa, I stood witness to Don Andong's conversion while listening to the tumult of the demo at the gates, only myself knowing I had a hand in *both* happenings. Power was nothing new to me, but this kind of power, yes. My life had been multiplied by two. I was this Christian devoutly witnessing an act of faith and at the same time I was the anti-Christian at the gates reviling that act of faith.

At that moment I saw what road lay before me. Not for me to counter Don Andong's conversion with a sensational apostasy of my own. Enough that suddenly completely I was pagan in my heart. I could do more for the heathen cause by staying in the Church and seeking to undermine it from within. Besides, the secrecy gave my every moment such a terrible aliveness, as if my senses were doubled. (p. 253)

Here speaks the pure hubris of multiplicity, an articulation of Desire as the disjunctive synthesis of two determinations affirmed by their difference. Pocholo's exulting in secrecy dissolves past and future in the intense present: the body resurrected, nature triumphantly redeemed.

All the elaborate moves to give flesh to the ideals of Don Andong and Alex Manzano should now be seen as a structural counterpart to Pocholo's project: an attempt to comprehend the antagonistic forces, grasp their singularities, and coalesce them in a movement of self-becoming. Pleasure springs from the flux of desire, exercising its nomadic distribution of energies throughout the social body. An orgasmic sensation of self-fulfillment and self-detachment overwhelms him. His sense of "terrible aliveness," the climax of the revitalization efforts, stimulates a narcissistic fervor needed to regenerate the Philippine wasteland (circa 1960-72), a zeal co-extensive with the self-proclaimed will to manipulate contradictory forces in the political arena. This aspiration to transcendence comes first before his specious and self-serving arguments about the restoration of paganism to save the Filipino. Note, however, that for all his sense of self-sufficiency—his alternating roles underwrite his joy of illusory self-presence—Pocholo's identity rests on his image reflected in the obedience of his subalterns: "Only he and Ginoong Ina knew who I was."

The intrusion of Nenita Coogan into this hitherto unconfessed realm of self-presence (based on a pattern of domination/subordination) hints at a fissure in the system. What is at first surprising is Pocholo's perplexity about how Nenita died—he doubts whether she was suffocated in his car's luggage compartment—but his transporting the body into the cave is meant to reanimate the legends textualized earlier. "Now can I be said to have killed her?" Pocholo asks. Is this a question of agency or causality? He is not deterred by any sense of culpability or guilt; on the contrary, he vehemently asserts his ruthlessness on the face of "the importance of our movement." Pocholo's notion of expediency in fighting Christianity with violence reveals, to be sure, a total ignorance of the working of ideology, a naïveté exceeded only by his fallacious belief that the "true heathen Filipinos" will be made "great by paganism as the Japanese were made great when a revived devotion to Shinto turned them into a world power at the turn of the century" (p. 258). Parodically, this will to repeat and thus fashion the incongruous begins to problematize the status of Platonic models.

What is significant in Pocholo's misrecognition of heathenism and the dynamics of power is not its fatuous crudity but its value as a symptom of a pervasive *ressentiment* in Pocholo's character typical of deracinated fractions of the middle stratum. He betrays this when he tells Jack Henson his relief at "a narrow escape"—why this if he has already confessed everything to Jack? The past—the utopian space of secular romance, not the immediate punctual past—has been permanently exorcised:

Whew! For a moment there, my father almost got even with me! But the anitos are on my side, protecting me all the way. It was the anitos that prompted you, Jack, to say yes, let's burn the letter. They're coming back, they *have* come back. This is their Second Coming. The future belongs to *us*. As for the past, if the Manzanos stand for my father, or the world of my father, I've had my revenge. The house of the Manzanos had collapsed. (p. 258)

With this vengeance-cathected vision of a new order, whatever Jack Henson does can only further the will of the founding ancestors: everything is predetermined. But the ultimate refutation of this voluntarist and fatalist (paradoxical but logical twin) belief comes with Isagani Segovia's revelation that he is the guardian of Pocholo's secret, the truth-monopolizing informer in the bosom of the conspiracy. Not a "practical joker" but a "practical pagan" for whom "anything goes," he confides to Jack:

I got sick and tired of his thinking I was his creature, his tool, his devil's apprentice. Now he knows better. When he came here the night before he disappeared, I told him everything: that it was I who exposed him to Nenita and Yvette and Alex Manzano. Man, was he stunned! I think that's what really drove him underground. The poor devil realized who between us really was master. All the time he thought he was being oh so ruthless and satanic, somebody else was beating him at being diabolical, and for no reason at all. (p. 268)

Is this gratuitous deviltry the mask of Christian freedom sprung from the womb of pagan fatalism? Isagani seeks to encode the surface of the text with the despotic style of barbaric and imperial representation (to use Deleuze-Guattari's term), but since his motive is anarchic, he can be interpreted as the embodiment of the unconscious as desiring-machine geared to dissolving all representations, all identitary logic. Jack's compliment to Isagani (a drifter hired by Pocholo) that he was "never the lesser evil," an evil born from "gratuitous" malice, seems an acknowledgment of a new reality in which the infinite play of difference unleashes its phantasmagoric seductiveness. We enter a world where hierarchy and coherence have dissolved and the flux of endless substitutions and incessant displacements now reigns supreme. In effect, the logic of Pocholo's aestheticist vitalism, the desperate effort of the alienated petty bourgeois politician to achieve a totalizing grasp of a fragmented and reified society in order to transcend it, succumbs to its immanent truth: the glorious past of the ilustrado can only return hidden in Nature's vengeance against Faustian rationality. Isagani may be read then as the herald of the resurrection of the body—all that has so far been silenced, marginalized, repressed.

Populist Hermeneutics

From the logocentric plenum and self-contained immediacy of Pocholo's concluding testament (part 4) to the vertiginous disclosure of the modern-day civilized but polis-less citizen Isagani Segovia (a pun on the Archbishop's See of Nueva Segovia), we have reached the limit of intersubjectivity where finitude, the death of God, and erotic transgression stare us in the face. Speech proclaiming the self-identity of the sovereign and autonomous ego becomes exhausted, terminates in a silence to which only a woman's fecund body can respond, hence Jack Henson's panicked pursuit of Chedeng only to discover the futility of a self-ingratiating and deluded mimesis: "She didn't want to force my hand; so she wouldn't even let me know where she was hiding." Here Jack's desire exhibits its Hegelian essence in its derivation from the supposed desire of the other, the reciprocal desire for recognition: "But this morning, when I saw her, she knew I knew she was waiting and that I would come for her" (p. 269).

Reminding him of "living in the shadow of something ugly"—his wife captured by the Christian imperialist—Jack Henson collapses. This outsider from the fringes of the neocolony seeks the vessel of promise and possibility in the person of Monica (the *virgo intacta* of the defunct Manzano clan) whose charity lies in preventing the mutual ruin of Jack and Chedeng. It is Monica, the female survivor of the fallen world, who incarnates at this juncture the principle of discontinuity, the instrument of Jack's "salvation." For Jack, at the moment of departure, still harbors the illusion of free will, the presumption of a self-activating ethical subject circa 1972: "But *why* should they be past and *why* should they be carried away if he chose not to be? Not all the monuments had vanished" (p. 271). But the last caretaker of La Alejandria only offers the protocol of a refusal through her maid: "'Maybe being prized as a monument was not Monica's trip,' Jack ruminates, resigned to a final departure from the past." Having transgressed boundaries and penetrated through the blocked passage between the heathen matrix (the cave) and the Christian (chapel), Jack bears the stigmata of emptiness and of repetition ineluctably oriented to the future.

Conceived as a repository of relics and monuments, can the past of personal and collective history be liquidated by the physical/geographical remoteness of Davao from Manila? Since the early seventies, Mindanao has emerged as the most fiercely contested piece of real estate in the whole archipelago, a battleground where the Bangsa Moro Army and its political leadership the Moro National Liberation Front has waged unremitting struggle against landgrabbing transnational corporations and the fascist state. But how explain Joaquin's blindness to this except through a parochial chauvinism that vitiates Joaquin's reading of pagan and Islamic history? In the late seventies and early eighties, clusters of towns surrounding Davao City, now the most beleaguered metropolis in the whole country, have been temporarily occupied by the New People's Army, so that in Jack's pastoral retreat, the past indeed returns as the long-repressed suffering and convulsive defiance of millions of Muslim and Christian peasants and workers deprived of any goddess parasitic on a patrocentric theology but nourished by the inexhaustible fertility of the earth and the procreative richness of revolutionary praxis.

Is the birth of the centered monadic subject, Jack Henson the "lonely man" flying back to exile (note the allusion to his Icarian/Luciferic image), thus aborted? Unable to possess or subordinate the female Other (wife, housekeeper, mistress), foiled by the women's (Chedeng, Monica) subterfuge, a gesture which repeats inversely Alfreda's original act of distancing, our inquisitorial agent of truth wrests the final answer from Monica but is thwarted from responding: "Then think it over, Jack—but don't let me know" (p. 271). Consequently the specular or Imaginary identity of truth is barred, hysteria forbidden. But because a demarcation has been established (Jack as progenitor of "heartless women"), he becomes the charisma-filled performer of ritual acts of defilement even as he himself has to violate boundaries and prohibitions to discover links, connections, passageways, attracted and repelled at the same time by the power of what Kristeva calls "the abject."[53] Unknowingly, Jack becomes other than what he thinks he is, differentiated largely by the circumstantial thickness of his milieu.

In part 5, Isagani Segovia purveys the empirical data on the origin of Ginoong Ina by repetition: "Urduja, born of a T'boli datu." He adds that "she's a myth because she wasn't an individual but a series of persons.... Who she is, as she herself would say, is irrelevant" (p. 519). We are caught in an endless chain of signifiers without beginning or end. It is this quasi-mythical speaking subject, an actantial mirage functioning as stand-in for what cannot be represented by realistic narration, that the text presents as the reliable authority on what really happened to Nenita Coogan. But this verbalization of the purported truth comes to us as a transcript (a parallel script) of Nenita's voice performed by another subject, vivid testimony to the relevance of Freud's theory of "deferred action" (*Nachtraglichkeit*): the recollection of the past depends on the intentionality of one's present project. In this context, the repetition and transmission of messages from one person to another, one generation to another, historicizes the myth just as the epiphanies of the Goddess textualized in the "flashback" interruptions of the chronological sequence may be considered as a counter-memory, a repudiation of Platonic recollection. Nature is now regarded as an archive of discourses, with writing performing this eccentric de-Platonizing strategy.

What the Ginoong Ina describes as the miraculous appearance of the numen (the Earth Mother of fertility and generation) to Nenita is the communication of a message, her passing from the profane to the sacred sphere (a reinsertion into the womb) where the alien is naturalized or nativized, the "American" becomes "Filipino":

And Nenita understood she was likewise being called to offer herself in love, so that a different rain might cleanse the land, and a different fertility enrich it, and a recalled race be returned to its roots, all its foreign disguises discarded at last. Nenita understood—and she gave her fiat. At that moment she became purely her Philippine blood.... The cave was open. And the goddess told Nenita she was free to go back to the world if she wished. But all wish for movement was gone from the girl. She felt herself full of stillness and love and the desire to stay. All she wanted now was the stillness of love. And she replied by going back to the inner cave and lying down again on the rock. That was when she became one with the goddess. (p. 265).

Is this how Joaquin cures the sin of Alfreda and the impotence of Jack Henson? The rewriting of the lacuna in the text by Ginoong Ina is disbelieved as "one possibility" by Jack whose inner isolation becomes pronounced when he is disabused of Pocholo's version of the crab-and-ghost scenario, the priestess avatar tracking down the absence of Yvette as the presence of Nenita manifesting herself to the hunted, personalized "private detective." The Lockean *tabula rasa* experiences a tremor: "Jack sat silent, unable to control a feeling of helpless dread."

What the Ginoong Ina does here within the precincts of the temple is to displace the analytic consciousness (the monadic ego caught in the narcissistic Imaginary double-bind) and shift the ground of communication to the mother-son level (the "Hen/son" metaphor resonates here) whereby the Goddess' "reason" becomes either immanent or structural:

> You have felt her touch, who do not believe—which is more than can be said for a believer like Pocholo, who prefers claptrap. . . . You have been called, Mr. Henson. You may run away now but you will find your way back in time. (p. 266)

Desire dies in the unfolding of time as remembrance while the dis-membered self becomes re-membered. A transitive reflection ensues when Jack prophesies "the revival of the old myth," the joint reappearance of "the renegade Christian and the pagan priestess" which the Ginoong Ina conceives of as "destiny." While Jack may be considered the hermeneutic decoder of the interludes on the pagan resistance to Christian monotheism, he disclaims any mandate, lacking "charity," the will to "take sides." But what the text enacts before the priestess exits is the production through matriarchal prophecy of a subject emptied of presuppositions, stripped of empirical ballast—the embryo of primal narcissism whose position of not taking sides accurately defines the domination of the Imaginary in the semiotic rhythm of the maternal-child union (time as repetition; degraded lived time renewed in the flux) where positions are exchangeable or alternating:

> It was the first time he had seen her smile and suddenly all these things that had happened were but as the sound of lyres and flutes.
> Hand on the doorknob, she stood in afternoon sunlight, in her purple plaid wrap-around and transparent blouse, her long black hair streaming down her back; and it seemed indeed as if from her face smiled four centuries of myth and mystery. (p. 267)

It is at this juncture where we can elucidate the cryptic, dispossessing figure of Nenita Coogan and the metamorphic Goddess whose epiphany the text reenacts by juxtaposing them with Jacques Derrida's suggestive commentary on Nietzsche, "The Question of Style." Derrida's remarks on woman's powerful impact as (in Nietzsche's phrase) "action at a distance" clarify the absences and discontinuities of Nenita, Alfreda, and Chedeng:

> Woman's seductiveness operates at a distance, and distance is the element of her power. . . . There *must* be (we *need*) distance; we must keep our distance from that which we lack, from that which we fail to do. . . . "Woman" is *not* just any thing, *not* just an identifiably determinate appearance that is imported at a distance from

> somewhere else, an appearance to draw back from or to approach. Perhaps, as non-identity, non-appearance, simulacrum, she is the *abyss* of distance, the distancing of distance, the thrust of spacing, distance itself—distance *as such,* if one could still say that, which is no longer possible . . . .
>
> The opening, separation or spread brought about by distancing gives rise to truth—from which woman separates herself in turn.
>
> There is no essence of woman because woman separates, and separates herself off from herself. From the endless, bottomless depths, she submerges all essentiality, all identity, all propriety, and every property . . . . There is no truth about woman, just because this abysmal separation from truth, this nontruth, is *the* "truth."
>
> Woman (truth) does not allow herself to be possessed. The truth about woman does not allow itself to be possessed.
>
> That which truthfully does not allow itself to be possessed is feminine.[54]

In this light, Ginoong Ina's smile transfixed by the disenchanted gaze instances what Derrida regards as the simulacrum, nonidentity, "the abysmal separation" and distancing which are also intimated by the divorces, earthquakes, gaps, hiatus, non sequiturs, chasms divulging apocryphal news.

We now come to the point of the narrative closure.

In contrast to the customary dénouement of romance where innocence is restored, the symbolic law of the Father reaffirm, and the moral order sustained, we witness here the construction of a subject-position which is open (Jack is a disillusioned non-believer), still unformed, susceptible to the interpellations of new historic forces displaced onto the scene. For, if we ask, what knowledge will Jack Henson transmit to Alfreda, the expectant Other in the land where the instruments of violence come from, we can only surmise that it is the experience of multiple dispossession, of the primal lack, which may be the allegorical equivalent of the opportunity seized by the September 1972 coup, delivering to us an authoritarian pseudopatriarch with his own paraphernalia of myths and hoaxes to mimic the Archbishop and the Princess. How this could happen given the inertia of the state apparatuses and the self-reproducing equilibrium of class forces depicted in the novel, may be accounted for by the dialectic between the imaginative will to textualize four centuries of myth and the racial unconscious into some intelligible linear / evolutionary form, and the perpetually exfoliating series of incidents and intersecting lives constituting the narrative quests and ordeals of the individual characters.

What I would argue in the rest of this chapter is that the subversive potential of the collective myths becomes sublimated if not discharged in the cathartic wish-fulfillment of art itself, or else becomes virtually encapsulated in hypostatized symbols and images broken from their concrete historical moorings, up for grabs by contending forces in real life. Because human need expressed as demand is not fulfilled by reality, desire becomes repetition—uninterrupted cultural revolution. This is the utopian vision inscribed in the economy of the psyche and insistently rendered by the form of the narrative.

From Disenchantment to Provocation

It will now become clear that Joaquin's project of blasting the continuum of a reified and homogenized history by the dialectics of a deconstructive narrative method—the annalistic commentaries embody the disruptive alterity of a past that, because forgotten and repressed, condemns the reader / writer to compulsively reject it—is open (by another hermeneutic operation) to the historicist idealism of a Hegelian idea translated as the energies of the Virgin Mother's numen unfolding in the populist, millenarian sects and movements in our history. Prised from the subterranean archives of the past, these anecdotes and images are retrieved with all their untarnished aura, evoking a hypnotic spell by its erotic promise and provocative lacuna. Of course, the reconstructed lineage of Ginoong Ina and the Archbishop is not pure mimicry but quasi-mimetic displacements in the archaeology of the narrative.

Still Joaquin seems vulnerable to the pathology of mere antiquarian nostalgia: "Just as a man lying sick with fever transform all the words which he hears into the extravagant images of delirium, so it is that the spirit of the present age seizes on the manifestations of past or distant spiritual worlds, in order to take posession of them and unfeelingly incorporate them into its own self-absorbed fantasies."[55] On the other hand, in a self-referential gesture, the text immunizes itself against that delirium when the Hermana in part 4 dismisses with her dying words the phenomenal whirligig as "All only shadows in a cave .... Oh, fly me outside!" But where is outside? When the torrents of rain after the fateful birthday revelations precipitate a landslide, the inside of the inner cave becomes an outside where the naked corpse of Benjie, the youthful activist, is exposed as gratuitous shrine offering while André Manzano's body is swallowed up by the angry river below.

Sabotaging the homogeneous and axiomatic time of the ruling class illustrated in the social relations of the Manzano family, Pocholo's office, etc., the "deferred impact" of the excavated and disinterred bodies (not only Nenita's but also the other ascetic virgins) suggests that the past cannot be safely sealed in the auratic halo surrounding fetishized objects like the touristic *santos,* or the cameos and bric-a-bracs populating Joaquin's *Almanac.* Like the empty cave, emblem of the unconscious and the tabooed *jouissance* of the female, the repressed traces of popular revolts and utopian wish-fulfillments exhumed by the text preserve their emancipatory force because, first, they resist a one-to-one correspondence with the manipulated Samahang Anito cult (its parody performs an eccentric reflection of the prophetic impulse); and second, they convey the possibility of the complete healing of the female body's wounds (the earth) and the recovery of what has been lost: the harmony of nature and civilization.

From another perspective, the time of the Now, Walter Benjamin's *Jetztzeit* "shot through with chips of Messianic time," is registered in the superimposition of the sacrificed bodies (Nenita, Benjie, André: deaths enabling symbolic exchange to proceed) on the moment of Adamic carnal awakening experienced by the Archbishop in his nuptial rites with the native princess in part 8, this conjugal liaison being the prelude to the insurrectionary offensive against the colonial intruders who had just defeated the Dutch in 1646—for Joaquin, the inaugural event of Western Christian victory over heresy and paganism:

> They were together all day long and it seemed to the Archbishop that his loinclothed body was waking from long sleep and had woken up young, to recovered wonder and this outlandish August. The heat was a new experience and so were the abrupt rains of the tropics. Nothing was not new, nor anything quite recognizable: bird or beast or flower or sensation. Earth was happening to him as a novelty, astonishing his senses, as though he had lost all memory or had exchanged earths, being now an Adam tasting mangoes and bananas for the first time, and black salted berries that stained the mouth violet, and gold-skinned lanzon that had a sweet meat the color of water and a bitter green seed.
>
> He watched the heathen at boisterous worship and could well have believed that here where nature was glut and riot the idea of One God became preposterous. Over the shouting and dancing worshipers hovered mountain had been trained to think of religion as urbanity but, watching the priestess at worship, could not but feel how right it was that she should look as wanton and sinister as the rite itself, as the jungle itself.
>
> That night he became her lover.[56]

While the Archbishop dominates this scene, it is in part 6 where the Edenic age of the Goddess judges the present time as fallen or corrupt, where the signifying practice of the text rewrites the past by denying the immanent telos of a spirit animating history: the discursive labor of selecting, cutting, editing, arranging of quotes, citations, testimonials, etc. This rhetorical practice, a creative destruction of paradigms and Platonic models, annuls the historicist mode of identifying a positivist self-becoming of an essence; its antiteleogical thrust counters the deductive-inferential, unilinear evolution of the plot where Jack Henson (enthroned Reason) charts the causality of events, digs up hidden motivations, and attempts to synthesize all the parts into a coherent and intelligible whole. The interruption of the realistic "thriller" plot of causality by bits and fragments of the utopian or archaic moments in the past shatters the bourgeois continuum of everyday life, unhinges the complacent ego, and initiates that fleeting moment of danger which Benjamin considers requisite to articulating the past historically, a process which "means to seize hold of a memory as it flashes up at a moment of danger," to seize a past "which unexpectedly appears to man singled out by history at a moment of danger" (see Jack Henson immured in the cave). The credible picture of the past, adds Benjamin, "can be seized only as an image which flashes up at the instant when it can be recognized and is never seen again."[57] This follows because "history is the subject of a structure whose site is not homogeneous, empty time, but time filled by the presence of the Now [*Jetztzeit*].... For every second of the time was the strait gate through which the Messiah might enter." [58] Simulacrum without genesis, the messiah here in Joaquin's text is woman, the disinheriting/ fructifying feminine principle symbolized by the twin figure of Demeter-Persephone.

From Inwardness to the Logic of Difference

We can now reposition the theme of sexual politics I noted in the beginning within the problematic of discontinuity and free play versus the anxiety for a central locus of meaning, being as presence.

Given the immanence of the discontinuous in the narrative, does history then wind up and dissolve into a timeless universal myth where the female messiah reigns supreme? No categorical answer can be given. One discerns a sustained tension in the narrative structure between the constative or declarative mode of representation (irreversible sequence, fixed attributes, etc.) and the interrogative or performative mode: for example, Jack Henson's "I promise Alfreda [or his other eclipsed double] to find out the truth about...." Coeval with this is the tension between the Enlightenment idea of secular progress as a cumulative development and an archaic conception of life as repetition of a model, an exemplary paradigm. In the space of the hiatus one can locate Joaquin's prophetic deconstruction of the present, his strategy of reinscribing desire into an institutionalized past and a consumer-oriented but equally reified future.

In the general economy of the novel, the utopian vision I alluded to above is refracted by the contradiction between the unilinear unfolding of the detective plot (the odd-numbered parts) which strives to purge the pollution / guilt implicating the whole society so as to restore a primordial innocence, and the tortuous intertextual labor of the hermeneutic sleuth (the even-numbered parts). Each one interrogates the other. The detective (Jack Henson) fails to grasp an apodictic knowledge, an unequivocal truth: *aletheia* radiant in conscience. Redemptive apocalypse is aborted. Such is the fate of the Cartesian ego and instrumental reason. But his specular counterpart, the archival anthologist and quoter of texts (memoirs, documents of the missionary orders, folk legends, rumors, etc.), succeeds in identifying an elusive "presence" or its traces, the ghost of a generative life-force metamorphosing in history. Contradictions, permutation of surrogates, parallelisms, and tropes of rebirth or resurrection function as the matrix of the signifying process. We observe how the archival decoder reenacts for the characters (and for readers) what they cannot think or imagine: recurrence, causal successions becoming simultaneous substitutions. There is no discernible beginning or ending in the subtext, in the evolving menippean plot of the Filipino people's quest for liberation and wholeness.

In the vicissitude of reenacting what has transpired—an act of disinterring or exhuming the body for an inquest, the narrative generates an incommensurable paradox: the arrow of time reverses itself, boomerangs.

We encounter a moment of undecidability: if the moral fable involving Jack Henson and his complicitous circle hinges on the Christian doctrine of personal responsibility within the context of time as a pilgrimage to redemption, then this fable is inescapably subverted by the cyclical or, more precisely, asynchronic returns characterizing our recollection of the past. There is no origin, telos, or unmediated presence in the intertextual space of recovered history to ascribe guilt or innocence to; there is only the already inscribed terrain of *deus absconditus*, a permanent sliding of the signified under the signifier. Gaps and fissures in the metonymy of discourse ceaselessly generate possibilities, dissimulations, analogies, prefigurations. To be sure, part 8 concludes with the reputed reincarnation of the native priestess in the 1896 uprising; and the allusion to La Hermana Beata returns us to the beginning: the ongoing struggle over the cave, the interdicted womb. This gesture of recapitulation and reversal operates on the level of national allegory, with individual psychology marginalized so that the instrumental logic (the metaphysics of rational prudence) of part 9 suffers the vertiginous pressures and dissonances of the text's infinite duplicity. This yields an aporia whose configuration sutures the time shifts of the alternating chapters and the reconstituted body/cadaver of Helen/Nenita Coogan. In this interweaving of synchrony and diachrony, does the Ginoong Ina have the last say after all?

What has enabled this ingenious dialectic of temporality between a chiliastic view of life and the countervailing belief in recurrence is the inaugural sacrifice of Nenita Coogan. Her death and the mystery surrounding it, reduplicated by Henson's vision and the caesural intertexts, initiates the exchange of signifiers and the corresponding play of interpretations. This circulation of signs would be chaotic if it were not circumscribed by the cave, the sacred milieu, over which various social-ideological forces struggle. Written large, this cave is the Philippines, the body inhabiting power or *socius* whose identification is now the object of sharp political contestation. The text's project of reconstructing the past, the genealogy of the cave and its occupants, may be read as Joaquin's attempt to diagnose our contemporary predicament as the clash between the patriarchal rationalism of the elite (La Alejandria) and the creative imagination, the revolutionizing impulse, of the masses (personified by the Goddess, her avatars and hierophants), between the technocratic and hierarchical West exemplified by Henson's thinking and the egalitarian impetus of the native resistance. If the cave (the telluric matrix, the chthonic opening) supersedes everything, the earth itself splitting and uncovering what has been buried by layers of accumulated legalisms, chicaneries, and expediences of custom, then history and the anticipation of fundamental changes are undermined. Space is bargained for time: the strategy of protracted people's war.

Whose side is Joaquin—or his persona—on? Perhaps this question is gratuitous and irrelevant. In any case, only a judgment of the relative weight of antithetical parts of the text (both syntagms and paradigms), of the subject of discourse (hypostatized egos, events as given) vis-à-vis the speaking subjects (the praxis of a versatile ventriloquism) can supply the answer. On this topic of the "political unconscious" of the text I devote the concluding section of this reading.

Celebrating the Breakthrough

Construing this novel as the fullest expression of Joaquin's vision of history as a fable of the messianic breakthrough, we can now define the nature of the narrative's performance as an ideological representation of the crisis suffered by the Filipino middle stratum caught between the more intense predatory exactions of U.S. transnational interests and the accelerated growth of radical egalitarian mass insurgency in the late sixties and all throughout the seventies. This crisis is particularized in the collapse of the Manzano dynasty and its patriarchal authority, with the alien (U.S.) power absorbed or domesticated in the naturalization (in all senses) of Nenita Coogan and its role as haven for both Alfreda and Chedeng Manzano. At the same time, the text provides a mode of indispensable fantasizing by which the individual subject (Jack Henson; the narrator, reader) can invent and map its lived relationship with the hegemonic systems and institutions (family, church, state, etc.) and thus, through a network of rhetorical devices and constraints, attain an illusion of stable self-identity, an illusion because the two promises Jack makes (one to Alfreda, the other to Chedeng) are left unfulfilled, thus opening up this authorial channel to the ellipses and sliding of a signifier endlessly repositioned by successive interpellations (by Ginoong Ina, Isagani Segovia, etc.).

Precisely because it deconstructs the ratiocinative and valorizing intentionality of Jack Henson and frustrates the happy traditional closure of families reunited, alliances repaired, and contracts salvaged, the narrative generates that self-estrangement of the narrator conducive to the messianic intervention of the repressed, a *peripeteia* underscored by the violence of the storm, flood, earthquake—signs of molecular flows, quanta of intensity that cross and recross the threshold of the cave, the hymen of time and consciousness.

From this angle, the cave becomes not the Platonic theater of illusions or the Freudian womb where Jack, like Alice in Wonderland, discovers the connection between the pagan past and the Christian present, but the magical space of transformation. It becomes a locus where the molar nodes of patriarchal power interact with the molecular pulsations of "polymorphously perverse" bodies and the nomadic, destiny-defying line of the repressed energies disclosed in folk traditional practices, arcane scripts, and revitalization rituals whose latest filiation is the Sambahang Anito. The cave may be read as an *a-topia*, a place outside the Law, shut down by the government (a figure for the 1972 imposition of martial law), the refuge of transcendence and the crucible/fountainhead of virginal *jouissance*.

If the children's sacrifice in the struggle to reopen (deflower) the cave symbolizes the release of the phallus (not the penis but the Lacanian phallus designating the symbolic "lack" necessary for communication and exchange in society to be established), the threshold or "hymen" of the cave itself—the site of the conflict of forces—may be the antithesis of oedipal castration, the emblem of the undecidable addressed by Derrida in *La Dissemination*. Derrida perceives the "hymen" as what subverts hierarchies of power and refutes the fallacy of representation:

> The hymen, confusion between the present and nonpresent . . . "has taken place" in the *between*; it is the spacing between wish and fulfillment, between perpetration and memory. . . . Hymen—consummation of differents, continuity and confusion of coitus, marriage—becomes confused with what seems to be its place of derivation: hymen as protective screen, casket of virginity, vaginal partition, thin and invisible veil that, for the hysteric, maintains itself *between* the inside and the outside of woman—hence between the wish and its fulfillment. It is neither the desire nor the pleasure but between the two. It is the hymen that the desire dreams of piercing, of bursting, with a violence that is (either, both or between) love and murder. If the one or the other had taken place, there would be no hymen—but even if they had not occurred, there would still be no hymen. Hymen, with its completely undecidable meaning, hasn't happened except when it has not happened, when nothing *really* happens, when there is consummation without violence or violence without thrust, or thrust without mark, mark without mark (margin), etc., when the veil is torn *without being* torn; for example, when someone is made to die of laughter or happiness.[59]

Like Joaquin's Virgin Mother and the androgynous Santo Niño, in a sense undecidable figures, the cave signifies the elision of desire, transitional point between a past convulsed in its death-throes and a future struggling to be born: the interregnum of the hymen. Of course, as Pierre Bourdieu has shown in *Outline of a Theory of Practice* (1977), the polysemous richness of discourse and actions, their complicities and reappropriations, rests on the specific practices of material existence, the *habitus*, circumspect movements of everyday work.[60]

Associated with the cave is the figure of the Virgin, matrix of fertility, who incarnates a utopian vision of fulfilled desire exemplified, for example, by one American Indian chief's enunciation of totality: "We and the earth, our mother, are of one mind."[61] If the myth of the archaic mother counters the plenitude of an annulled tradition, the absence/separation of Alfreda (wife/mother), the absent/present corpse (become cadaver under the gaze of male authority) of Nenita Coogan, and the detached/attached position of Chedeng Manzano all serve to body forth the fantasy of narcissistic completion that defines the persona Jack Henson. In contrast, the text practices Joaquin's ecosystemic strategy (mediated through the Goddess and her multiple understudies) and endeavors to redeem the unmanned Jack, the *ressentiment*-filled Pocholo, the self-castrated Alex, and the anguished Don Andong with its dislocating impact: the mystery of Nenita Coogan's death and her invasion of the cave's sanctuary may be taken as the irruption of distance and difference, the cutting up of the space for heterogeneity, semiotic novelty, and carnival. In this prophetic perspective, history now articulates itself as a series of breaks generated by internal contradictions, exorbitant inadvertencies that the text strives to resolve through various rhetorical maneuvers:

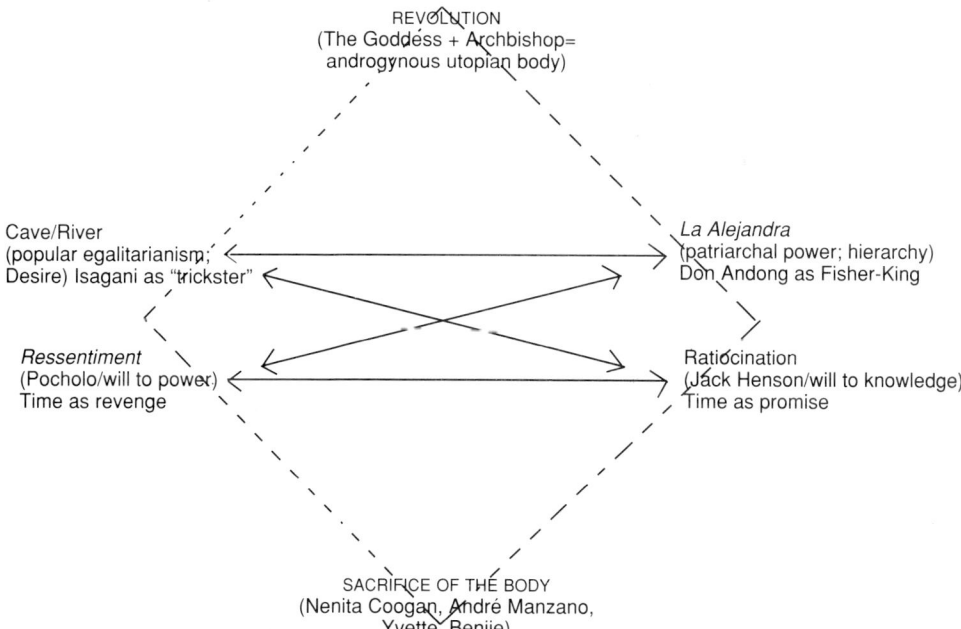

As for Alfredo Coogan and Chedeng Manzano, and the lack of an equivalent for the Archbishop's place vis-à-vis Ginoong Ina, we can suggest that the two mothers betoken the nomadic force, the woman who has torn free from the terminalistic reign of the patriarchs and has migrated to the decoding and deterritorialized realm of capitalism, "a relativity without recourse." Into the Archbishop's slot we can insert Pocholo, the shaman/trickster who manipulates, and Isagani Segovia, the hieratic unmasker and demystifier; in effect, the Archbishop is one instance of the actantial function of Joaquin's Faustian hero mobilized to unfix Original Sin and overthrow the patrocentric State of property-owners by an act of dispossession. Or could it be that this function has now been appropriated by the theologians of struggle and the partisans of an indigenous, local "nihilism"?

Within the framework of the initiation ordeal and education of Jack Henson, the fantasy of revenge (and its sadomasochistic ambivalence) embedded in the chronicles and in Pocholo Gatmaitan's reactive cunning as well as in Isagani Segovia's anti-Platonic ruses, is played out in a scandalous catharsis: Jack's awe at the purificatory spectacle of Yvette's killing after the "live show," an implied foil to the "Eleusinian" mystery and the ascetic practices of the cave. The final blow of decentering comes when the torrential flood wrests André's body from Jack's grasp. We no longer find here the nostalgic for a self-evident "truth" intertwined with the "navels" of Connie Vidal.

Now shorn of the famous exotic and flamboyant style of *Prose and Poems*—here the Latin idiom finds a modulated tone in the archival interludes—with a self-effacing protagonist imbricated in an astringent style, Joaquin's practice finally negates the ascribed "heroism of repentance." It now introduces the collective enunciation of the oppressed in a disabused, exteriorizing discourse produced by a messianic sensibility, flows of an ever oscillating libidinal economy, a montage no longer of the ego recuperating a lost or mutilated identity (the hegemonic Western ideologeme) but of ceaseless transformations where the moment of *peripeteia* discloses the misrecognitions of the subject (protagonist, empathizing reader, implied author) and its self-betrayals.

What the novel *Cave and Shadows* ultimately renders then is an erasure of genesis by repetition and parallel scripts: who can tell the origin of the myth, the prime mover of Nenita's entombment/enwombment? And, together with that, an abolition of telos or preconceived, informing purpose: What has Jack Henson gained? Does he return back to the same position as before? The dominant intertextual strategy negates origin and telos by deploying a de-Platonizing counter-memory through the triangulation of desire among the various characters: for example, Jack, Pocholo, Isagani Segovia, Pocholo, Alex Manzano, Jack Henson, and so forth. An analogous triangulation may be discerned in an understudy of this novel,

"Balikbayan" in *Joaquinesquerie: Myth a la Mod* where the American-born Billy (like Nenita) becomes the field of struggle between the mother Mrs. Daryo and the spirits of the ancestral town-fathers, with matriarchal filiation winning and capitalist deterritorialization circumventing the old order.

Certainly, in this novel and also *The Woman Who Had Two Navels* the ecosystem has been severely disturbed, the artifice-ridden emplotment of actors revealed by the earthquake as anchored to complex material practices. Ultimately the Judaeo-Christian Faustian will (which explains Joaquin's fascination with mechanics) incarnate in Pocholo and Jack Henson is defeated by the artifices of the feminine and its principle of semiotic multiplicity or intertextuality bereft of the castration (oedipal) trauma. If the Judaeo-Christian antiphysis ideology is responsible for the dualism of humans and nature (flesh / evil versus soul / good), in which a Platonic rationality controls nature for the sake of spiritual transcendence, here we see how asceticism, self-mortification and other worldly sublimations are contravened by the anti-Platonic Virgin worship of the heretical movements seeking to rehabilitate nature, replace alienated production by communal reciprocity, and sanction a pantheistic Joachite regime. Patriarchal supremacy and the fetishism of Reason are subverted all throughout by the ironic mystifications and the menippean heteroglossia of the narrative. Refusing the rule of the Fathers and affirming the resurrection of bodies, the millenarian sects (recall the Adamic conspiracy in "The Order of Melkizedek") evoke not the nostalgia for origins, not an orgiastic craving for nirvana and the apotheosis of the pleasure principle as against the reality principle, not even the Virgin Mother; but rather the enigmatic figure of Walter Benjamin's *Angelus Novus*—perhaps Nick Joaquin's double—face turned toward the past where "one single catastrophe" piles wreckage upon wreckage before him; he would like to stay, awaken the dead, recompose the debris, but "a storm is blowing from Paradise which irresistibly propels him into the future to which his back is turned, while the pile of debris before him grows skyward."[62] We may call this storm (circa the last quarter of this century) the raging Filipino people's national democratic revolution.

8 Demystifying the Past, Unfetishizing the Present, Reinventing the Future

The Golden Age, which blind tradition has placed in the past, is in the future.

—Henri Saint-Simon

The real genesis is not at the beginning, but at the end.

—Ernst Bloch

Sòyez realiste, demandéz l'impossible!

—Communal demand, Paris, May 1968

IN HIS FAMOUS DISCOURSE "What Is an Author?" Michel Foucault argues that in order to limit "the cancerous and dangerous proliferation of significations" and polysemous meanings, post-Cartesian scholarship in the human sciences has prioritized the author as the "principle of thrift." Frightened by the glut of meanings, Western culture invented this ideological figure of the author, this disciplinary agency of the author, in accord with the sanctity of private property and the authorizing power of the individual entrepreneur in the "free" market. Bourgeois norms dictate that if someone could own and transgress, he could also be punished, fined, imprisoned, etc. Foucault observes further that "the author is not an indefinite source of significations which fill a work; the author does not precede the works; he is a certain functional principle by which, in our culture, one limits, excludes, and chooses; in short, by which one impedes the free circulation, the free manipulation, the free composition, decomposition, and recomposition of fiction."[63]

One way of circumventing this logocentric strategy of postulating the author as creator of autotelic art is to invoke the mediation of personal testimony and the criteria of the empirical inventory.

Seizing the temporary absence in Manila of his brother-in-law (then visiting Spain where he met "those dark-eyed señoritas from romantic La

Palma de Mallorca") as an opportunity to respond to persistent requests, Sarah K. Joaquin wrote a rare "profile" of Nick Joaquin for *This Week,* issue of 13 March 1955, presumably solicited by the editors. Her account renders in a series of recollections not so much the psychology of the author as his "death" in the figural sense that Roland Barthes gives it in his essay, "The Death of the Author," and in the process captures via montage and spatial mapping the writerly ambience which gives the lie to the myth of the artist's self-identical, autochthonous genius.

Nicomedes, Onching, Nick, the playwright of "Portrait," the ad hoc composer of the Far Eastern University (FEU) hymn, etc.—the putative integral self disappears, even the masks disintegrate, dispersed over the scene of writing constituted by those oscillating instants where presence and absence meet. Where is the original self or psyche of which the public personae are mere reflections? We get a premonition of this effect in Sarah's initial warning: "For Nick has a special hatred for pictures—his pictures." Indeed, what can a photographic image reveal? As she insightfully puts it, it was print that produced Nick, separated "Onching" from the author, and then distributed the remaining fragments to a discontinuous, aleatory series in which three items may be selected as heuristic "spots of time": first, the dialogical quest for the father, a reconciling gesture addressed to the vanished patriarchal ethos—"When he did not have anything to read he would get his father's law books, which were in Spanish"; second, the break with formal schooling (school should be considered here as the prime institution of U.S. colonialism to guarantee cooptative bourgeois hegemony) and its replacement by churches as the alternative if not oppositional site where the games of time may unfold; and third, the return of the repressed when Sarah finds herself "six years later . . . cast in the very play which I thought was impossible to stage." This return of the "play" of language and writing, destroying the author's monadic identity or its illusion, finally assumes a collective presence at one moment of "emergency" when Nick's lyrics become the memorized FEU hymn sung by generations of students and thus explodes the idiosyncratic, unrepeatable subjectivity of "Onching/Nick" into anonymous bits and fragments—voices interpreting signs whose origin and metaphysical genealogy have been irretrievably lost. But Sarah, after manipulating the device of the family testimony and the deposition of peer and colleague, escapes the ghost of the paternal surrogate: "I am trying to get this written and published before he comes because I know he would never have allowed me to do this if he were here."

So "Nick Joaquin" appears in and through his absence, a trace whose tenor is perpetually deferred. Desacralized, emptied of any positive referent, the scriptor of our texts now becomes a subject-position, an intertextual score ready to be performed and enunciated by us (readers here, now). Let us explore further the problematic of biography and its implications to elucidate the crisis of the author-function from another perspective. It may be appropriate to transcribe here a few facts: Born in Paco, Manila, in 1917, Joaquin studied in the public schools. After his father's death—his father was a colonel in the revolutionary struggle against Spain—Joaquin is said to have lived with his sister-in-law and, after the Japanese occupation, worked as stage manager for her acting troupe, the Filipiniana Troupe. After submitting his essay "La Naval de Manila" (October 1943) to a contest sponsored by the Dominicans, he was awarded a scholarship to St. Albert's College in Hong Kong in 1947 to study for the priesthood. But he left in 1950 with a knowledge of Latin and a rich experience in the seminary. His story "Guardia de Honor," which won the *Free Press* short story contest in 1949, together with the publication of *Prose and Poems* in 1952, placed him in the first rank of Philippine writers. His first cited story, "Shooting Stars," was published in 1943 in *Graphic*. From 1950 on he was a staff member of the now defunct *Philippines Free Press*. He has won several awards: Rockefeller grant, Journalist of the Year, and finally National Artist of the Philippines.[64]

When the *Free Press* asked him for his biography, Joaquin's reply took the form of a telegraphic communiqué:

I was born in Paco, where I spent an extremely happy childhood . . . I have no hobbies, no degrees; belong to no party, club or association; and I like long walks; any kind of *guinataan;* Dickens and Booth Tarkington; the old Garbo pictures; anything with Fred Astaire . . . the *Opus Dei* according to the Dominican rite . . . Jimmy Durante and Cole Porter tunes . . . Marx brothers; *The Brothers Karamazov;* Carmen Miranda; Paul's *Epistles* and Mark's *Gospel;* Piedmont cigarettes . . . my mother's cooking . . . playing *tres-siete;* praying the Rosary and the *Officium Parvum* . . . I don't like fish, sports, and having to dress up . . .[65]

In this piece of apparent veridical testimony, we confront the epitome of Joaquin's modernizing sensibility: spatial ordering, comic montage, a decentering intertextuality. The juxtaposition of the Marx Brothers with Dostoevsky's masterpiece, of the Gospel with Carmen Miranda and Piedmont cigarettes, etc. is of course not intended to be naive parody, systematic burlesque, or satiric undercutting. This method inheres in what I have pointed out earlier as the subliminal drive of the discourse to effect an imaginary unity of self out of a hypothetical or assumed coherence in culture and society.

In *Understanding Media*, one of Joaquin's scriptural sources for his scientistic reductionism, Marshall McLuhan notes how modernist art—from Baudelaire and Flaubert to Joyce's *Ulysses*, symbolism and surrealism—appropriated the structural mode of the newspaper "to evoke an inclusive awareness" and "effect a complex many-leveled function of group-awareness and participation such as the book has never been able to perform."[66] McLuhan's "progressivism," however, confesses its regressive, dehumanized kernel when he comments on the Vietnam War: "As a crash program of Westernization and education, the war consists of initiating the East in the mechanical technology of the industrial age."[67] In any case, the ethos and design of the newspaper serves as one influential model for the erstwhile journalist-editor in which to graft the analogical mentality of a former novice learned in patristic hermeneutics with the serializing and at the same time homogenizing dynamics of the electronic media today.

The preceding chapters may be taken as an extended meditation on the feminine *mythos* as figure and discursive principle in Joaquin's art. I may add here that the pagan correspondence of the Virgin with the Demeter-Kore (Persephone) mythologeme which lies at the heart of the Greek Eleusinian mystery rites—the authentic model of the tatarin feast—indicates how, again, Joaquin sublimates the urge to return (the *apocatastasis*) to the miraculous origin or beginning in an acceptable orthodox form. This resembles the hierophant's experience of "being in death" as he celebrates the showing forth of the sprouting of seed into blossom and fruit; in this context, the artist assumes the hierophantic persona.

The other mythologeme which supplements and complements the Virgin is the Santo Niño child cult which, like the Kore (Demeter/Persephone), evokes the cosmogonic deity of archaic religion as hermaphrodite. Carl Jung and K. Kerenyi have investigated thoroughly the archaeological background and psychological significance of both the Kore and the Primordial Child in their book *Essays on a Science of Mythology*. Jung has observed how, parallel to Christ's androgyny in Catholic mysticism, the divine child (Santo Niño) is the archetypal symbol for the creative union of opposites, the *coniuncto* of male and female, the conscious and unconscious, thus a primordial image of hierogamy (the marriage of female and male deities). The divine child symbolizes the wholeness of primordial being; in gnosticism and other metaphysical practices, this anthropomorphic archetype—also imaged in the funerary child icon as sepulchral phallus—functions as a unifying and healing emblem, connecting for example the preconscious (the child before coming to reason) and the postconscious (rebirth after death) phases of existence.[68] In his essay, "The Santo Niño in Philippine History," Joaquin interprets the image of the divine child, which is now conflated with the Virgin in the androgynous Nenita Coogan, the absent-present protagonist of *Cave and Shadows*, as our rightful national emblem, this image being inherently "revolutionary": "The Santo Niño represents the new, the novel, the revolution we underwent with the coming of Christianity, and the national culture we now proudly call Filipino. He is the pagan in us, and he is also the Christian; he is our past, and he is also our present, he is the old, and he is also the new; he is the conservator, and he is also the revolution."[69]

As against the segmental bureaucratic procedures of the twentieth-century technopolis and the capitalist chronotope theorized by Poulantzas, Joaquin contraposes the emblem of the Santo Niño, the bridge or transitional liaison between past, present and future. If anything, the modernist impulse in Joaquin moves him to orchestrate experimental decreations, the elliptical avant-garde style of stream-of-consciousness and plural perceptions, witty reflexive texture, T.S. Eliot's luminous symbol outside time, and fugal arrangements, with a compulsive predilection for an art of the hieroglyph, rebus, and charade. Such emblematic art, suturing the image, motto and explanation together (as in the *Almanac*), is programmed to produce silent parables and portentous talismanic signs that distort surfaces to unveil forever deferred origins. This may explain Joaquin's obsessive quest for beginnings, as in tracing the mass to "the oldest and most primitive of human rites—the eating of a chieftain's flesh and the drinking of his blood—to Christ's adaptation of it in the sacrament of the Last Supper."[70]

We are always tempted to repeat what previous critics have said about Joaquin's seemingly incurable fixation on the Catholic Spanish past, as for instance Armando Manalo's opinion that in Joaquin's stories "the past exist as a standard, a norm, with which to compare and against which to judge the imperfect present."[71] On the other hand, if the present is so degraded, what point is there in closely monitoring and recording it? In his introduction to Jose Lacaba's book *Days of Disquiet, Nights of Rage,* Joaquin valorizes that most ephemeral accounting of the quotidian, testimony and reportage: "Because literature today—when involved, engaged, committed, militant—itself becomes a 'hurrying of history.'"[72]

Consequently I would suggest that there is no such thing as the timeless past, the fetishized primal scene, in Joaquin which is not invaded, recaptured, and assimilated by a present that is hostage to the future. One can hazard the proposition that, faced with the now stereotyped crisis of representation whereby realist, ego-centered conventions no longer seem adequate to express history defined as a "process without subject," Joaquin is forced to adjust his metaphysical-idealist *Weltanschauung* with empirical notations (McLuhan), or explode the presumed unity of the transcendental ego, the post-Cartesian rational psyche, with the enigmas of the body, the "polymorphous perverse" drives once invested in archaic rituals and myth-laden memory. The subject (ego-centered consciousness) is thus put on trial when sexual difference, the reproduction of gendered subjects, power and meaning through sacrifice of one kind or another to establish the socio-symbolic contract, occupy the focal concern of the narrative. With the notion of a fixed identity exploded and temporality pluralized, the texts begin to constitute a fluid and heterogeneous subjectivity or subject-position that questions phallocratic power and class oppression.

In many stories whose theme has been formulated as the conflict between Christian freedom and pagan fatalism ("Three Generations" or "Guardia de Honor," for instance), we see time transformed from *chronos* to *kairos*. We perceive a demystification of present circumstance as a fall, a corrupted web of false appearances prefiguring an eventual redemptive exposure and discovery, a trial to be enjoyed and suffered; an affirmation of the present as the truthful fulfillment of the past, a working out of grace by violence, guilt-exorcising actions, revenge and repentance; and a witnessing to the truth of how the present cannot be saved, understood and mastered unless the unconscious/the body as psychosexual process and historical construct takes center stage and overrides the hubris of Western reason, the discourse of phallocentric metaphysics, the sexism of capital.

In the process of trying to recuperate the libidinal potency of the past, Joaquin is caught in the trap of what Lacan calls the "mirror phase of infancy," the Imaginary state where the scopic drive or perceptual passion predominates: every other is seen as the same as the subject. In this stage, exclusion and difference do not exist. It resembles the life of the bourgeois individual who operates on a spontaneous natural code (ideology), unable to envisage the other as different. In negotiating a break from this impasse, Joaquin may have learned from Rizal's distantiating technique, his defamiliarizing mode as shown for example in chapter 3 of *El Filibusterismo* where Fr. Florentino's recounting of the tale of "Doña Jeronima" is framed within the conflicting perspectives of his listeners, "the others," who constitute the specular truth of the narrative.

Is it believable that, as the title of one of Joaquin's discourses says, "The Past Always Returns?" In what sense should we take this "return"?[73]

Postulating that the artist "creates the cultural community," begets his kind of audience, and that art "is a wedding, the result of intercourse between artist and audience "—a dialectical conception removed from the elitism of Pound's belief that artists are "the antennae of the race"—Joaquin goes on to describe instead the dependence of artists like Shakespeare and Emily Dickinson on the material infrastructure and cultural milieu in which they find themselves. He contends that "because there was an audience for 'proletarian' literature, 'proletarian' literature was produced—and its finest works will survive as universal literature because, again, the artist and his audience both felt the need to express at a particular time the specific circumstances then of the human condition." So then art endures, instructing and delighting because it transcribes, discriminates, and renders judgment on the contemporary and urgent problems of the time.

Joaquin goes on to confess that when he wrote about what was then familiar to him in the immediate prewar days, his readers considered him strange, "baroque" with an "outlandish theology and . . . barbaric style and language." He explains this asymmetrical relation as due to the fact that "the American Occupation had so alienated Filipinos from their past that they could no longer even see what of the past will have survived in those days." But times have changed, the alienation has somehow been purged, and Joaquin insists that his function after all has been to make explicit what was hidden and that he merely expressed a subterranean impulse in his audience who in secret was preparing to acknowledge him as their spokesman in the collaborative forging of the historical conscience of the nation. This populist self-assessment (circa 1977) of Joaquin's writings vis-à-vis an audience whose problematic identity lapses into the Imaginary, is rare and deserves to be quoted at length:

> Any minute now I expect some breathless critic to discover that the outlandish extravagant barbaric style of Nick Joaquin is no more and no less than the style of, say, the Morong Church, or the jeepney, or the Ati-Atihan, or the embroidery on the *barong tagalog.*
>
> In short, I had found an audience; and maybe I had created that audience or had helped to create the climate for such an audience. A Nick Joaquin story no longer looks outlandish in the era of *santos* as artifacts and of processions as culture.
>
> ... I repeat my initial dictum: the artist is the audience. I think there was bound to be a reaction against the Americanization of Filipino culture during the American era. The past we rejected was bound to come back because, after all, it had been our culture for some 400 years.
>
> I think it was this reaction, this obscure yearning or nostalgia for what we had set aside in favor of Hollywood and Manhattan, that was bound to break out sooner or later. I just happened to be around when it was bound to happen.
>
> The audience was there, waiting to be expressed—though I might have thought at first there was *no* audience. But it seems now that I was expressing a more or less general impulse. We were all wanting to be reminded that the Filipino has a grandfather, that the Filipino didn't begin with Dewey's Battle of Manila Bay.
>
> I merely brought back that grandfather. Of course, when he first appeared in my early stories, nobody could make head or tail of him in the same way that nobody could see a Picasso until Picasso had trained the eyes of an audience to see a Picasso. This may sound immodest—but it's the standard process in art.
>
> You couldn't see me either when I first started writing, nor could I, alas, see you—but in this era of La Plaza and La Azotea and what have you, in all the chi-chi hotels and art galleries, we realize that you and I were wanting to express what had to be expressed—if Filipino culture is to achieve a reintegration. If we are to rediscover our grandfather: you and I, driven by the same impulse.[74]

What comes out here are two contradictory positions: the first, postulating that a turnabout in thinking and taste has occurred in which the artist may have participated (his role is hypothetical) so that now the writer's style and themes are fully appreciated; and the second, a self-aggrandizement of the artist's vatic and combined Orphic/Apollonian role as the tribune of the "general impulses" of the nation, the agent of "reintegration" mediating what the society unconsciously felt and what the writer consciously wanted. Less inconsistency or equivocation, this ambivalent stance is symptomatic of the tension in Joaquin between the passive (the female register) and the active personal—Jack Henson, Chitong Monzon, Connie Vidal, etc.—but it does not confirm the thesis that "The past always returns" unless this past is nothing but the unconscious that demands to be heard—what I denominate as the "subversions of Desire." Can a revival of antiquated forms and outmoded mentalities release the repressed?

In "Popcorn and Gaslight," Joaquin bewailed the endemic "social amnesia" which he felt afflicted his compatriots, "our apathy to and even contempt for our own past"; and because the native stage traditions depended on the continuity of Spanish culture, when that culture declined in the twenties, the native theater also died. [75] By association, then, to revive Filipino theater must one revive the zarzuela and the *moro-moro*? Formalism need no more eloquent exponent than Joaquin here. So what happens to the ceaselessly mutable "general impulse" in society that artists should apprehend and flesh out in appropriate practices? And what of the artist's creative and innovative function in shaping tastes, criteria of judgment and aesthetic values?

It is remarkable how Joaquin's vehement antiecumenical hostility against Moro culture and Moro claims to independence and integrity can only be matched by his equally intolerant animus toward the vernacular, specifically Tagalog writing, as shown in "What Price Our Writing in English?"[76] Here the argument displays the same hedging and equivocations as in "The past always returns" when Joaquin seeks to explain that Jose Garcia Villa, although a writer in English, was also produced by "400 years of a particular kind of historical process and cultural development" as the Spanish intellectuals. But this same history somehow excludes the vernacular writers whose oral style, unaffected by the superior visual tradition of Spanish and English writing, possesses no "sense of history," lacks detail and irony, prompting him to hand down the verdict: "For good or ill, our literature in English is the standard against which our literature in the vernacular will have to measure itself." Paradoxically, when he begins to describe the complex harmonies in English fiction, his metaphors—"quiet of tone," "noisy," "louder," "very noisy," "very garrulous" which ascribe positive virtues to writing in English—are all aural, the dire stigmata of the oral culture of the vernacular bards and storytellers. No longer are we concerned with the audience nor with "general impulses"; this self-appointed Devil's Advocate in an aristocratic peremptory gesture now subordinates language, art and literature to the paramount business of "living," "life itself."

This is, I think, the moment to note that Joaquin's crusade to defend and eulogize an irrevocably dead Hispanic culture encounters the more preponderant secular code of acquisitive individualism enforced by the State which, in the era of monopoly capitalism, is the only force that can establish a viable relation between history and territory, individualizing the people-nation within a segmented, serial, divided time-space matrix. The material organization of capitalist historicity for the Filipino people is inescapably the nation-state; whether we like it or not, territorial-national traditions can be concretized only within the confines of the Nation-State on the face of imperialist ethnocentrism and chauvinism whose spurious claim to catholicity is backed by arms, dollars, and the weight of self-reproducing tradition and habits.

Because the Philippines is still struggling to construct its identity as a sovereign nation-state, the *socius* still remains fluid, the object of competing and antagonistic interpellations one of which is Joaquin's, the other the powerful U.S. technocratic consumer rationality, and the last the popular revolutionary culture developing in the midst of concrete struggles. Schematically viewed, Joaquin is the residual; the U.S., the hegemonic or dominant; and the popular discourses, the emergent culture; the present conjuncture may be grasped as a complex heteroglotic interpenetration of all three. Because Joaquin's discourse is a heady mixture of the *ilustrado* aristocratic and the popular, he suffers a division signalled by his adoption of a mask: "Quijano de Manila." This is not a quixotic double or alter ego, a legal ruse or parodic evasion; it resembles a Yeatsian mask which, following the tradition of Diderot and Hobbes, enables us to objectify ourselves, to become "actors of ourselves" and imitate the life which, according to Hobbes, we "create first in dreams."[77] Such impersonation, artificial and counterfeit for the puritanical ethos and for romantic sensibilities like Rousseau, is required by the fragmented and mutilated condition of modern urban existence. The Dostoevskyian double and Baudelaire's schizoid *flaneur*, like Quijano de Manila, mirror the volatile antinomies and fluctuating dissonances of the modern crisis; but unlike Quijano de Manila, their *métier* of producing a mask of persona in the public sphere does not require the desideratum of fetishizing the past. On the contrary.

I have discussed in the introduction Joaquin's project of reinventing a public sphere in which the private, interior self can be allowed free play; a sphere where the Aristotelian division of *nous* (mind) and *psyche* (emotions) can be bridged, where the Augustinian antithetical cities can intersect and at least conduct a dialogue. His discursive strategy is to outline a genealogy of the city, Manila, by invoking the Spenglerian Faustian hero which inaugurates urban anomie and capitalist reification. In an article celebrating Manila, "400 Years a City," Joaquin contemns Islamic culture and lauds Western ingenuity: "Where a Magian maze had been, a cluster of arabesques, Legazpi implanted Faustian geometry."[78] It is here that Joaquin explicitly defines his conception of history as "the self-consciousness that recognizes events . . ." which are recorded "in proper chronology and specific detail"; such self-consciousness, coeval with "a literate culture," of course can be identified, as he does in "History as Culture," with the minority elite, the *ilustrado* or *principalia*, which now become founding culture heroes. A shrewd strategic move. This now explains why Joaquin has deliberately fetishized 1521 and 1565 as the origin of "Filipinoness" in that the diachronic sequence traced by Joaquin, following McLuhan and Spengler, punctuates the rise of the ilustrado, the propertied and educated elite, as the hegemonic class. This version of history can be clearly seen actualized in *A Question of Heroes*, *The Aquinos of Tarlac*, and practically all the journalistic "historical" pieces that in general describe the cultural and psychic metamorphoses of the pettybourgeois, middle strata. In the synchronic organizing of single instants or vertical cross-sections of time patterned on the newspaper, as I have noted earlier, the *tour de force* performances are the *Almanac* and also the *The Aquinos of Tarlac* with its homologizing morphology. In both "an eschatological framework helps conservative politics masquerade as ethics in an ostensibly aesthetic enterprise."[79]

The individualistic Faustian model that displaces the Virgin and occludes the Santo Niño in Joaquin's discursive grammatology may be deemed a function of the baroque sensibility sensitized to a decaying social structure brought about by the capitalist division of labor, alienated work, and insidious commodification of everything including the psyche. Joaquin's vision of history may be termed "baroque" in that it denotes simply a chronicle of recurrent events, a relentless turning of fortune's wheel, where people are motivated chiefly by perverse discontent and other humours. In *A Question of Heroes* and *The Aquinos of Tarlac* "history" unfolds as the conspiratorial maneuverings of villains and heroes, mere succession without development, an architectonic frieze. Concealing the concrete ground, the infrastructure of socioeconomic processes, and transcribing only the surface dance of passions, reflexes, wills, Joaquin's "history" strikes us more as a baroque funeral pageant adorned with all the mesmerizing finery of a Renaissance triumphal procession.

By a supreme irony, Joaquin's history translates into mythical thinking when we realize that the Faustian culture heroes function as allegorical devices, allegory being defined as the will to reconcile spirit and objects in contrast to symbolism which can be grasped as the confirmed reconciliation of consciousness and the world. In the modern urban, postindustrial world where things have been separated from meanings, from spirit, from authentic life, allegory becomes the dominant and privileged mode of expression. We decipher the import of every moment, painfully endeavoring to restore some organic continuity to the chaotic series of instants that were once fused in a highly cathected, single moment in the symbol. The Virgin, Santo Niño, Faust, the three kings in "The Order of Melkizedek," etc.—these are all emblems or scripts in Joaquin's discourse which, in a world grown lunatic, empty, a veritable wasteland of ruins, corpses, demonic instinctual forces, remain the surviving key to some still unprofaned realm of truth, community, plenitude—the long awaited apocalypse of freedom, justice, equality, *jouissance*. Against the ruins of Intramuros and the duplicitous carnival of treachery and violence in *The Woman Who Had Two Navels* and *Cave and Shadows*, Joaquin, the disenchanted chronicler of paraliturgical practices, rituals and other telltale symptoms of the unconscious, stages the allegorical drama of our national existence. The power of this art is perspicuously elucidated by Walter Benjamin:

Allegories are in the realm of thoughts what ruins are in the realm of things. . . . Where the symbol as it fades shows the face of Nature in the light of salvation, in allegory it is the *facies* hippocratica of history that lies like a frozen landscape before the eye of the beholder. History in everything that it has of the unseasonable, painful, abortive, expresses itself in that face—nay, rather in that death's-head. And while it may be true that such an allegorical mode is utterly lacking in any "symbolic" freedom of expression, in any classical harmony of feature, in anything human— what is expressed here portentously in the form of a riddle is not only the nature of human life in general, but also the biographical historicity of the individual in its most natural and organically corrupted form. This—the baroque, earthbound exposition of history as the story of the world's suffering—is the very essence of allegorical perception; history takes on meaning only in the stations of its agony and decay. . . . The amount of meaning is in exact proportion to the presence of death and the power of decay, since death is that which traces the jagged line between Physis and meaning.[80]

If Joaquin is our allegorist *par excellence*, his amateur, ad hoc theorizing can now be linked to "theory" in its Greek sense of "theater," and to "theorist" as referring to: envoy sent to visit the oracle in search of divine communication and interpretation of the god's message; state ambassador delegated by one polis to attend another's sacred festivals and games; spectator at games and foreign exotic places.[81] The theorist then described and appraised oracles, festivals, and games that comprised performances revealing the truth (*aletheia* = unhiddenness) in an attitude of wonder, puzzlement and canny susceptibility. Such performances constitute the drama whose signifiers an audience (*theoria*) can read and interpret for the shrouded truths (*aletheia*) they incarnate. In all these senses, Joaquin's art may be assayed as a profound theorizing of our spiritual predicament, our collective destiny, as a people in which the theorist, like this critic and everyone else, is as fatefully and urgently implicated.

In "The Virgin and the Dynamo," W.H. Auden distinguished the "Natural World of the Dynamo" where "freedom is the consciousness of Necessity" from the "Historical World of the Virgin" where "Necessity is the consciousness of Freedom."[82] One can sum up Joaquin's writing as an intensely haunting dialogical play of the imagination with such differences, a dialectic of theory (in the Greek sense) struggling to celebrate the dreamed-for and much prophesied wedding of nature and history.

Notes

1 *The Education of Henry Adams* (Boston: Houghton Mifflin, 1961), pp. 383-89.

2 *Religion in the Secular City* (New York: Simon & Schuster, 1984), p. 170. See also Cox's earlier books *The Secular City* (New York: Collier, 1966) and, for a revaluation of festivity and fantasy, *The Feast of Fools* (New York: Harper, 1969).

3 Alan Watts, *Myth and Ritual in Christianity* (Boston: Beacon, 1968), pp. 107-13. See also Mircea Eliade, *Myths, Dreams, and Mysteries* (New York: Harper, 1960), pp. 155-230. Joaquin evinces knowledge of "mariolatry" in *Almanac for Manileños* (Manila: Mr. & Ms., 1979), pp. 118-20.

4 Watts, p. 108.

5 Ibid. On the notion of history and the sacred, see Michael Harrington, *The Politics at God's Funeral* (New York: Harper, 1985), pp. 132-37.

6 *The Second Sex* (New York: Grove, 1952), p. 193. De Beauvoir is seconded by Mary Daly, *Beyond God the Father* (Boston: Beacon, 1973), pp. 90-92.

7 *La Naval de Manila and Other Essays* (Manila: Alberto S. Florentino, 1964), p. 30.

8 Ibid., p. 28. Of relevance are these historical resumes: Carmen G. Nakpil, "A History of Maynila," *The Philippines Quarterly* (March 1976), pp. 3-5; Teodoro Agoncillo, "The Last Years of Intramuros," *Archipelago* (1975), pp. 15-22.

9 Edward Said, *Orientalism* (New York: Pantheon, 1979). A critique of U.S. "Orientalist" discourse on the Philippines may be found in my *Crisis in the Philippines: The Making of a Revolution* (South Hadley, Mass.: Bergin & Garvey, 1985).

10 Quoted in Edward Said, *Beginning* (New York: Columbia University Press, 1985), p. 203.

11 Quoted in Edward Said, *The World, the Text, and the Critic* (Cambridge, Mass.: Harvard University Press, 1983), p. 111.

12 Nick Joaquin, "Culture as History," *The Manila Review* 3 (1975), p. 13. Except for the elaborate enumeration of tools, etc. inspired by McLuhan's reductive technologism, this long essay conflates the basic idea of "La Naval de Manila" and other later pieces collected in *Discourses of the Devil's Advocate and Other Controversies* (Manila: Cacho Hermanos, 1983).

13 Julia Kristeva, "Women's Time," *Feminist Theory*, ed. Nannerl O. Keohane, et al. (Chicago, 1982), p. 35.

14 "The Art of Ancient Egypt," *The Philippines Quarterly* (December, 1960), p. 25.

15 Joaquin, "Culture as History," p. 25.

16 Nicos Poulantzas, *State, Power, Socialism* (London: Verso, 1978), pp. 101-3. Cf. Raymond Williams, *The Country and the City* (New York: Macmillan, 1973), pp. 1-12, 279-306.

17 Poulantzas, p. 107. On spatial politics, see Michel Foucault, *The Foucault Reader* (New York: Pantheon, 1984), pp. 239- 56.

18 Poulantzas, pp. 108-9.

19 Lewis Mumford, *The Culture of Cities* (New York: Harcourt, 1970), pp. 71-72. See Gideon Sjoberg, *The Pre-Industrial City* (New York: The Free Press, 1960), pp. 327-28: "The periodic religious ceremonies, in which a large segment of the community may participate, are one of the few mechanisms the city possesses for integrating disparate groups in an otherwise segmented community."

20 Marshall Berman, *All That Is Solid Melts Into Air* (New York: Simon & Schuster, 1982), pp. 142-66. On the city as festival, see Henri Lefebvre, *Everyday Life in the Modern World* (New York: Harper, 1971), pp. 122-24, 205-6.

21 Quoted in Fredric Jameson, *Marxism and Form* (Princeton, N.J.: Princeton University Press, 1971), p. 73.

22 See Paula Webster, "Matriarchy: A Vision of Power," *Toward An Anthropology of Women* (New York: *Monthly Review*, 1975), p. 147; see also Rayna Rapp, "Gender and Class: An Archaelogy of Knowledge Concerning the Origin of the State," *Dialectical Anthropology* 2 (1977), pp. 309-16; also S. Ortner, "The Virgin and the State," *Michigan Papers in Anthropology*, Vol. 2 (1976).

23 Paul Ricoeur, "Narrative Time," in *On Narrative*, ed. W. J. T. Mitchell (Chicago and London: University of Chicago Press, 1980), p. 176.

24 Carl Jung, *Four Archetypes* (Princeton, N.J.: Princeton University Press, 1959), pp. 35-36.

25 On the "phallic mother," see Julia Kristeva, *Desire in Language* (New York: Columbia University Press, 1980), pp. 191-200, 238-42.

26 On "transitivism," see Jacques Lacan, *The Language of the Self*, trans. Anthony Wilden (Baltimore and London: Johns Hopkins University Press, 1968), pp. 27, 159-60.

27 On the concept of "chora," see Julia Kristeva, *Desire in Language* (New York, 1980), pp. 6, 133, 174, 284-87); see also her *Revolution in Poetic Language* (New York: Columbia University Press, 1984), pp. 25-28; *Powers of Horror* (New York: Columbia University Press, 1982), pp. 1-89.

28 Louis Althusser. *Lenin and Philosophy and Other Essays* (London: Verso, 1971), p. 204. For an exposition and critique of Althusser's theory of ideology, see Paul Hirst, *On Law and Ideology* (Atlantic Highlands, New Jersey: Humanities, 1979), pp. 1-74.

29 On the intertextual relations between "The Legend of the Dying Wanton" and its historical sources, see Florentino Hornedo, "The Source of Nick Joaquin's 'The Legend of the Dying Wanton,'" *Philippine Studies* 26 (1978): 297-309.

30 All quotes from the plays are from *Tropical Baroque* (Manila: National Book Store, 1979).

31 See Francis Barker's account of the constitution of the Cartesian (bourgeois) subject which sheds light on Bitoy's bifocal consciousness in *The Tremulous Private Body* (London and New York: Methuen, 1984).

32 For an exposition of Lacan's "Imaginary Order," I recommend Anthony Wilden, *The Language of the Self* (Baltimore: Johns Hopkins University Press, 1968), pp. 159-77.

33 On *jouissance*, see Julia Kristeva, "Women's Time," *Feminist Theory: A Critique of Ideology*, ed. N. O. Keohane, M. Rosaldo, and B. Gelpi (Chicago: University of Chicago Press, 1982), pp. 31-54.

34 Nick Joaquin, "Beatas: the Intrepid God-seekers of 17th Century Manila," *Archipelago* 3 (1976), p. 11.

35 Ibid., p. 16.

36 For the ideology of the folk-carnival in European literature, see M. Bakhtin, *The Dialogic Imagination* (Austin: University of Texas Press, 1981), pp. 167-205.

37 In addition to *The Secular City* (New York, 1965), Cox has updated his critique of metaphysics in describing the "theology of liberation" in *Religion in the Secular City (New York, 1984)*.

38 *Beyond God the Father: Toward a Philosophy of Women's Liberation.* (Boston: Beacon, 1974).

39 *Sexism and God-Talk: Toward a Feminist Theology* (Boston: Beacon, 1983), p. 134.

40 Quoted in Ann Rosalind Jones, "Writing the Body," *The New Feminist Criticism (New York: Pantheon, 1985), p. 365.*

41 Ibid., p. 370.

42 Michael Hollington, "Baroque," *A Dictionary of Modern Critical Terms*, ed. Roger Fowler (London: Routledge Kegan Paul, 1973), p. 21

43 On "expressive realism," see Catherine Belsey, *Critical Practice* (London: Methuen, 1980), pp. 7-14, 46-47.

44 "Feminist Theory and Dialectical Logic," *Feminist Theory*, p. 107-9.

45 Ibid., p. 109.

46 For the concepts of "deterritorialization," "desiring-production," and so forth, see Gilles Deleuze and Felix Guattari, *Anti-Oedipus* (Minneapolis: University of Minnesota Press, 1983). For *jouissance* and the "phallic mother," see Julia Kristeva, *Desire in Language* (New York, 1980), pp. 15-16, 192-95, 242-43; *Revolution in Poetic Language* (New York, 1984), pp. 75-81, 142-51, 178-91, 204-12.

47 A suggestive guide to the novel is Regina Garcia-Groyon, "Joaquin's Connie Escobar: Fall and Rise," in *Philippine Fiction*, ed. Joseph Galdon (Quezon City: Ateneo de Manila University Press, 1972), pp. 25-45. See also in the aforementioned collection Josefina D. Constantino, "Illusion and Reality in Nick Joaquin," pp. 13-24. Other studies are: Abdul Baksh, *The Filipino Novel in English* (Quezon City: University of the Philippines Press, 1970), pp. 110-14; and Laura S. Oloroso, "Nick Joaquin's La Vidal': A Study in Characterization," *The MST English Quarterly* 13 (1963): 1-6.

48 For "Symbolic" and "Imaginary," see Jacques Lacan, *Ecrits* (New York: Norton, 1977), pp. 65, 180-87, 191-97; also Lacan's *The Four Fundamental Concepts of Psycho-Analysis* (New York: Norton, 1978), pp. 279-81. For commentaries, see Anthony Wilden, *The Language of the Self* (Baltimore, 1968), Anika Lemaire, *Jacques Lacan* (London: Routledge Kegan Paul, 1977), Juliet Mitchell, *Psycho-Analysis and Feminism* (New York: Vintage, 1974) and Jane Gallop, *The Daughter's Seduction* (Ithaca, New York: John Hopkins University Press, 1982), pp. 18-55, 80-89, 129-30.

49 Deleuze and Guattari, pp. 130-38. See also Michel Foucault, "Theatrum Philosophicum, *Language, Counter- Memory, Practice* (Ithaca, N.Y.: Cornell University Press, 1977), pp. 165- 98. For a Marxist objection to *Anti-Oedipus*, see Henri Lefebvre, *The Survival of Capitalism* (London: Allison & Busby, 1976), p. 34.

50 Francis Barker, *The Tremulous Private Body* (London & New York, 1984), p. 105.

51 Gilles Deleuze and Felix Guattari, *Anti-Oedipus* (Minneapolis, 1983), pp. 329 ff. I am indebted to this work for concepts I've used throughout this book: "desiring-machine," "desiring-production," "decoding," "deterritorialization," etc. See also Gilles Deleuze and Felix Guattari, *On the Line* (New York: Semiotext(e),1983), which contains "Rhizome" and "Politics." Cf. Jean Baudrillard, *The Mirror of Production* (St. Louis: Telos, 1975) for a critique of Marxist productivism, especially "Judaeo-Christian Anti-Physis."

52 Alexandre Kojeve, *Introduction a la lecture de Hegel* (Paris, 1947), p. 368, quoted in Anthony Wilden, *System and Structure* (New York: Tavistock, 1972), p. 66.

53 Julia Kristeva, *Powers of Horror* (New York, 1982), pp. 1- 2, 14.

54 Jacques Derrida, "The Question of Style," in *The New Nietzsche* (New York: Dell, 1977), pp. 178-79.

55 Quoted in Terry Eagleton, *Walter Benjamin* (London: Verso, 1981), p. 52.

56 Nick Joaquin, *Cave and Shadows* (Manila: National Book Store, 1983), pp. 220-21.

57 Walter Benjamin, *Illuminations* (New York: Schocken 1973), p. 255.

58 Ibid.

59 Jacques Derrida, *La Dissemination* (Paris, 1972), pp. 237- 41, translated by David Allison, p. 189.

60 Pierre Bourdieu, *Outline of a Theory of Practice* (Cambridge: Cambridge University Press, 1977), pp. 72-95, 114-58. For a historical survey of "the patriarchal system" *(tota mulier in utero)*, see Evelyne Sullerot, *Woman, Society and Change* (New York: McGraw Hill, 1974), pp. 19-42.

61 Quoted by Anthony Wilden, p. 487.

62 Walter Benjamin, pp. 257-58. On the symbolism of the cave as cosmic "center," see Mircea Eliade, *Images and Symbols* (New York: Harper, 1969), pp. 27-56; on the theme of initiation, see *Mircea Eliade, Rites and Symbols of Initiation* (New York: Harper, 1958), pp. 61-80.

63 *The Foucault Reader,* ed. Paul Rabinow (New York, 1984), pp. 118-19. See also his *Language, Counter-Memory, Practice,* ed. Donald Bouchard (Ithaca, 1977), pp. 113-38; Janet Wolff, *The Social Production of Art* (New York: New York University Press, 1984), pp. 117-36.

64 Data culled from: Nick Joaquin, *Tropical Gothic* (St. Lucia, Queensland: University of Queensland Press, 1972), pp. vii- viii; Antonio Manuud, "Joaquin, Nick," *The Penguin Companion to Literature* 4 (London: Penguin, 1969), p. 264.

65 Quoted in Maximo Ramos and Florentino Valeros, eds. *Philippine Cross Section* (Quezon City: Phoenix-Alemar's, 1964), p. 128.

66 McLuhan, *Understanding Media* (New York: New American Library, 1964), p. 193.

67 Quoted by McLuhan's most trenchant critic Sidney Finkelstein in his *Sense and Non-Sense of McLuhan* (New York: International Publishers, 1968), p. 117.

68 Carl Jung and Karl Kerenyi, *Essays on a Science of Mythology* (New York: Harper, 1949), pp. 92-98. See also Mircea Eliade, *Myths, Dreams and Mysteries* (New York: Harper, 1957), pp. 155-89.

69 *Discourses of the Devil's Advocate and Other Controversies* (Manila, 1983), p. 118.

70 Quoted in Antonio Manuud, ed., *Brown Heritage* (Quezon City: Ateneo de Manila University Press, 1967), p. 784.

71 Quoted in Lourdes Busuego-Pablo, "The Spanish Tradition in Nick Joaquin," *Philippine Fiction,* ed. Joseph Galdon (Quezon City: Ateneo de Manila University Press, 1972), pp. 59-66.

72 Jose Lacaba, *Days of Disquiet, Nights of Rage* (Manila: Salinlahi Publishing House, 1982), p. 10.

73 *Archipelago* 4 (1977): 13-16.

74 Ibid., p. 16.

75 *La Naval de Manila and Other Essays* (Manila, 1964), p. 45.

76 *Discourses of the Devil's Advocate,* pp. 65-74; also in *Philippine Quarterly of Culture and Society* (1978), pp. 118-24.

77 Excerpt from *Leviathan* in Richard Sennet, ed. *The Psychology of Society* (New York: Vintage, 1977), p. 21.

78 *Philippines Free Press,* 2 January 1971, p. 38.

79 Fredric Jameson, *Marxism and Form* (Princeton, N.J.: Princeton University Press, 1971), p. 324. On a critique of the technocratic account of culture, see Armand Mattelart, "Introduction" and "Communication Ideology and Class Practice," *Communication and Class Struggle*, ed. Armand Mattelart and Seth Siegelaub (New York: International General, 1979), pp. 23-72, 115-23.

80 Quoted in Jameson, pp. 72-73.

81 Stanford Lyman and Marvin B. Scott, "The Drama of Social Reality," *The Psychology of Society*, ed. Richard Sennett (New York, 1977), pp. 110-11.

82 W. H. Auden, *The Dyer's Hand and Other Essays* (New York: Random House, 1962), pp. 61-62.

Index

A

Abel, 170
Abraham, 97, 98
Achilles, 122
Acquisitive individualism, secular code of, 20
Activism, secular, 63
Adam, 97, 98, 100, 184
Adamic conspiracy, 191
Adamic hearth of the vestal virgins, 90
Adams, Henry, 1, 2
Adonis, 34
Advice to Girls in These Parlous Times," 64
Aestheticism, 15, 49
Agamemnon, 107
Agape, 76, 127
Age of the Father. *See* Old Testament
Age of the Son. *See* New Testament
Agon, 11, 126
Agricultural societies, 34
Agueda, Doña, 28, 29, 30, 31, 32
Agueda and Don Badoy, case histories, 28
Aguinaldo, Emilio, 11, 99, 152, 154, 155, 156, 157
La Alejandria, 174, 179, 186, 189
Aletheia, 202, 203
Alexandrian masculinist supremacy, 173
Alice in Wonderland, 188
Almanac for Manileños, 7, 8, 9, 13, 183, 196, 201
Alvaro, 119
Amada, 35, 36
American (s), 35, 53, 54, 156, 157, 162, 171, 180

Anabaptist rebellion, 97
Anagnorisis, 173
Anarchy, 104
Anchises, 122
Angelus, 112
Angelus Novus, by Walter Benjamin, 191
Anglo-Saxon culture, 136
Anti-Christ, 96, 97
Anti-Kafkaesque motive, 91
Anti-Oedipal decoding, 167
Anti-Oedipal schizoid, 145
Anti-Platonic Virgin worship, 191
Anti-Virginal secularization, 2
Antipolo, 90
Antiquity, 10, 13
Antonia, 127, 128, 129, 134
Aphrodite, 34, 111
Apocalypse, redemptive, 185
Apocatastasis, 195
Apollonian structure, 6
Aquino, Benigno Jr., 170
The Aquinos of Tarlac, 201
Arcanae of Florentine Neo-Platonists, 141
Archaic rite, cult of, 32
Archaic societies, 13
Archbishop, 72, 73, 74, 75, 131, 132, 133, 183, 184
Archbishop's See of Nueva Segovia, 178
Arché, 175
Archetype, dynamism of the, 49
Aristeo, 119
Aristotelian division of *nous,* 200
"The Ancient Art of Egypt," 8
Asia, 133
"Asianization of the Filipinos," 6
Astrology, device of, 8

"At the Sign of the Milky Seed. Deck Six," 97
Ateneo de Manila University Press, 105
Atheists, 7
Atlantis, Cathay, 133
A-topia, 188
Attis, 34
Auden, W. H., 174, 203
Augustinian, 96, 143, 200
Authority, subversion of, 39
Autonomy, 5
Autotelic art, 192
La Azotea era, 198
Aztec fertility goddess, 2

B

Baal, 97
Babel, 59, 64
Babylon, 17, 85, 89
Bacon, Roger, 46
Badoy, Don, 29, 30, 31, 32, 33
Baguio, 92
Bakhtin, 145, 169
"Balikbayan," 191
The Ballad of Five Battles, 111
"Ballad," 110, 116
Baltazar, 99, 100, 101, 114, 115
Banaag, Mrs., 92, 95, 97, 101
Bangsa Moro Army, 179
Banzon, Chayong, 59, 60, 61
Banzon, Tony, 59, 61, 63, 121, 122, 123, 124
Barbara, 131
Barker, Francis, 173
Barros, Maria Lorena, 134
Barthes, Roland, 193
Bathala, 97
Baudelaire, Charles, 15, 16, 194, 200
Beata (s), 130, 132, 133, 155
The Beatas (play), 3, 27, 125, 126, 128, 130, 132, 133, 134, 141
"Beatas: The intrepid God-seekers of 17th century Manila," 125
Beaterio, 125, 126, 128, 131
Beauvoir, Simone de, 4
Being-with-Others, 38, 39, 43
Belief, superstructure of, 46
Benjamin, Walter, 16, 119, 184, 185, 191, 202
Benjie (youthful activist), 183
Berman, Marshall, 15
Bernini's Saint Theresa, 141

Bernini's Saint Theresa, 141
Bessie, 26, 138, 139, 141
Biak-na-Bato, Pact of, 155
Bildungsroman, 57
Bilibid Viejo, decline of, 8
Biliken, 145, 147, 148, 149, 156
Billy, 191
Black Christ in procession, 157
Black Death, 97
Blake, 63, 126
"Body of God," 48, 49
Bonifacio, Andres, 8
Bontoc, 92
Book of Daniel, 96, 98
Borges' Library, 8
Borja, Sonya, 84, 85, 86, 87, 89, 92, 93, 95, 99, 101, 102
Borromeo, Conching, 154, 164, 165
Borromeo, Esteban, 147, 151, 157, 164
Bourdieu, Pierre, 188
Bourgeois, the, 22, 109, 170, 171, 173
Brecht, 142
Bureaucratic alienation, 84
Bureaucratic dependency of foundations, 174
Bureaucratic-military corruption, 27
Bureaucratic power, 101
Byron, 30, 136

C

Cabrera, Angel, 59, 60, 62, 63
Cabrera, Lulu, 59, 62, 63, 64
Cabrera, Noe, 59
Caesar, 107
Cain, 170
Calezon, Fray, 85, 91, 97, 100, 101, 102
Calvin, 4
"Calvin's shadow," 5
Camacho, Bitoy, 61, 62, 117, 118, 119, 120, 121, 123, 124, 125
Candida, 119, 120, 121, 122, 123, 124, 125, 141
Candido, 77, 78, 79, 80, 81, 82
"Candido's Apocalypse," 12, 76, 84, 174
Capital, sexism of, 197
Capitalism, 10, 40, 61, 65, 83, 98, 190, 200
Capitalist (s), 10, 12, 18, 20, 27, 33, 54, 76, 102
Caravaggio's painting, 141
"Carnal Christ," 86
Carnal church, 96
Carretela King, 139

INDEX

211

Cartesian cogito, 91
Cartesian ego, 174, 185
Cathedral, 94
Catholicism, 34, 35, 77, 79, 195
Cave and Shadows, 3, 8, 11, 12, 13, 14, 15-16, 76, 84, 103, 135, 136, 190, 195, 202
Ceres, 34
Charismatic power, 101
Chartism, rise of, 28
Chauvinism, 57, 200
Chavez, Dr., 49, 51, 52, 53
Chavez, Fe, 49
Child-Deity, 58
Chinatown temple, 148
Chinese, 8, 11, 145, 155, 157, 168
Chinese Moon, 145, 150, 153, 163, 166
Christ, 3, 10, 34, 71, 90, 96, 97, 98, 99, 106, 109, 110, 114, 132, 154
Christian, 13, 45, 134, 179, 181, 188, 196
Christian doctrine, 100, 186
Christian faith, 66, 76
Christian freedom, 5, 39, 143, 145, 178, 197
Christian humanism, 63, 149, 151
Christian mythology, 3, 30, 115
Christian Revelation of Saint John of the Apocalypse, 96
Christianity, 4, 7, 10, 13, 34, 45, 98, 101, 125, 177, 195
Christianization of the native, 7
Christmas, 115
Christology, 132
Christos (female), coming of, 126
Christos messiah, 101
Christos-redeemer, 98
Chronos, 31, 198
Church, 2, 46, 96, 127
Circumcision, feast of the, 90, 102
"Citizen of the World," 151
City, liberation of the, 12
"City of God," 96
Civil power, 6
Cixous, Helen, 135
Class, 3, 12, 84
Classical/feudal matrices, 9
Cogito, 173
Cold war, 58, 76, 104
Coleridge, 78
Collected Verse by Joaquin, 105
Collective Desire, flows of, 102
Collective destiny, 38
Colonial Hispanic World, 46

Colonial politics, 164
Colonial society, 19, 146
Colonial tyranny, 126
Colonial virgin, 67
"The Comment Ungallant," 112, 115, 116
Commodity exchange system, 146
Commonwealth era, 52
Communal faith, 28
Communal form of society, 34
Communal society, primitive, 33
Communal solidarity, 5, 124
Communal territory, spirit of, 33
Communal tribe-house, 5
Communist, 106
Communist China, 146
Communist victory, 100, 105
Communist Manifesto, 28
Comprador capitalism in U.S. colony, 120
Comprador class, 88
Comprador-landlord-bureaucratic ruling block, 11
Concha, Doña, 53, 55, 56, 57, 58, 167, 168
Conquistador (es), 46, 72, 100, 113
Constitutional authoritarianism, 27, 173
Contra mundum, 120, 124
"Contribution to the Critique of Hegel's Philosophy," 64
Coogan, Alfreda, 135, 171, 172, 173, 174, 180, 181, 182, 185, 190
Coogan, Nenita, 8, 12, 13, 171, 172, 175, 177, 178, 180, 181, 183, 186, 187, 189, 191, 195
Corpus Christi, 102
Corregidor, fall of, 8
Cox, Harvey, 2, 76, 129
Crane, Hart, 114
Creation of the world, 46
Crisis in the Philippines, 10
Cross and Conquistador, 75
Crucifixion, pilgrimage to, 149
Cultural artifacts, 58
Cultural codes, 91
Cultural community, 197
Cultural development, 199
Cultural relativism, 53
Cultural revolution, 182
Cultural ritual, 3
"Culture," 2, 46, 58, 66, 144, 199, 200
"Culture as History," 2, 6, 9
Customs, 29, 79
Cybele, 34

D

Dacanay, Chedeng, 50, 51, 52, 53, 174, 178, 179, 181
Daly, Mary, 131, 133
Daryo, Mrs., 190
Dasein, 43
Davao, 12, 174, 179
Days of Disquiet, Nights of Rage, 196
De Losada, Luisa, 128
De Salcedo, Mariana, 126
De Santa Maria, Sebastiana, 127
De Vera, Ana, 70, 71
"Death Be Not Proud," 107
Death, metaphysics of, 173
"The Death of the Author," 193
Death-worshipping technocratic machine, 102
Deity as a child, 56, 57
Del Espiritu Santo, Francisca, 128
Dela Cruz, Apolinario, *Cofradia* of, 126
Deleuze, 102, 103, 145
Deleuze-Guattari, 161, 165, 178
Delilah, 30
Demeter, 34
Demeter-Kore, 195
Demeter-Persephone, 137, 158, 185
Derrida, Jacques, 6, 181, 182, 188
Desire, 25, 31, 35, 39, 40, 42, 83, 126, 159, 165, 176, 188
Desire, *écriture* of, 95
Desire, phenomenology of, 155
Desire, subversions of, 83, 199
Deus absconditus, 186
Deus ex machina, 175
Devil's advocate, 200
Dickinson, Emily, 197
Diderot, 200
Diffused Law, 53
Dionysian/Bacchic frenzy, 35
Dionysian celebration of the Spanish Renaissance, 69
Dionysian *materia*, 6
El dios pobre, 96
"La Dissemination," by Derrida, 188
Diwata, 76
Doctrine of Divine Election, 14
Dogmatism, 28
Domingo, Father, 126, 127, 128, 129, 130, 132, 133
Dominican (s), 20, 68, 194
Donne, John, 126
Dostoevskyian double, 200
Dostoevsky's masterpiece, 194
Dualism, 82
Dutch defeat in 1646, 184
"Dynamic National Uplift" (Commonwealth election rally), 60
Dynamo, 9

E

Earth mother, 180
Easter, 115
Eastern and western mores, 155
Ecclesiastical authority, 128
Economy, libidinal, 135
Eden, 91, 99, 108
Edong (son of Doña Concha), 54, 55, 57, 58
The Education of Henry Adams, 1
Ego cogitans, 170
Egyptian art, 8
1872 Cavite Uprising, 8
1896 revolution, 15, 17, 52, 140, 151, 165, 186
1899 Filipino-American war, 1
The Eighteenth Brumaire, 84
"Eleusinian" mystery, 190
Eliade, Mircea, 3
Elijah, 74
Eliot, T. S., 83, 141, 196
Elisa, Aunt, 40, 42
Elite, 7, 202
El (Zaduk), 97
Engels, 33, 100
Enlightenment, 12, 140, 141
England, 72
English writing, 199
Entoy, 136
Episteme, 65
The Epistle to the Hebrews, 100
Eros, 49, 106, 111, 126, 172
Escobar, Connie, 145, 146, 147, 148, 149, 150, 151, 152, 153, 155, 156, 157, 158, 159, 161, 163, 165, 166, 167, 168
Escobar, Macho, 12, 145, 146, 150, 151, 154, 156, 157, 161, 162, 163, 166, 168
Essays on a Science of Mythology, 195
Establishment power, 95
Esteban, 39, 42
Estiva, Sid, 85, 86, 87, 88, 89, 90, 91, 92, 93, 94, 95, 96, 97, 98, 99, 102, 171
"Eternal Feminine," 136, 164

"Eternal gospel," 96
"Eternity," 7
Ethical dualism, 19
Ethnic grouping, 7
Ethnocentrism, 55
Eucharistic analogy, 107
Europe, 4, 5, 28, 29, 72, 133, 141
Eve the sinner, 4
Exodus, 98
Explication du texte, 17

F

Faith, victory over technology, 97
Fall and salvation, 10
Fall, Bernard, 58
False Apostles, sect of, 96
Family, 38, 39, 80, 172
Far Eastern University (FEU) hymn, 193
"Farewell to flesh," 127
Father's Law, 125, 130, 134, 145, 146, 167
Father Master, 8, 26, 68, 106
Fathers and Sons, 25, 26, 27, 135, 138, 141
Faulkner, 19
Faust, 203
Faustian hero, 15, 190
Faustian culture, 201
Faustian individualism, 14
Faustian scientist, 46
Faustian spirit, 6, 9
Felix culpa, 150
Female, 2, 7, 127, 135
Femme couchant, 157
Fernando, Brother, 66, 67, 72
Ferrer, Adela, 85, 86, 88, 94
Ferrer, Santiago, 86, 93
Ferrer, Sid, 101
Ferrero, Andong, 40, 43-44, 79, 189
Ferrero, Natalia, 40, 42, 43, 44
Fertility, cult, 145, 169
Fertility, matrix of, 189
Festival of the Oppressed, 15
Festivities, religious calendar of, 9
Feudal oligarchy, 162
Feudal patriarchy, 20
Feudal social formations, 9-10, 17
Feudal spatial matrix, 10
Feudal survivals, 20
El Filibusterismo, 197
Filipiniana troupe, 196
Filipino (s), 3, 6, 7, 14, 45, 51, 91, 120, 125, 145, 155, 156, 157, 172, 177, 179, 180, 198

Filipino culture, 7, 198
Filipino identity, 6, 172
Filipino insurgents (Fil-American war of 1899-1902), 54
Filipino masses, 174, 187
Filipino people, 15, 186, 191, 200
Filipino subjectivity, sacramental constitution of, 9
Filipino theater, 199
"Filipinoness," origin of, 201
"First Quarter Storm," of 1970, 12, 83
Fisher-King, 141
Flagellant movement of 1260, 96
Flaubert, 194
Flesh, 20, 25, 96
Florentino, Father, 197
Folk customs, 38
Folk festivals, 7, 127
Folk memory, 173
Folk myths, 48
Forbes Park capitalists, 27
Forster, E. M., 50
Foucault, Michel, 6, 76, 192
"The Fourteen Stations of the Cross," 108, 109, 111, 116
Francisca del Espiritu Santo, 126, 133
Franciscan doctrine of Christ, 97
Franciscan spirituals, persecution of the, 96
Free individual, 65
"Free" market, 192
Free Press, 59, 194
Freedom, 129
French Revolution, 28, 51
Freudian mode, 92
Freudian womb, 188
Freud, 159
Freud's *Nachträglich* effect, 63
Freud's theory of deferred action, 180
"From Intramuros to the Liberated City: Salvaging the Aesthetics of the Polis," 10
Fuente, Francisca, 126, 133
"The Future's rapping at the door," 106

G

Gaspar, 100, 107, 114
Gatmaitan, Alfonso, 12, 171. *See also* Gatmaitan, Pocholo
Gatmaitan, Pocholo, 12, 75, 174, 176, 177, 178, 180, 181, 183, 190, 191

Gerard of Borgo Sar. Donnino, 96
Germany, 97
Gigi, 101
Ginny, 101
Ginoong Ina, 12, 13, 14, 173, 175, 177, 180, 181, 182, 183, 186, 187, 190
God (s), 82, 99, 105, 109, 114, 115, 120, 125, 126, 133, 154
God, death of, 178
God, love of, 21
God, scourge of, 110
God, submission to, 20
Goddess, 7, 181, 184, 187
Godoy, Natalia, 38, 39, 44
Goethe, 9, 30, 136
Good and evil, moral conception of, 59
Gough, Kathleen, 33
Gramsci, 169, 170, 171
Graphic House, 104
"Great American dream," 158
Great Mother's revenge, 126
"Great Pan," 110
Great Schism, 97
Greek epic, 148
Greene, Graham, 141
"Guardia de Honor," 13, 32, 45, 95, 126, 198
Guattari, 102, 103, 145
Guerrilla warfare against the Japanese, 162
Guia, 84, 85, 86, 87, 88, 89, 90, 92, 94, 95, 97, 101, 102, 103
Guiang, 87, 101
Guido, 35, 136
Guilt, body politic of, 89
"Gypsy from India," 127

H

Happy Valley, 105
Harvest, abundance of, 34
Hawthorne, 30
Heathenisms, 100
Heavenly dynamo, 9
Hegel, 71, 95, 134
Hegelian idealism, 183
Hegemonic hierarchy, 83
Hegemonic law, 82
Heidegger, 38
Heideggerian phenomenology, 39
Henson, Jack, 12, 13, 14, 79, 90, 135, 169, 170, 171, 172, 173, 174, 175, 176, 179, 180, 182, 184, 186, 187, 188, 189, 191, 199
Hera, 34

Heraclitean river, 72, 75
Heredia, Bobby, 77, 78, 79, 80, 81, 82, 83
Heretics, 4
La Hermana Beata, 186
Hindu, 157
"Historical World of the Virgin," 203
"History as Culture," 2, 7, 201
Hobbes, 65, 200
Holland, 72
Hollywood, 198
Holy Child, 63
Holy Cross, 157
Holy Ghost, 99, 126, 134, 135, 163
Holy Spirit, 9, 86, 98
Holy Virgin. *See* Virgin Mary
Hong Kong, 11, 38, 104, 145, 154, 155, 156, 167
Hong Kong, exile, 161
Humanistic empiricistic positivism, 91
Hyde, Mr., 176

I

IMF. *See* International Monetary Fund
Ideological-political domination, 18
Ideology, 9, 12, 19, 71, 112, 144, 177
Ifugao, 92, 93
Igorots, 7
Ilustrado (s), 7, 174, 201
Image, 5
Imaginary, 29, 36, 73, 79
Immaculate Conception of the Virgin, 4, 59, 63
Immortality, emblem of, 48
Imperial power, 67
Imperial Spain, 68
Imperialist ethnocentrism, 200
Imperialist hegemony, 94
In illo tempore, 100
Incarnation, theology of the, 88
Independence, 18, 22
India, 34
Individual freedom, 62, 84
Individual hedonism, 64
Individual will, 39
Individualism, ordeal of, 52
Indo-China in 1800, 100
Infinity, a symbol of, 1
"The Innocence of Solomon," 111, 115
Institutional differentiation, networks of, 76
Insurgents, 132
Insurrection, 28

Intellect and Progress, worship of, 60
International Monetary Fund, 76
Intramuros, 8, 59, 94, 117, 124, 146
Ishtar, 34
Isis, 34
Islam, 4, 10
Islamic culture, 201
"Ivory tower," 112

J

Jacinta, Hermana, 129, 130
Jameson, Fredric, 83
Janus (Roman god), 8, 45
Japanese, 8, 58, 107, 110, 177
Javier, Tony, 118, 119, 141
Jeronima, Doña, 71, 72, 73, 74, 75, 175, 197
Jerusalem, 10, 11, 59, 63, 98-99, 133
Jesus sacrifice, 109
Jetztzeit, 184, 185
Joachim, 86, 96, 98, 100, 101, 134
Joachite, 134, 191
Joaquin, Sarah K., 193
Joaquinesquerie: Myth a la Mod, 191
Joel, 134
John the Baptist, 135, 137
John XXII, Pope, 96
Josie, 38, 39, 40, 41, 42, 43, 44
Jouissance, 15, 39, 81, 110, 125, 137, 147, 150, 156, 172, 183, 188
Joyce, 19, 83, 144, 194
Joycean palimpsest, 18
Juana, 128
Juanito, 136
Judaeo-Christian antiphysis ideology, 191
Judaeo-Christian tradition, 132
Judaism, Pauline renunciation of, 129
Judas, 29
Jung, Carl, 49, 50, 195
"Jungle of slums," 118

K

Kabataang Makabayan, 76
Kafkaesque hero, 86
Kali, 34
Kairos, 31, 166, 173, 197
Kansas, USA, 85, 94
Katipunan, 29, 126
Kerenyi, K., 196
Kinship-based organization of society, 33

Kore, 196
Kristeva, Julia, 7, 69
Kwan Yin, 145

L

Labor, 33, 36, 185
Lacaba, Jose, 196
Lacan, 24, 29, 58, 78, 123, 157, 197
Lacanian moment of the Imaginary and the Symbolic, 170
Lagman, Dr., 85, 91, 98, 99, 101
Landgrabbing transnational corporations, 179
"Landscape without Figures," 106, 109, 111, 115, 116
Lao, Father, 85, 87, 89, 90, 94, 95, 97, 101, 102
Laocoon, punishment of, 66
"Last Farewell," by Rizal, 101, 116
Last Judgment, 13
Last Supper, sacrament of the, 196
"The Laugh of the Medusa," 135
Lawrence, D. H., 19, 65, 78, 89, 92
Lawrencian harangue, 60
"Laws of God & Man," 131
Leacock, Eleanor, 33
Legacy, Hispanic, 79, 96
Legaspi, 68, 201
"The Legend of the Dying Wanton," 68
"The Legend of the Virgin's Jewel," 3, 66, 68
LeGuin, Ursula, 65
Lem, Stanislaw, 65
Lent, 127
Lepanto, 4, 5
Lepanto Lady and Queen Mother of Manila, 5
Liberalism, 57, 79, 81, 139
Libertarian, ecumenical cultural politics, 16
"Liberation," 20, 47, 57, 58, 186
Liberation, theology of, 2
"Liberators," 54
Liberty in Christ, 129
"Life and Letters," 109, 110, 116
Life, renewal of, 34
Lingam, 34
Lockean *Tabula rasa*, 181
Logos, 3, 4, 7, 125
Lopez, Currito, 69, 70, 71, 72
Lopez, Rita, 151, 155, 156, 160, 167

Lord (s), 10, 114, 128, 136
Lorenza, Hermana, 127
Lorenza (servant), 128
Lorenzo, Don, 117, 118, 119, 120, 123, 127
Lost Eden, by Rizal, 65
Luddite reaction, 78
Lupe, Doña, 135, 137
Lupeng, Doña, 35, 36, 37

M

Macao, 154, 156, 160, 165
McLuhan, Marshall, 6, 194, 195, 196, 201
Madonna, 68, 69, 70, 71, 158
Magdalene, 138, 153
Maggie, 135
Magian maze, 201
Magic Mountain, by Thomas Mann, 144
Makati, 86
Malaga, 70
Malays, 110, 157
Male, the 4, 18, 24, 33, 37
Manalo, Armando, 196
Manhattan, 87, 89, 198
Manichean dualism, 69
Manicheanism, 82
Manila, 11, 45, 57, 72, 76, 86, 133, 154, 155, 159, 171, 179, 192, 201
Manila, destruction of, 109, 156
Manila, image of, 94, 153
Manila, reminiscences of, 162
Manila vs. Davao City, 170
Manila Bay, Battle of, 8, 198
Manila, "400 Years a City," 201
Manileños, 8
Mann, Thomas, 34, 144
Manzano, 83, 173, 179, 187
Manzano, Alex, 174, 175, 178, 189, 190
Manzano, Alfreda, 187
Manzano, André, 183
Manzano, Chedeng, 187, 189, 190
Mao, 105
Marasigan, 119, 120
Marcuse, 77
Maria Cristina, reign of, 28
Marian figure, 7
Marikina, 8
Mario (Natalia's lover), 39, 42, 43, 44
Marital bondage, 31
Marital-parental love, 81
Maypole dance in Europe, 34
Maytime rituals, indigenous, 8

Media, accumulation of, 7
Medieval Manila, 75
Medieval spatial matrix, 10
Medusa, 28, 112, 167
Melchor, Father, 85, 86, 87, 88, 89, 90, 91, 93, 94, 95, 96, 97, 98, 100, 101, 102, 103
Melchor de la Epifanio, 100
Melkizedek, 91, 97, 98, 99, 100
Menchu, Tita, 80, 81
Merchandiser, 59
Messiah, 137, 185
Messianic faith, 129
Micaela, 135, 136, 137
Midas, 54
Military *coup d'etat*, 28
Minotaur, 104
Mindanao, 179
Minnie, 145
Monica, 179
Monogamous coupling, 33
Monogamous family, 24
Monogamy, upholding of, 20
Monson, Chitong, 18, 19, 20, 21, 22, 24, 25, 26, 27, 138, 139, 140, 199
Monson, Dr., 48, 144, 145, 147, 151, 152, 153, 155, 157, 160, 162, 163, 166, 167, 168
Monson, Pepe, 145, 150, 155, 160
Monson, Tony, 168
Montesquieu, 140
Monteverdi, 141
Montiya, Badoy, 28
Mont-Saint-Michel and Chartres, 1
Monzon, Marcelo, 27, 28, 138, 139
Monzon, Zacarias, 26, 27, 138
Moors, 88
Moral crisis, 69
"A Morality," 111, 116
Morality, 19, 22, 143
Morel, Pompoy, 78, 80, 81, 82
Mores and customs, 20
Moro, 199
Moro-Moro, 199
Moro National Liberation Front, 179
Morong Church, 198
Morris, William, 78
Mother Archetype, 78
Mother Goddess, 34
Movement for the Advancement of Nationalism, 76
Multiracial nationalist movement, 7
Mumford, Lewis, 4

Munzer, Thomas, 97, 100
"Mysteries of the Rosary," 150
Mystery Man, 126, 127, 128, 131
Mystical community, 128
Mysticism, Self-indulgent, 130

N

Nation-State, 200
National consciousness, 7
National culture, 116, 195
National destiny, 5
National identity, 4
National liberation and freedom, 155
Natural world of the Dynamo, 203
Naturalization, 187
Nature and Culture, 154
Nature/Culture, dualism of, 144
Nature's vengeance against Faustian rationality, 178
"La Naval de Manila," 2, 3, 5, 6, 15, 37, 38, 118, 119, 122, 124, 194
Nazarene in Quiapo, feast of, 8
Nazareth, prophet of, 2
"Necessity is the consciousness of Freedom," 203
Nena, Tia, 22, 25, 26
Neo-Aristotelian perspective, 17
Neocolonial inheritance, 173
Neocolonial society, 170
Neocolony, 179
"Neolithic caves," 106
Neo-Platonic tradition, 19, 74
New Critical perspective, 17
New England, 134
New People's Army, 134
New Salem community, 100
"The New Science," 6
"Now Sound the Flutes," 108, 116
New Testament, 96
New Year, 46, 47
New Yorker, 106
Newman, Andrew, 53, 54, 55, 56, 57, 58
Nietzsche, 6, 100, 181
1972 Martial Law, imposition of, 188
Nixon doctrine, 76
"The Noble and Ever Loyal City," 118
"The Noble and Ever Loyal Intramuros," 153
Noe, Father, 60, 62, 63, 64
Nominalism, 14
Non-Christian World, 68
Nostradamus, 46
Nous, 172
Nuclear armageddon, between U.S. and Soviet Union, 104

O

O'Brien, Mary, 142
"O Death Be Proud," 107, 111, 113, 116
Obando, 34
Odysseus, 122
Oedipal coding, 167
Oedipal crisis, 78
Oedipus, 103
Oedipus complex, 66, 138, 166
Old Manila. *See* Intramuros
Old Testament, 24, 96, 129
Oligarchic elite, 171
"On Public Speech," 107, 109, 111, 116
"The Order of Melkizedek," 12, 76, 83, 84, 114, 134, 174, 191, 202
"Orientalism," 5
Origin of the Family, Private Property and the State, 33
"The Original Manila," 119
Original sin, 190
Orphic/Apollonian role, 199
Orthodox doctrine, 7
Orthodox faith, 7
Osiris, 34
Otis, General, 99
Our Lady of Guadalupe, 2
"Outline of a Theory of Practice," by Pierre Bourdieu, 188

P

Paeng, Don, 34, 35, 36, 136, 137
Pagan cults, 47, 101
Pagan fatalism, 143, 178, 198
Paganism, 47, 66, 72, 75, 90, 98, 99, 177, 188, 196
Pakil, 34
La Palma de Mallorca, 192-193
Papal-imperial wars, in Italy, 96
"Parallel lives," 144
Parental authority, 78
Paris Great Exposition of 1900, 1
Paris Spleen, 15
Parochialism, 133
"Pascua Flamenca," 112, 114, 116
Pastoral adoration, retablo of, 47

Paternal power, 6, 188
Patriachs, 102, 114, 190
Patriarchal authority, 17, 122, 126, 163, 164, 175
Patriarchal domination, 172
Patriarchal law, 27, 75
Patriarchal wills, 18, 25
Patrocentric state, 190
Patron saints, cult of, 4
Patroness of Columbus, 67
Paula, 119, 120, 121, 122, 123, 124, 125, 141
Pauline Era, 133
Pax Romana, 117, 123
Pearl Harbor, 109
Peasant (s), 27, 96, 99
Peasant War in Germany by Engels, 100
Penitence, dignity of, 56
Pentecostide, 108
Pepang, Doña, 54, 56, 58, 118, 119, 120
Pepita, Doña, 42, 43
Perico, Don, 119, 123, 124
Peripeteia, 173, 187, 190
Persephone, 34, 112, 195
Petrarchan sonnet, 112
The Phenomenology of Mind, 71
Philippines, 5, 10, 15, 39, 58, 66, 84, 117, 133, 144, 151, 160, 167, 186, 200
Philippine crisis, 144, 162
Philippines, formation of, 27, 84, 102, 139, 163, 171
Philippine society, 39, 84
Physis, 202
Picasso, 198
"Picture of the Founder," 85
Pilar, 131
"A Pilgrim Yankee's Progress," 53
Platonic *chora*, 125
Platonic ideas, 156
Platonic models, 177, 184
Platonic recollection, 180
Platonic theater of illusions, 188
Plenum, Logocentric, 178
The Plumed Serpent, 65
Poe, 30
Political authority, 130
Political crisis, 69
Political organization of the polis, 10
The Political Unconscious, 83
Politicoeconomic structure, 60
Politics, egalitarian, 134
Pop anthropology, 6

"Popcorn and Gaslight," 199
Populism, demagogic, 173
A Portrait of the Artist as Filipino, 3, 13, 27, 63, 117, 193
Post-Cartesian scholarship, 192
Post-Constantinian faith, 4
Post-Enlightenment radicalism, 134
Post-Oedipal, 82
Post-Renaissance individualism, 143
Poulantzas, Nicos, 9, 10, 12, 13, 14, 196
Pound, Ezra, 114
Poverty, absolute, 96
Power, 2, 10, 91, 107, 172
Power-bloc, 172
Power elites, 107
Pragmatism, 140
Pre-capitalist territories, 14
Pre-Christian community, 89
Pre-Columbian Aztec myths, 65
Pre-Counter Reformation, 63
Pre-Spanish aboriginal inhabitants, 4
Pre-World War II Manila, 85
Priapus, 97
Priestess, native, 186
Priesthood, vocation of, 21
Prieto, Captain, 130, 131, 132
Primitive mysticism, 11
Primordial child, 96
Principalia, 202
"Procession of the Holy Kings," 114
"Procession of the Holy Women," 115
The Profesora. *See* Dacanay, Chedeng
Progress, distrust of, 63
Proletarian literature, 197
Prophet-annalist, epistomological program, 175
Prose and Poems, 17, 104, 154, 190, 194
Prostitution, existence of, 26
Protestant doctrine of justification, by faith, 14
"Psychological Aspect of the Mother Archetype," 49
Puerta Postigo, 47
Puritan vs Royalist conflict, 91
Puritanical authoritarianism, 94
Puritanical idealism, 54
Puritanism, stereotyped, 53

Q

Quasi-Nietzschean reductionism, 76
Queen of the Most Holy Rosary, 4

A Question of Heroes, 201
"The Question of Style," by Derrida, 181
Quezon, Manuel, 162
Quezon-Osmeña generations, 154
Quezon-Osmeña *ilustrados*, reformist program, 51
"Quijano de Manila," 200

R

Rabelaisian festival deity, 166
Rabelaisian humanism, 107
Rabelaisian vision, 102
Radical feminism, 134
Radical humanism, 63
Rafael, 136
Realism, 28, 70, 81, 118
Reality, quest of, 72
Reason, fetishism of, 191
Reconciliation of consciousness, 203
Recto, Claro, 76
"Red, White and Blue Ball," 60
Religion, sacramental view of, 78
Religious control, 129
Renaissance, 51, 75, 76, 201
Repentance, heroism of, 190
Republic's downfall, 154
"Retrato del Artista Como Filipino," 122, 123
Revolutionary culture, 200
Revolutionary Republic of 1898, 151
Ricoeur, Paul, 38
Rios, Eden, 62
Rizal, Jose P., 94, 108, 111, 155, 197
Roman Catholic church, 17, 96
Roman Catholic teaching, 7
Roman epic, 148
Roman religion, 45
Roman state, 123
Romance, customary dénouement, 182
Rome, 10
Rosa (daughter of Capt. Prieto), 130, 132, 136
Rousseau, 140
Ruether, Rosemary, 134
"Rule of Saint Augustine," 105, 106

S

Sacramental past of old Manila, 38
Sacred bodies, superimposition of the, 184

Sacred heart, 152, 156
Sacred transcendental power, 6
Sacrifice, 4
Sacrifice of female bodies, 130
Sadomasochism, 159
Sagada, 92
Said, Edward, 5
Saint Albert's College in Hong Kong, 106, 194
Saint Andrew's monastery atop Holy Cross Hill, 145, 168
Saint Augustine, 47
Saint Bernard, 19
Saint Catherine of Siena, 132
Saint Francis, 96
Saint James, 88
Saint John, feast of, 34
Saint John of the Cross, 72, 126
Saint John the Baptist, 105
Saint Paul, 97
Saint Simonian, 134
Saint Sylvester, 45, 46, 47, 48
Saint Teresa, 126
"Saint Thais," 111, 112, 115
Salcedo, 68
Salem House, 90, 103
Salemites, 84, 87, 88, 89, 91, 92, 95, 97
Salgado, 69
Salome, 30
Salvation as a woman, 56, 57
Sambahang Anito, 183, 188
Santa Ana, 8
Santacruzan, legend of, 8
Santo Domingo convent of Manila, 66
Santo Niño, 8, 188, 195, 196, 201, 202,
"The Santo Niño in Philippine History," 7, 9, 195
Santo Rosario, 68
Santos, 183, 198
Sartre, 130
Sartrean existentialism, 76
Sebastiana, Hermana, 126, 128, 129, 133, 134
Second World War, 164
The Secular City, 129
"Secular Communion of Saints," 126
Secular individualism, 120
Secularization, 129
Segovia, Isagani, 175, 178, 180, 187, 190
Semicolonial Philippines, 157
Semifeudal capitalism, 18
Semifeudal oligarchy, 174

Semiotic *chora*, 69
September 1972 coup, 182
"Servant of the Lord," 4
Sexism and God-Talk: Toward a Feminist Theology, 134
"Sexual economist," 85
Sexual politics, 169
"Sham World," 147
Sheba, 111
Shinto, 177
Shiva, 34
"Shooting Stars," 194
Simulacrum, 185
"Sinai," 113
"Six P.M.," 104, 112, 113, 114, 115
Slavery, sensual, 109
"Social Amnesia," 199
Social atomism, 14
Social changes, 82 65
Social classes, 12, 20
Social decorum, 25
Social development, 27
Social-ideological forces, 186
Social life, 39
Social solidarity, 7
Socialist political organization, emergence of, 28
Society, 56, 65, 128
Socioeconomic formation, 19
Socratic drive, 172
Sofia, Doña, 18, 23, 25, 26, 138, 139, 140, 141
Solidarity among women workers, 24
Solomon, 111
"Song Between Wars," 104, 107, 108, 111, 116
Sophia, 69
Sorge, 38
Sovereign nation-state, 200
Space, production of, 3, 11
Spain, 4, 5, 28, 66, 156, 192
Spaniards, 110
Spanish-American War of 1898, 54
Spanish colonial domination, 4-5, 28-30, 66, 162
Spanish culture, 199
Spanish naval victory of 1646, 4, 67
Spengler, Oswald, 6, 201
Spirit, 96
"Spirit Christologies," 134
Spiritual enlightenment, 21-22
Spiritual hunger, 109

Spiritual purification, 19
Spiritual struggle, 21
Spiritual transformation, 3
State, 11, 95
State, Power and Socialism, 9
"Stowaway," 77
"Stubbs Road Cantos," 104, 106, 111, 116
Subject-on-trial, 134
Suez Canal in 1869, opening of, 119
Suffrage in the Philippines, 125
"The Summer Solstice," 37, 135
Surrealism, 195
Sybilline writings, 96
Symbolic law, of the Father, 182
Symbolic order, 23, 62, 76, 82, 124, 148, 157
Symbolism, 194

T

Tabula rasa, 174
"Tadtarin," 32, 33, 34, 35, 36, 37
Tagalog writing, 199
Tammuz, 34
"Tatarin," 135, 136, 137, 138, 141
"Tatarin" feast, 195
Taylorist division of labor, 10
Technology, negative, 81
"Technology: The Philippine Revolution," 2
Telos, 175
Temporal-spatial matrices, 12
Tenorio, 69
Territorial-national traditions, 200
Texeira, Mary, 156, 160, 161, 167
Texeira, Paco, 11, 12, 145, 148, 151, 155, 156, 157, 158, 159, 160, 161, 166
Textuality, utopian moment of, 48
Theoria, 204
Third Age of the Holy Spirit, 100
Third World, 2, 65, 83
Three Generations," 17, 23, 25, 27, 32, 37, 135, 197
Three Kings, 84, 86, 93, 97, 98, 100, 202
Three Marias, 115
Time-space matrix, 169, 200
"Tiny Rome growing up by the Pasig," 4
Tirad Pass, Battle of, 11, 157, 162
Tonantzin, 2
Tony, Father, 145, 151, 155, 166
Totalitarianism, modern, 12
Totem and Taboo, 137

Tour de force, 201
Tradition, 38, 84
Traditional oligarchy, 173
Traditional paradigm, 4
Transformation, space of, 188
The Transposed Heads, 34
The Tremulous Private Body, by Francis Barker, 173
Tribal custom, 4
Tribal obedience, 5
Tribal order, 27
Tribe of Tarsus, 133
Trojan prince, 122
Tropical Gothic, 17
"Trouvere at Night," 113
Troy, 122
"True Heathen Filipino," 177
Turk in Africa, 137
Twelve Apostles, 99
"Twin Caves of Christ's birth and burial," 115

U

U.S. *See* United States
Ulysses, by Joyce, 144, 194
Un-Christian Chinese New Year, 168
Understanding Media, 194
United Nations in New York, 86
United States, 9, 11, 18, 51, 54, 58, 59, 65, 118, 119, 151, 155, 162, 164, 172, 187, 193, 200
United States imperialism, 15, 55, 144
United States sovereignty, 154, 187
Universal Spirit, 96
Urban anonymity, 170
Urban insurrections, 12
"Urbi et Orbi," 126
Urduja, 180
Utilitarian morality, 22
"Utopian," 2, 3, 27, 78, 116, 172
Utopian-Anarchistic sects, 65

V

Valero, Pepe, 49, 51
Venus and Virgins, 1
Vera, Señor, 70
"Verde Yo Te Quiero Verde," 105, 110, 111, 112, 115
Verfremdungseffekt, 142
Vico, 6

"La Vida," 2
"La Vidal," 84, 145, 160, 161, 163
Vidal, Concha, 144, 145, 146, 147, 150, 151, 154, 156, 158, 160, 162, 163, 164, 165, 166
Vidal, Connie, 11, 15, 166, 190, 199
Vidal-Escobar, Connie, in Hongkong, 167
Vidal, Manolo, 118, 119, 120, 125, 151, 155, 163, 164, 165
Vietnam War, 76, 86, 195
Villa, Jose Garcia, 199
Virgil, 122
Virgilian *pietas,* 141
Virgin (s) 3, 9, 10, 11, 14, 15, 16, 70, 125, 126, 141, 142, 189, 195, 201, 202
Virgin, animation of the, 67
Virgin, cult of, 4, 5, 7
Virgin, Igorot style, 90
Virgin, miraculous intercession of, 39
Virgin of Guadalupe, 15
Virgin of the Rosary, 43, 44
Virgin of Zaragoza, 167
"The Virgin and the Dynamo," by W. H. Auden, 203
La Virgin del Carmen fiesta, 8
Virgin Mary, 4, 7, 34, 68, 99, 120, 145, 153. *See also* Virgin Mother
Virgin Mother, 7, 64, 66, 68, 69, 124, 125, 130, 183, 188, 191
Virgo intacta, 179
Virtù, 75, 139
Visayan sugar plantation, 146
"The Visitation," 108, 116
Vocation, experience of, 18
Voltaire, 28, 140
Voltairean skepticism, 32

W

Walled City, 47
War-devastated Manila, 121
"Warm responding flesh," 113
Watts, Alan, 3, 4
"Weakness of the Flesh," 19
Weber, Max, 91, 138
Weltanschauung, 196
Western Christian Victory, 184
Western colonialism, 125
Western culture, 192
Western fashion styles, 82
Western ingenuity, 201
Western technology, 158

Westernization crash program, 195
"What Is an Author?," 192
"What Price Our Writing in English?," 199
Whore of Babylon, 96
Wittig, Monique, 137
Woman (en), 19, 24, 27, 32, 33, 36, 37, 44, 142
Woman: Mother/Lover, 25
The Woman Who Had Two Navels, 8, 11, 15, 63, 84, 144, 191, 202
Women's Liberation Movement, 25
Wordsworth, 78
Wordsworthian/Proustian "spot of time," 164
World War II. *See* Second World War
Worthy victims, 129

Y

Yahweh, 97
Yankee, 47, 54, 57, 110
Yanquis of MacArthur, 99
"The Years," 111, 116
Yeats, 83
Yeatsian epigraph, 118
Yeatsian mask, 200
Yvette, 171, 178, 190

Z

Zaduk, 97
Zarzuela, 199
Zeitgeist, 62
Zhdolajczyk, Francis Xavier, 46, 47, 48